BLUE WATER,

a year in the ocean.

By Julianna Lembeck

Author's Note

This book contains sensitive topics around violence, substance abuse, emotional abuse, depression, anxiety, and suicidal ideation that some may find triggering or upsetting.

If you or someone you know is feeling suicidal, call the **National Suicide Prevention Lifeline** *immediately at* **800-273-8255**. *You can also call* **911** *or go to a hospital emergency room.*

If you or someone you know is in crisis—whether considering suicide or not—please get help. Reach out to others for support—family members, friends, 12-step program community members, sponsors, mentors, teachers, school counselors, or anyone you have a safe and trusting relationships with. If no one comes to mind, understand **you are not alone**. *Below are a few **free** resources.*

National Suicide Prevention Lifeline
Call 800-273-TALK (8255) to speak with a trained crisis counselor 24/7

Crisis Text Line
Text NAMI to 741-741to connect with a trained crisis counselor to receive free, 24/7 crisis support via text message

The **NAMI HelpLine** can be reached Monday through Friday, 10 am–6 pm, ET.1-800-950-NAMI (6264) or info@nami.org

---

If you are not in crisis but still struggling with mental health, substance abuse, or stuck in an unhealthy relationship, please seek support, and understand there is no shame in asking for help. In fact, it's the opposite. It takes strength and courage to advocate for your mental wellness.

I created an app I wish existed during my healing journey:

taurus | Holistic Mental Health App
https://www.tauruswellness.io/

Other resources that have helped me along my healing journey:

Dr. Nicole LePera | Widely known as The Holistic Psychologist
https://theholisticpsychologist.com/
https://www.instagram.com/the.holistic.psychologist/ (Free content)
https://www.youtube.com/channel/UCtEWTaMjqOH8J1Gy06Ey0Yg (Free content)

Dr. Kelly Brogan, MD | Holistic Psychiatrist
https://kellybroganmd.com/ (Free content)
https://kellybroganmd.com/ownyourself/ (Book)

Psychology Today | Find a Therapist, Psychologist, or Counselor Near You:
https://www.psychologytoday.com/us/therapists

Copyright © 2023 by Julianna Lembeck
All rights reserved

First Edition
Book Cover Design by Fanny Peault.
Book Cover Photography by Ryan Selewicz.
Editing by Nina Denison.
Written by Julianna Lembeck.
Published by Steady Ground LLC.

Library of Congress Cataloging-in-Publication Data

Lembeck, Julianna
BLUE WATER, a year in the ocean. / Julianna Lembeck
ISBN: 978-1-7363952-0-2
1. NONFICTION

No part of this book may be reproduced, stored in a retrieval system, or transmitted by any means, electronic, mechanical, photocopying, recording or otherwise without written permission from the author.

BLUE WATER, *a year in the ocean.*

For all the Jordans

Julianna Lembeck

BLUE WATER,

a year in the ocean.

Julianna Lembeck

Did it become your identity or your lesson?

Perhaps both.

Julianna Lembeck

TABLE OF CONTENTS

PART I: FIRE, *a natural disaster of human proportions.* 13

    APRIL 2007, *when the floor falls away.* 15
    DECEMBER 2008, *ablaze.* 17
    JANUARY-APRIL 2009, *you, me & our pretty little problems.* 25
    MAY 10, 2009, *Mother's Day & other sorts of flowers.* 45
    JUNE 3, 2009, *high as high-school Prom.* 51
    JUNE 12, 2009, *under the sun; wrestling restlessness.* 60
    JULY 7, 2009, *home is where the beach is.* 68
    JULY 9-12, 2009, *heatstroke strikes; again and again and again.* 72
    JULY 14, 2009, *happy pills.* 82
    JULY 15, 2009, *These Days. This Day.* 86
    JULY 16, 2009, *let's break it down; she broke down.* 92
    JULY 18, 2009, *show & tell.* 96
    AUGUST 7, 2009, *like boyfriend, like girlfriend.* 101

PART II: FLOATING & *other things to do in limbo.* 130

    OCTOBER 2009, *a punch of finality.* 132
    MARCH 2010, *carefully choosing college.* 135
    AUGUST 2010, *what do you mean, she's mean?* 139
    OCTOBER 2010, *what do you do in a dead sea? Float.* 153
    APRIL 2011, *pick your poison.* 155
    JULY 2011, *a penny for your thoughts.* 165
    2012, *ring around the rosie* 176
    2013, *a pocket full of posies* 181
    2014, *ashes! Ashes!* 188
    2015, *we all fall down.* 194

PART III: BLUE WATER, *a year in the ocean.* 200

    AUGUST 26, 2016, *whiplash in my ponytail slash.* 204
    SEPTEMBER 3, 2016, *hey, hi, how do you do? How do we do this?* 209
    OCTOBER 5, 2016, *you're doing that thing you do.* 225
    OCTOBER 29, 2016, *Halloweeney & Vee.* 227
    NOVEMBER 2016, *candied darkness.* 237
    DECEMBER 2016, *holding, getting, gaining.* 239

JANUARY 12, 2017, *stupid happy.* 247
JANUARY 21, 2017, *levity; light as air, breath, and laughter.* 255
FEBRUARY 2017, *missing, memories, loss. Things to think of when you're not thinking of me.* 261
MARCH 2017, *why are we doing This?* 272
APRIL 2017, *the sun shifts without you.* 288
MAY 2017, *the magic. Oh, oh, oh.* 294
JUNE 2017, *we're easy to name and hard to hold.* 296
JULY 2017, *I miss you when you're sober. But only when I'm drunk.* 298
AUGUST 2017, *you tell me to turn off my emotions, but don't you know that's what keeps you around?* 299
SEPTEMBER 2017, *it ain't me.* 304

PART I: FIRE,
a natural disaster of human proportions.

Julianna Lembeck

APRIL 2007,
when the floor falls away.

If they were home, it was hard to tell.
Bedroom curtains drawn, door locked.
No, not just at night. 24/7.
What—your parents didn't do that?

Took a few years to learn
to keep that
to myself.

She eventually left, and things went quiet.
The house, my dad, my brothers, me.
Our familial frequency askew.

Bit by bit, our foundation shifted.
Not by explosion—
by erosion—
water to the rocks.

No matter.
Invincible am I,
adorned in adolescent armor.
I simply shift my focus.
    School validates my intellect.

Julianna Lembeck

    Peers, my identity.
        Alcohol, that it's easy to forget.

Welcome home.
Do what you'd like.
No one's watching.
Big freedom.

DECEMBER 2008,
ablaze.

It's winter break, Aslyn's dad is out of town, and we're throwing a huge party.

When Aslyn's parents split during our sophomore year, her dad stayed in the family house. He goes away on weekends all the time, for god knows what, and since the house is basically a bachelor pad anyhow, the girls and I take full advantage for parties when he leaves.

Like this weekend.

I'm sitting on the countertop in Aslyn's kitchen, drink in hand, slowly but surely entering my stage of buzzing bliss, looking out at the sea of people jammed into the living room and spilling outside into the backyard. It doesn't take long for Kolton to spot me, and when he does, he bee-lines it straight for me.

Ballsy.

I didn't even know who he was until two weeks ago.

Didi dated Kolton's best friend, Tobi, the year before, so when I asked her about Kolton a few weeks ago, she had the goods. Her dish on Kolton, animated and wild with fascination, rings through my mind.

When I was dating Tobi, I was with those guys all the time.
They're crazy.
Kolton was adopted at birth so his whole family's white—parents, brother, all of 'em.
Super rich, too.

And he was in this really bad car accident when he was fifteen, so he has all these gnarly scars on his face and hands.
He also went to juvie for a few months. I can't remember what for.
But they're nuts.
We'd be driving, and you know those red trays from In-N-Out? Tobi kept one in his truck, and they'd straight up just do line after line of coke when we'd be driving around. Like, in the middle of the day.
So fun. So many drugs.
He got kicked out of Canyon High School for whatever that juvie incident was about.
So now he's starting at Elmo after winter break.
Pretty sure he's been in rehab at some point, too.
But he's hot. You should totally go for it.

Didi's right. With light-black skin, a solid build, and a frame over six feet tall, he's easily attractive. I'm playing her words through my mind as Kolton plops himself next to me on the counter, his red plaid jacket so fluffy and huge it's brushing my long-sleeve shirt. The furred hood so close that it's tickling my cheek.

"What are you drinking?" He pushes closer to me as he leans in, peeking his head in my cup. He smells incredible.

"Vodka," I answer with an amused smile, pulling my cup away from his face. I can't get over the way he smells, clean and inviting.

"Straight? Damn, didn't know you got down like that," he chuckles.

"It's mixed," I say with feigned disinterest, swinging my dangling legs back and forth, peering aimlessly out into the party. His body is only a few centimeters away from mine, and I'm getting hit with his scent through every breath.

"So, were you gonna ignore me all night?" He turns to look at me directly.

I slowly turn my head toward him, letting my eyes follow lazily at the last second like a cat's.

"What? You just got here," I practically purr, looking up at him through half-closed eyes, firmly holding his stare like a challenge. His gaze is penetrating and intense. People don't look at people like this.

"Ahhh, so you *were* keepin' your eyes peeled for Big Slice," he says as he extends and raises both arms in front of him, palms up toward the ceiling like he's jeering a crowd to get rowdy.

"Who the hell is *Big Slice*?"

He puts his arms down, turns to me, and pauses dramatically as if he can't believe what I just asked.

"Me," he answers through a smile that spreads slowly, blooming from the right-side corner of his mouth.

I break into my own smile and wait for him to brush my arm and tell me he's joking. I wait for him to explain that he doesn't actually refer to himself in the third person—by some douchey nickname nonetheless—but he doesn't do any of that. And I burst into laughter.

"Seriously?"

"Seriously, what?" He seems confused.

"What kind of name is *Big Slice*?"

"Tobi gave me that nickname. Slice, like the basketball player. I ball, too," he explains as he flicks his wrist, pretending to shoot an imaginary basketball, "and I'm good."

"You're ridiculous," I shake my head at his unshakeable confidence, giggling despite myself.

"Let's get out of here," he says, looking at me with no hint of a smile. He's not so much asking, but directing, like he knows I'll go.

I don't know at which point in the last few minutes I became willing to go, but when he hops down from the counter without a word, not waiting for my yes, I, too, know I'd go. He turns his body toward mine, stands tall and steady, and chugs the rest of his drink. He keeps his eyes on me from behind the rim of his plastic red SOLO cup. Once he's finished, he places the empty cup on the counter, still holding my stare. When he reads the yes in my eyes, he grabs each side of my hips to gently hoist me down from the counter.

A splash of my drink escapes my cup and explodes on the floor as my feet hit the ground.

I still haven't said anything, and neither of us have broken our stares.

Everyone else at the party fades away, like background music.

It's just us.

He turns now, ready to maneuver through the swarm of people, throws his hand back without looking like he knows I'll grab for it. I do. He leads the way with his red plaid jacket, fluffy and huge, splitting the crowd, our hands locked, me following effortlessly behind him.

"Where are we going?" I ask him as I shiver, the December air cold for California's standards.

"Does it matter?" he asks back.

"Guess not," I respond, eager to be out of the chill.

We walk to his parked car, a silver Mercedes Benz sedan, and he opens the passenger-side door for me. Together, we glide away from the party, the car humming without resistance as he accelerates. He keeps the windows down but blasts both the heat and music, some type of rap hitting through the speakers.

I can't get enough of *right now*. My face smiles with drunken stupor. My stomach tickles silly from the car's speed and ease. My mind takes note of Kolton's attentive glances. My thoughts are occupied by a jagged scar on his face, loosely in the shape of a boomerang, and how closely it falls above his right eye. My own eyes drink in the pinpoints of white light where the stars break through the black blanket of night sky.

We're going nowhere, but no matter.

I don't mind being nowhere with him.

Today, Kolton picks me up for smoothies, and invites me back to his house after.

When we pull up to his big, black iron gate, he punches out a code in a box to the left, and the gate opens horizontally. He drives forward across the pavement toward the back of the property, where I see a garage and a huge, long house to our left.

We enter his house through a back door, and I'm immediately welcomed by the scent of patchouli, pepper, and laundry detergent. There are other scents I don't recognize, but I like all of it. I'm a sensitive sniffer, and smell is big for me. Feels like one of the ways my body says yes or no to people.

Like me, Kolton also lives in Orange Park Acres, a small, upscale equestrian community with enormous properties.

Unlike me, Kolton's home is clean and feels occupied. Safe. Warm.

I hear a loud, raspy cackle drifting from somewhere further away and look up at him curiously.

"My mom," he responds as we maneuver through the house. We make our way toward a pair of double doors. Before he opens one of the doors, he simply says, "By the way, my family's white."

"Okay," I nod, already aware of this detail thanks to Didi.

The double doors open to a backyard patio, and sitting around a table are who I presume to be his parents.

"Kolton! We were just talking about you," his mom exclaims. "And who's this?" she asks me directly, standing up from her chair. I take her in as she stands to greet me. She's wearing light-colored Levis, a big, comfy button-up flannel paired with an even bigger and longer fuzzy, gray-teal cardigan. She's shorter than me, maybe five feet, and her wild, wiry hair spills loosely from a ponytail. Bangs wrap her forehead, and she's wearing black-framed glasses, medium in thickness. Her feet are covered in thick socks and tucked into loafers with no backing, which kind of look like Crocks without the holes. She has a smile that looks like a laugh.

"Jordan," I beam back at her, extending my hand to shake hers.

"Oh, we don't shake hands here." She playfully swats my hand down and wraps me in a hug. I hug her back and want to stay there, wrapped into the coziness of her flannel and oversized cardigan. Her clothes smell just like the house with a hint of smoke.

"Welcome, honey. I'm Nancy," she drips in her raspy voice and smiles another laugh of a smile.

"Did you guys eat?" she follows up immediately.

I look to Kolton. "We got smoothies," he answers, calmly.

"Oh, that's nice. From where?"

He lifts up his Styrofoam cup in place of an answer.

"Ahhh, Jamba Juice," Nancy observes. "Well, that's just a smoothie. Do you guys want food?"

Kolton looks at me in question. "Oh, no thank you. I'm fine, really," I say.

"We're good," Kolton concludes.

"Okay, okay. Oh, Jordan, honey—this is my husband." She points behind her to the quiet man, who offers a warm, gentle smile in return, moving to stand and greet me as well.

"I'm James. So nice to have you over," he says as he wraps me into a hug. He's much taller than Nancy. He's wearing worn cargo pants and a plaid flannel. Dressed similarly, the two certainly look like a couple. Like Nancy, James has glasses, too, his with a much thinner wire frame. His hair parts on the side of his head, both sides sprouting forth thick, full, peppered-gray tufts. I notice a rounded copper bracelet on his right wrist. He, too, smells like the house—patchouli, pepper, laundry detergent and all. He strikes me as someone who would teach college-level English.

Nancy, sunken back in her patio chair, brings a plastic off-white cigarette filter to her mouth, which is encased around a cigar as thin as a cigarette. She takes a drag and continues her original thought before the introductions.

"So. Before you guys got home, I was talking about that time we went to Europe—and of course took a million pictures only to drop the camera in that waterfall before flying back. Do you remember? Oh my god, we were devastated."

Nancy alternates looking at Kolton and me excitedly. When she doesn't get much of a response from him, she fixates on me, obviously not off-put by his lack of enthusiasm.

"So, before we went home, we stopped at a convenience store to buy one of those little disposable cameras and asked a random person to take a picture of all of us. We were so bummed about losing all our other photos, though, that we all just looked lousy. But the one picture was better than nothing, so guess what I did?"

"Extended the trip to take more pictures?" I try.

"Nope. I framed it. Framed that god-damn photo. Just the one. Lousy expressions and all." Nancy bursts into the same raspy cackle I'd heard minutes ago.

I find myself wrapped up in her laughter and begin laughing, too.

"You want to see it?" She stands up, takes one last drag of her thin cigar, and ushers me behind her without waiting for an answer. "Come on, I'll show you."

I follow Nancy back through the house and into the kitchen, Kolton staying behind with James.

"You want a sandwich, honey?"

"Oh no, I'm okay."

"Right. You said that already. Okay, so here we go." She picks up a frame sitting on the kitchen windowsill. Sure enough, everyone looks miserable. I take the frame in my hands, laughing again and pointing to the kid with the bright blonde hair, looking at Nancy in question.

"Ah, that's Kolton's brother, Cyler. Must have noticed by now that Kolton was adopted. Did he mention it?"

"Kind of," I answer.

"No surprise there, Kolton doesn't give much information in general," she says, laughing easily.

"What are you talking about over there?" Kolton walks back in the house, his dad behind him.

"Nothing, honey, just showing Jordan the picture I was talking about."

"Uh huh. She tryin' to talk your ear off or what?" Kolton teases. "She'll talk for hours if you let her," he continues.

"Well someone's gotta do the talking around here. We all know it won't be you," Nancy teases back.

"Nope," Kolton says, shaking his head through a cocky smile.

"We're going to the grocery store. I'm picking up some cran-grape juice and peanut butter for you. Need anything else?"

"Ooooh. Get those Uncrustables sandwiches. Those are the business."

"Alright, we'll be back." And just like that, Nancy and James are out the door, and the house quiets.

We make our way to Kolton's room, and I sink down on the suede duvet cover, taking in the checkered pattern of alternating reds. His room smells different than the house—better, even. Although there are still some hints of the house in his room, I also notice tones of clean ocean, like one of those candles named "Sea Salt" or "White Sand."

He removes his jacket, the same red plaid one he wore last night, so fluffy and huge—the one with the furred hood that tickled my cheek when he sat next to me. That was only last night, but I feel like I've known him longer.

He hangs the jacket on a wooden hanger. I notice all the hangers are the same, and all the shirts, flannels, and jackets are color-coordinated. The organization soothes the Type A in me. Next, he removes his shoes, a pair of black Vans with three big Velcro straps across the top, and places them on the floor in his closet next to two rows of over a dozen pairs of shoes—not including the chunky basketball shoes I notice trailing away to the other half of the closet, covered by mirrored sliding doors, both pushed to the left.

He turns on the TV, flips the channel to an NBA basketball game, and doesn't do much else.

He's lying down completely horizontal, but I'm sitting up, a pillow propped between my back and the wall. We're close, but we're still not touching. Like a magnetic force, my skin tingles with an itch to be closer to him. Within this proximity, his scent grows sharp and clear, and it takes everything in me not to curl up under his arm and kiss him.

Do you taste as good as you smell? I wonder silently to myself.

"So, you're starting at Elmo this semester?" I ask instead.

"Yup."

"Why switch half-way through senior year?"

"You don't want me to go to Elmo?" he deters from the question.

"I don't care. Just wondering why you'd switch halfway through, especially your senior year. Seems weird."

"I got kicked out."

"For what?"

"You always ask this many questions?" he chuckles, looking at me sideways through an amused smile.

"Yes," I frown back firmly.

"Oh maaaaan," he says, locking eyes with me, still amused.

He pulls me from propped-up to horizontal, parallel with his body.

Next, he pulls me in, body to body, and like swallowing flames, we're ablaze.

What do I mean?

Ever seen wildfire swallow an entire hillside of dry brush?

Ablaze. Instant. Exactly.
That's us.
Not even together a whole twenty-four hours and we're already ablaze.
Touch after touch, kiss after kiss.
We do everything except sex, and by the time he drops me off back at home, I toss around two things in my mind:

1. I'm still a virgin
2. Yet, something is lost.

Not even twenty-four hours, and he's already everything I didn't know I was waiting for.

♪
Music picks up where words fall short:
["Nineteen" by Tegan and Sara]
♪

JANUARY–APRIL 2009,
you, me, & our pretty little problems.

    We establish our rhythm like a dance we were born knowing. Kolton's attention is constant and pressing, but I eat it right up.

    hi. Always his swooping opening over text.
Good morning ☺. I'm sweet as candy.
wat r u doin
Just in my Stats class. This teacher practically puts me to sleep. And she smells like death.
lol the grim reaper
Hah exactly. What's your 1ˢᵗ period?
dont have one
Why not?
didnt need it
Ahh, well, lucky you.
i miss you
I miss you too. I'll see you at nutrition though, right?
yee but still
    These conversations play on repeat the entire week. And I feel found. I'm here, and he's here.
    I feel seen, heard, felt. Found.
    I could practically curl up in his *i miss you* morning texts and *come over* post-basketball practice texts.

Except Thursday, that is.

Saw him Wednesday night. We did our back and forth Thursday morning; saw him at nutrition, our high school's fifteen minute, mid-morning snack break; again at lunch, and, as usual, I knew he had basketball practice after school today. At 5:17, he finally texts me.

hi

How was practice?

stupid wat r u doin

Just some Stats homework. What are you doing?

bout to eat dinner. text you after

Alrighty, sounds good.

It's odd he didn't invite me over yet. Monday, Tuesday, Wednesday, he would have already invited me over by now. Give it a few minutes more, and we'd be sitting with his parents at that point, eating dinner.

6:17.

7:17.

Still nothing.

I text him.

Hoping you didn't choke on some chicken. You alive?

8:17

9:17

10:17

A whopping nothing, and I go to bed anxious.

Finally, at 7:13 this morning, a text from Kolton pings through my phone.

sorry i fell asleep.

My stomach flips upside down with relief as I reply.

No worries.

I thought…I don't know what I thought, but I'm relieved. That was odd, not hearing back from him, since he typically texts back at the speed of light and always wants to know what I'm doing. But he's back. He just fell asleep. No big deal.

I'm here, and he's still here.

We're on.

Later in the day, I'm in Yearbook class chatting away with Shayla. Shayla's a year older, and we're not super close anymore, but we were on the dance team together during my sophomore year. We're still acquaintants, and we run in the same party circles.

"Are you going to the basketball game tonight?" she asks.

"Probably, what about you?" I return.

"Duh."

"'Kay, well if I go, I'll probably drive with Didi, Aslyn, and Britney, so let me know if you need a ride."

"'Kay, I will."

"And oh, girl. *Speaking* of basketball, guess what?" I gush.

Shayla's eyes perk up. Nothing like some gossip to get a high-school girl all wide-eyed and giddy, especially if the piece of information might lend itself to boy talk.

"Ohmygod what?" She's all toothy smiled and giggly.

"So. Were you at Aslyn's party last weekend? I think you were. Anyway, Kolton's been harassing me party after party, and finally I hung out with him after Aslyn's party last weekend, and we've literally been talking and hanging out every day since. Well, except last night, but every—"

I stop mid-delivery because Shayla's face isn't all toothy smiled and giggly anymore. She's shifted to a look of apprehension, and I can barely contain myself, my stomach already tying up in knots.

"What!?" I demand.

"Girl, Jackie was at Kolton's last night."

"What do you mean? Jackie Haster? From volleyball?"

"Yeah, I was just talking to her at lunch. I guess they've been talking for a little while now."

"Dude, what the…" I practically spit.

"I'm so sorry. He's honestly an asshole. Don't even let it get you down. Screw him."

I immediately shoot off a text to Kolton.

Sleeping last night? Didn't know sleeping was code for screwing Jackie.

wat r u talkin about? who said that?

Doesn't matter. So it's true?

no it's not. dont be stupid.

Don't ever talk to me again.

wtf. ur so stupid for believing everything u hear. i was asleep

My stomach keeps dropping like I'm riding the Supreme Scream ride at Knott's Berry Farm—straight down, free falling. Except this isn't fun. And rather than the rollercoaster debriefing and bouncing gently up and down until the ride slows, the drop in my stomach reaches on endlessly.

When I don't respond to Kolton's text, he calls.

I ignore it.

He calls a second time, then a third.

And a fourth, then a fifth.
With each ignored call, I feel the slightest degree better.

Every weekend is pretty much the same.

Before every party, the girls and I stick together. We get ready together, pre-game together, and arrive together.

During every party, we disperse. All seeking something different to fill us up. Drugs. More alcohol. Thrills. Trouble. Attention.

After every party, it's a toss-up. Sometimes, we reunite and find a ride back to one of our houses. Sometimes, we just go home alone. Sometimes, we adventure to another party. Sometimes, we post up overnight at a dude's house.

Every-beezy-for-themselves kind of rules.

This weekend, we're getting ready at my house.

"Oh Joooooo-jooooo!" Didi sing-songs my name, announcing their arrival.

Aslyn walks into my room and throws her bags on the ground. "I gotta pee like a motha fucka." She storms away for the bathroom.

In middle school, before we were friends, I remembered Aslyn as the girl who printed her crush's name on the inside of her bra. She was also known for having a dildo and was rumored to have already lost her virginity. All the while I was busy being self-righteous with things like vowing to never drink or smoke, and winning *Most Likely to Succeed*. As student government secretary, I also spoke at our eighth-grade graduation.

We gained common ground the summer before freshman year when we both made the cheer squad. Despite both of our brown hair, brown eyes, beaming faces, and big personalities, we had enough differences to complement each other and quickly became best friends.

Aslyn introduced me to new songs like "Rainbowarriors" by CocoRosie, taught me how to brighten the corners of my eyes with glitter, and took me to get my eyebrows waxed and shaped for the first time.

I organized and renamed all the songs she'd downloaded for free in her iTunes music library, secured us our first joint babysitting job, and inspired her to journal more.

That was the first summer after my mom had moved out. My dad worked full-time, so I often got a ride to cheer practice from Aslyn's mom. With two-a-day practices, I ended up spending a lot of time at Aslyn's house.

"Where's Britney?" I ask Didi.

"Said she had to do the dishes so her mom would give her twenty bucks. She's coming after."

"Twenty bucks for dishes? Seriously? Must be nice," I scoff.

I shouldn't be surprised. Britney and I have been friends since elementary school, and her parents, although kind and well-meaning, have always semi-coddled her. She's the only one in our group who still has a normal family intact. The rest of us all live with just one of our parents and varying degrees of dysfunction in our homes. Despite her stable home life, Britney hates her body enough to feel troubled, so I guess that's reason enough to secure her spot in the group.

"What do you expect, Jojo?" Didi laughs and rolls her eyes, always laughing and rolling her eyes. I envy it. Seems so simple, not caring about much.

"Is Emily coming?" I ask.

"Ugh, you mean the other half of the anorexic duo? Perfect," Aslyn interrupts, walking back in from the bathroom.

It's true. Emily and Britney are both impossibly skinny.

Originally, it was *Aslyn* and Britney who bonded over their desire to lose weight. Out of all our girlfriends, Aslyn has the most attitude, the biggest bite, and the second-prettiest face after Didi's. But she's always been self-conscious about her weight. Stumbling upon their shared desire to lose weight, her friendship with Britney deepened during sophomore year as they began experimenting with laxatives and carrying around diet journals to record things like their daily allowance of almonds.

While Aslyn remained much the same, Britney succeeded in losing weight, even though I didn't think she had any weight to lose.

By junior year, Britney brought Emily into the group, and Emily is just one of those naturally lanky girls. A few months ago, Britney started to complain about her weight, and when Emily tried to echo those complaints, Aslyn shut it all down real fast. "If you anorexic bitches want to talk about how fat you are, then go in another fucking room."

"I think Britney is picking her up before heading over," Didi says, laughing.

"What? You know it's true. Britney doesn't eat a thing. And since Emily's her anorexic minion, obvi she doesn't eat anything either," Aslyn continues.

"I don't think I could be that skinny if I tried," Didi responds neutrally.

"Ohhooo, what up ladies?" Jackson pops his head in. Jackson is my younger brother, my favorite. There are four kids in my family, and my older two brothers, Jason and Justin, were best buds growing up. When I came third and Jackson fourth, we naturally paired off, too.

Jason, Justin, and I all have brown hair and brown eyes. Jackson came into the world as a tow head, hair so blonde it was almost white, with hazel green eyes. His hair darkened to a dirty blonde as he got older. At fifteen years old, he's beginning to fine-tune his charisma.

When Jackson was born, I was only two. According to my mom, I used to tell everyone he was *my* baby. There's always been an unspoken alliance between us. That's not to say I didn't join Jason and Justin in teasing Jackson when we were younger. As the only blonde in the family, my older brothers and I used to tell him he must belong to another family until finally he got so upset that my parents intervened.

"*Obviously*, you belong with us, dummy. You, Dad, and I all have the exact same nose," I'd told him as I'd wrapped my arm around his neck, only to have him shove me away while he continued to pout, tears streaming down his face.

Our alliance also didn't keep him from joining Jason and Justin in rolling me up in blankets as entertaining torture, knowing full well I'm claustrophobic. I'd be hyperventilating, kicking and screaming under the weight of the blanket, and they'd just be howling with laughter, shouting, "Our little burrito!"

Shits and giggles aside, Jackson and I know we're on the same team.

"Jackson, nice hair. You just wake up from a nap or something, you little bum?" Didi gushes at him.

We all know Didi's the only reason Jackson stopped in. Who doesn't have a thing for Didi? Half black, half white, with macchiato-colored skin, C-cup boobs, a bangin' booty, and yet a slender, toned body—courtesy of playing soccer all her life—she's easily the most beautiful of our five friends. Plus, she has those kind of teeth that are big and wide, forming a full, perfect smile. It's as though her personality shines right through that smile of hers, putting everyone at ease and sparkling with the charm of an effortlessly exotic model.

Didi's cool because she doesn't try to be. Guys love her. Girls love her. And Aslyn's overly possessive of her because they've been best friends since kindergarten. This doesn't stop Aslyn from picking up additional BFF's along the way (myself included for a period of time), but god forbid she'd ever allow Didi to do the same. My brothers are no exception to Didi's allure.

"Believe it or not, Didi, it's not easy being this good lookin'. Need my beauty sleep," Jackson gushes back, all sleepy eyes and smiles.

I just shake my head, laugh, and roll my eyes, in perfect Didi-style.

"Ohhhh, please," Didi chuckles.

"Seriously, shut up," I laugh and tease back at Jackson.

"So, what are we doing tonight ladies?" Jackson doesn't miss a beat.

"Some party. Jackson, you have an extra cig?" Aslyn presses.

"All out. Need to get some, myself." He shakes his head.

I bet he's lying.

"Helllllllllurrrrrr!" Britney calls from the other side of the house, slamming the front door behind her.

Jackson leans outside my bedroom door to greet her. "What up, girls," he nods.

Britney and Emily pour into my room, and Emily holds up a handle of Smirnoff vodka. "Look what I brought!"

"What the hell? How'd you get that?" I spill excitedly.

"I asked my mom to buy it. Surprise treat!" she squeals, proud of herself.

"Nice." Aslyn takes the handle out of Emily's hands. "Did you bring chasers?"

"Oh no! I didn't even think about that," Emily's face falls.

"It's fine. We should have some Naked Juice in the fridge. My dad just went to Costco," I say.

Aslyn walks out of the room with the handle, not even bothering to throw a "thank you" Emily's way. Since Britney brought Emily into the fold, I've been apprehensive about her, myself, but I'm not as outwardly callous as Aslyn.

Emily is an only child and lives with her mom full-time. Her dad's in the picture, and although he's sweet and goofy, he's also aloof and flakey, one of those never-grow-up kind of adults. Emily's mom spends weekends at her boyfriend's place, so Emily often has an open house, which makes it perfect for pre-gaming and even comes in handy for small parties when nothing else is happening.

She has long, dark brown hair and stunning green eyes. A year younger than the rest of us, she's sweet and a little shy. I don't mind shy, but it gets lost in the crowd.

We enter the backyard party, and I instantly feel Kolton watching me. I ignore his persistent stares and strike up a pointless conversation with an acquaintance. Just to be talking, doing something, and avoid dealing with his unmoving stare.

He eventually makes his way over to my group of friends. Judging by his movement and mannerisms, I know he's already drunk. The group disperses here and there to greet newcomers streaming in, and now it's down to Britney, him, and me.

"I want to talk," he starts, smiling and optimistic.

"About what?" I'm glaring at him, and Britney starts to laugh between sips of her drink.

"Over there. I want to talk over there." He nods his head to the side of the yard.

"About what?" I say, a little meaner this time.

"Just come with me," he says, chuckling at my meanness.

"Um. No." I whip my head sharply to face Britney directly.

"Oh, come on now, you're not that mad," he says through a few more chuckles, unfazed by any
of my resistance.

He touches my arm in question—*how mad are you?*

When I look up at him through slanted eyes, he already knows. He knows we're safe. He knows I'm not mad enough. I don't know which language we're speaking, but we're speaking the same one. It's all action and reaction. Words don't carry their weight in our language. In fact, it's mostly the things we don't say that we mean the most.

Britney senses it, too, because she laughs again, rolls her eyes, and makes her way for another group, leaving Kolton and me to ourselves.

"Okay. So, what? What is it?" I demand.

"I miss you."

"Well, who wouldn't," I roll my eyes, taking a sip from my cup.

"I wanna start talking again."

"Tough shit."

"You don't mean that."

"I do."

"But you don't."

"I do. Plus, I don't trust you," I try instead.

"I'll prove it to you."

"Prove what? I don't *trust* you."

"Nah, nah, nah. I'll prove it to you."

"You're drunk."

"No, that's—okay, well, yee, I'm a little sipped. But that's not why I'm sayin' this."

"Sure," I dismiss, growing agitated, wanting so badly for what he's saying to be true but wanting to rip him apart if he screws me over again.

"I'm serious. I'll call you tomorrow and say the same thing."

"Whatever." I go to turn but he grabs my arm.

"Jordan—I mean it."

"Okay, I know. I heard you."

"So…?"

"So, nothing. I said whatever, like, we'll see."

He likes this answer because excitement pops through his eyes, and a smile breaks across his face. "Yeeeeeee," he concludes that part of the conversation, nodding his head up and down in approval. "Okay, but for real, I need you to come with me," he redirects.

"Where?"

"To the side-yard. I have to pee."

"What?! No!"

"No, come on. Just come wait on the other side of the fence. Real quick, come on."

"Why? I don't want to watch you pee."

"Just come with me. It'll take two seconds. Come on."

"Fine."

It's a big party, and no one is allowed inside the house for fear someone will steal something, break something, or pee on a rug. Fair enough. So off to the side-yard we go.

I wait around the corner, drinking my drink, replying to a few texts, when suddenly I hear a few stumbles and then a thud. I rush over to the other side of the fence and see a deck that drops off to the dirt below. Kolton tumbled off the side of it. As I try and quickly assess how hurt he is, he starts laughing. Clearly, he's fine.

"You're an idiot," I say, laughing myself.

"Oh maaaaaaan," he responds.

"How did you even do that?"

"Oh maaaaan," he repeats through laughter, stands up, and wipes the dirt off his pants.

I shake my head back and forth in response, laughing more.

"You can't tell anyone," he pretend-whispers through fits of giggles like we're five-year olds.

"Oh, please. I'm definitely telling the girls." I laugh all over again.

For the rest of the night, Kolton won't leave my side, or rather, won't let me leave his. He sits down and pulls me on his lap. When I motion to stand up, he playfully pulls me back down. I pretend I'm placating him, but by the third time, I motion to stand, just to feel him tug.

Just to know,
    if I push away, will he pull me back?

Does he want me here as much as I want to be here?
Will he hold me even if I pretend I don't want to be held?
   Love me.
      Show me.
      Prove it.

Kolton texted me earlier today, just like he said he would.
Nothing elaborate.
wats up?
Just with the girls at my house.
cool r u goin to Brookes?
Yep.
me too ☺
I don't mention it to the girls, but I'm excited to see Kolton again.
Excited to push when he pulls.

When all I've wanted to do since we stopped talking is neither to push nor to pull, but to sink. Back into his arms. Back into his life. Away from mine.

I wasn't about to do that when we left things the way we ended.

I'd look stupid to go back.

Doesn't mean I don't *want* to go back.

But finally. He's coming to me.

This I can work with.

The girls and I arrive at Brooke's party and settle into a circle of loose acquaintances, some of them Kolton's friends. I see Kolton in my peripheral. Without moving my eyes away from the group, I notice his leaf-green shirt approaching us.

It's my turn to drink, so I ask Britney to hold the caps of the Smirnoff handle and the liter of Sprite while I take chugs from each, wincing as the liquid fire scrapes my throat, burning all the way down to my belly. I take another swig of Sprite, chasing the burn. Then another chug of the vodka, followed up with two more bouts of Sprite. Before putting the caps back on, I raise both the handle and the liter up in the air, motioning to the group—*anyone else?*

Kolton closes in on the circle, inserting himself between Britney and me.

"S'cuse me ladies. I'll have some of that," he says with a smirk.

Aslyn's all over it. "Don't you have your own, Kolton?"

"Aslyn, how many times have you beezies drank our shit?"

Aslyn rolls her eyes dramatically but lets it go.

Kolton chugs from the Smirnoff handle with no chaser.

"Ughhhhh," I say, scowling at him. "Gross."

"That's how Slice gets down, baby." He smiles, blowing out an exaggerated exasperation from the alcohol.

My heart jumps at him calling me "baby." I ignore it, take the caps from Britney's hand, and busy myself with screwing them back on the bottles.

"You know, I could teach you a thing or two. Baby."

"Don't call me baby." I glare up at him.

"You're not?"

"No, I'm not."

"Will you be?"

"What? No."

"You don't want to be my baby?"

"You're bugging me."

We're not any louder than any other noise or person at the party, but we've engaged a few people's attention. Britney, Aslyn, and even a few of Kolton's friends keep glancing over to see if he's serious.

"You can't stay mad at me forever," he coos.

"I'm not mad."

"Not for long."

"What does that—"

But Britney interrupts our banter. "Oh my god, just ask her out already!"

Kolton turns to Britney, surprised we had a small audience. He doesn't say a word, just smiles, and looks back at me.

"Don't." I shake my head, but I'm laughing.

"What are you waiting for? Get on your knee and do it! Get this thing over with," Britney promotes further.

By now, we've caught everyone's attention in the circle, and although most people are still carrying along their conversations, the buzz has quieted as they all wait to see what Kolton will do next. This *is* Kolton, after all.

Bitches a plenty.

Bitch to none.

Unbelievably, he gets down on his knee. Britney starts with her shocked squeals and fits of giggly, drunken laughter, soon followed by the other girls. Kolton's friends turn the squeals to roars with punches to the arms, hands to mouths, cupping and amplifying their *ooooooohs* like they're at a football game.

I can barely hear Kolton's request through our audience.

"Will you be my girl?" he asks in earnest.

Don't get me wrong…

I know we'll be messy.
I know because of the way we began.
But I don't care.
I want him still.
The constant and pressing attention is enough for me.
>Above all else, I want that. Need it.
>I haven't found it anywhere else.
>That thick attention, so deep, it pulses and ticks.
>So relentless, it pulls when I push.
>Coming back again and again. Reliable.
>>Attention that's:
>>Constant.
>>Pressing.
>>Thick.
>>Relentless.
>>Reliable.
>>Just what I'm looking for.

Clean and healthy won't do it for me.
I need to know how much I'm needed, wanted.
>Even if it's going to be messy.

I give one last shake of my head, bursting into tired, amused giggles, and answer with one word.

"Fine."

Didi tosses her head back, making room for her laughter to fall freely. Britney smirks, joins in Didi's laughter, and concludes with closing commentary: "Idiots." Aslyn walks away, likely bored or in search of a cigarette. It only takes Tobi a second before he exercises his gift for gab and drops his gem: "Alright, I see you, Cupcake Kolton! I see you." Kolton's friends all roar in comradery.

The rest of the party forgets us, but I don't.

Just like last night, he insists I stay with him everywhere he goes.
>With him to this group of friends.
>With him to that group of friends.
>With him to drink.
>With him to pee by the curb.
>With him, with him, with him. Everywhere.
>>And it's everywhere I want to be. With him, with him, with him.

When the party gets rolled by the cops, I invite a few people back to my house so we can continue the fun. My dad's gone for the weekend. Britney's driving, and we already have a full car, so I tell Kolton to meet us at my place.

When Kolton arrives at my house, I take one look at the blood dripping from his head and scowl. "Dude. What happened!?"

"A fight with these fucking douche bags," he says, loopy in slur, feet stumbling.

"Come with me." I drag him inside the bathroom, dabbing gently at his head with a warm washcloth.

"Does that hurt?" I ask.

"No." His eyes glaze over, and sure enough, he's not wincing a bit.

I continue to prod gently at his head, assessing the damage. The bleeding stops and it doesn't look so bad.

"This shirt is bad luck," he says.

"This green one?"

"Yeah, the last time two times I wore it, things went bed. The last time was this party in Santa Ana. Me and the boys had to smash some cars 'cause these bitches gettin' too rowdy."

"You smashed girls' cars?" I say in disbelief.

"No, these douche bags. Guys, not bitches."

"You said bitches."

"This shirt is bad, bad luck, Man. I gotta' get home. I don't feel so good." His eyes are still in a

haze, like he's reporting this to himself and not to me.

"I'll drive you."

"Can you drive right now?"

"Can you?" I flip the question.

We walk out of the bathroom, and he's heading toward the front door while I quickly inform the girls that I'll be right back.

I drive him home, walk him inside, and tuck him into bed.

I use his bathroom to pee, and by the time I'm out, he's already asleep. I grab the navy-blue hand-towel from the bathroom and lift his head gently from the pillow, placing the towel beneath it in case the bleeding starts again. He doesn't even stir, already dizzied into a drunken slumber, mouth slightly open with heavy breaths.

I quietly close his bedroom door and turn around to run straight into his parents.

"Oh!" I jump, not expecting them.

"Oh, sorry, honey. Didn't mean to scare you. Is Kolton okay?" James asks, both he and Nancy looking so concerned.

I don't mean to, but I laugh slightly, surprised by their genuine, considerate concern.

"He's fine. He got in a little scuffle at the party we were at, came back to my house, and just wanted to be home. He was pretty tired. He's already asleep, totally good to go."

"Ahhh, okay, okay. What kind of scuffle?" Nancy asks.

"I left the party before it happened, so I'm not sure," I answer truthfully. I'm also afraid to get Kolton in any trouble.

"This wouldn't be his first fight. You can tell us what happened," James reassures gently.

"I don't know. By the time he got to my house, he just said he got in a fight. I helped clean up the blood around his head and then just took him here." I'm still shocked, not only by their concern, but by their patience and non-reaction to the fact that Kolton was fighting, bleeding. Shouldn't they be mad?

Part of me basks in the slight heroics of the situation—me, the good one, returning their son home safely.

Another part of me wants to drop to the floor, banging my head on the way down, so when they look at me with those tender, warm faces of careful concern, the concern would belong to me and not to Kolton. I want those two faces pinched together for *my* sake, for *my* wellbeing.

"I got to get back to my house. I still have friends over." I smile at them, moving to make my way outside.

"Oh, of course," James says. "Yes, yes. Thanks, honey. Thanks for bringing him home. You're so sweet to do that. Drive safely, okay?"

James pulls me into a tender hug, and after releasing me, Nancy does the same, echoing James' gratitude.

I drive home, tossing Kolton's words around in my head:

This shirt is bad luck.

This shirt is bad, bad luck, Man.

I think of luck.

I think of Kolton.

I think of Kolton's luck.

I think how luck may not live in that leaf-green shirt, but it certainly lives in Kolton.

    Luck.

    Lucky.

    Adopted.

    Into a family like *that*?

    Dropped into a home with James and Nancy's careful, concerned faces?

    Sounds pretty lucky to me.

Spring break has arrived.
It's Friday.
It's my birthday.
It's my day.

Kolton comes by as we're all getting ready to go out for my birthday dinner. He pulls up bearing gifts.

Pink roses; I told him those were my favorite.

Little black stud earrings; thoughtful of him, but in the literal sense.

He had to have given thought to these earrings.

Rewind about two weeks prior. I had walked into his room and placed my cellphone down on his bedside dresser. I noticed his black stud earrings and mentioned how I was so sad because I had just bought a pair of black stud earrings and lost them the first night I wore them.

Clearly, he took note of the conversation.

My stomach does that little flippy thing.

I smile, reach up, latch my arms around his neck, and thank him.

He leaves because it's just the girls for dinner. He'll meet up with us at the party.

I make all the girls wear fairy costumes with chunky stripper heels. Because it's my birthday, and because I like all things fairy, they oblige. After all our leotards are tucked tightly into our tutus, wings on our back, Aslyn does our makeup, thick glitter underneath our eyes, fake eyelashes, and topping us off with stick-on-jewels trickling from the outside corner of our eyes.

We look ridiculous, like we're dressed for Halloween even though it's the end of March.

Before dinner, I drive to our drug dealer's meeting spot. When Britney gets back in my car with the ecstasy pills, she says giddily, "Diamonds." That's our favorite part of picking up. Discovering which logo's been stamped on the pills—typically it's just a smiley face, but we've gotten stars, rockets, and now, for the first time, diamonds.

Britney distributes the pills. Didi is about to pop hers in her mouth when I scold, "What are you doing?! We have to go to dinner first!"

"They take forty-five minutes to kick in. We'll be fine."

"I already took mine, too," Britney chimes in.

I contemplate for a second, and then ask, "Should we even go to dinner?"

Aslyn, Didi, Britney, and Emily answer in unison, "No."

We take our pills, skip dinner, drive to the party, park, and pass around a bottle of Smirnoff until it's time to get out.

The ecstasy makes me extra anxious for Kolton to arrive.

Waiting, waiting, waiting.

Text, text, text.

Call him. Call him again. Call him one last time.

Everyone's partying in the tennis court, and the drugs start to kick in, so I grab Britney and tell her we should go lie down and look at the night sky. She happily agrees. We lie down on our backs, link arms with each other, and tuck our knees into ourselves. We begin rocking back and forth, grinding our teeth, talking way too fast, and laughing all too loud.

But it's a party, and the music's loud, and people are drunk, so as long as we're not wildly obvious, no one's to be the wiser. Not that it'd be a huge deal. But people get judgey about drugs.

"I think I'm in love with Kolton." I giggle.

"You *think*?" Britney asks sarcastically.

"Well, it's weird. He's so weird. He's always texting me, asking me what I'm doing. But it never bothers me, you know? Sometimes when people do that, it's annoying. And creepy. And clingy. And then you're like blehhhh, over it, you know? But with Kolton, it's different. It's weird. Maybe I'm weird. I don't know, I just like him a lot." I'm talking a million miles a minute.

"Pahahahah, I can't believe he asked you out. On his knee. In front of everyone! Kid likes *you*, that's for sure," Britney comments.

"Dude, I couldn't believe that either. I know I tried to act like I didn't care, but I definitely cared. My stomach flip-flopped, even through the alcohol. I just really like him," I continue to spill.

"Well, duh. You think we didn't pick up on that? We all know you really like him. Please," Britney teases.

"Oh my god. Britney. Watch this!" I exclaim as I discover how fast I can move all five of my fingers, back and forth, back and forth, almost like there's ten fingers on one hand, because they're moving back and forth so quickly.

Britney bursts into laughter, and pulls my hand down towards our chests—"Dude, don't be obvious"—but she's giggling more than scolding, and by now, I'm squealing in my laughter.

We laugh some more, rocking ourselves back and forth.

Aslyn, Didi, and Emily hear our laughter and come lie down on either side of us.

"What are you bitches doing?" Aslyn asks, but she says it through a smile and a giggle of her own. She's in one of her good moods, albeit ecstasy-induced.

"Rocking," Britney says.

"And rolling," I add.

The five of us burst into laughter like we were the only ones at the party. For a few minutes, that's the way it feels. Just rocking and rolling, looking up at the night sky in the middle of a tennis court, tuning out everyone around us.

Woop. Except those people.

That's Kolton. And friends.

I jump up, heading straight for him, wrapping him in a huge hug.

"I'm so happy you're here," I gush.

"Oh yeah?" He pulls away slowly, slightly amused. I'm not typically so upfront, especially in public. As we separate from our embrace, I look up at him lovingly.

"Yes." I giggle.

He just shakes his head up and down slowly, a gentle smile.

I can tell he's already drunk, and he can tell I'm already rolling.

After an hour or so of shooting the shit, my friends with his, his friends with mine, we all grow bored and decide to take a field trip to another party. Tonight, being the kick-off to spring break, there are plenty of options.

First, we make a pit stop at In-N-Out. Between my friends and his, we monopolize the outside tables. I'm not hungry, but I wait patiently as Kolton and the guys devour their food.

Kolton looks up at me. "What are those dot things by your eyes?"

I smile expectantly. "My jewels? Aslyn put them on for us."

"Fancy pizazz for the birthday betch," Aslyn adds with a smirk.

"I don't like them," Kolton responds.

My smile melts, and I feel like I'm going to cry.

"You should take them off," he continues between bites of his three-by-three burger.

I hurriedly take them off without another word.

At the next party, I keep making attempts to be near him, just to be around him, but he's preoccupied with beer-pong.

I settle for a chair near the beer pong table. Matt, one of Kolton's best friends, is sitting in the chair next to mine.

He makes small talk. "So, are you and Kolton, like, a thing?"

"Yeah, since last week. He asked me out," I offer.

"That's cool."

"Yep. What about you and Courtney? I always see you guys together…"

"I don't know. We're good friends. She's chill, one of my best friends, helps me through shit, you know?"

"Yeah, no, I know what you're saying."

"Yeah, like when my dad died, she was there through everything."

"I'm sorry to hear that." Not-so-small talk after all.

"It's fine. He just—" he says as he forms his hand in the shape of a gun, pretending to pull the trigger and shoot himself in the head, implying his dad killed himself.

My heart catches a beat, and I take in his face, his features, his words.

I reach my hand out to softly and quickly pat his knee. "I'm so sorry, Matt."

"No, no, it's all good. Happens." He shrugs it off.

Even after Matt leaves, I remain in the chair, observing the beer-pong game.

After ten minutes, Kolton finally comes towards me.

I grow excited, eager for his attention.

He smirks. "So you and Matt, eh?"

My smile melts for the second time tonight.

"Fuck you," I growl at him.

He doesn't even flinch at my foul mouth. Instead, he chuckles as if he's amused, takes another sip of his beer, and strolls back to the beer-pong table toward a group of his friends.

Nights like this, he's hard to love.

Spring break means nonsense every night, and tonight is no exception, despite it being a Wednesday. We're headed to Matt's for a small gathering of shits and gigs.

In the car, Britney grabs the auxiliary cord to put her music on. "I got a good one," she boasts.

Dolla's "I'm Fucked Up" lyrics fill the car.

"Ohhhhh, Britney, this one *is* a goodie," Didi giggles, feeling the song, feeling her buzz, feeling herself, nodding her head in circles.

I like the song, too. I glance at Aslyn sitting in the passenger side. Looking out the window, I see her nod her head slightly. Another few seconds go by, and seeing as she hasn't ripped Britney's phone from the auxiliary cord, putting on her own music, I decide she probably likes the song, too.

"Ahhh, here comes the best part. Kitty caaaaat!" Britney yells from the backseat.

If we liked the song before, we *love* it now. Any mention of kitty cats and we're about it. Why? I don't know. Because we're a bunch of unruly girls, thinking ourselves different, special, fierce, bratty, loving attention but only on our terms.

Kitty cats.

We get to Matt's and walk into the open garage. There are about ten people meandering around, yelling above the blaring music, talking smack, passing around a joint.

Aslyn gets straight to business, locating a ripped-open plastic bag of red SOLO cups sitting on a random tool box in the corner of the garage. Emily's holding the handle, so Aslyn pulls her along to the back of the garage. Didi's hugging some of the guys, already laughing and rolling her eyes. I make my way to trail behind Aslyn and Emily—follow the drinks.

We open the handle of Smirnoff once more, half-empty now from our pre-game at my house, and make some crude mixed drinks, sloshing together the vodka with some Sprite from an open liter sitting next to the bag of SOLO cups.

Kolton stumbles into the garage from inside the house.

"Look who made it," he smiles, all googly-eyed and sipped up.

"Where were you?" I ask, sipping on my drink, wanting to catch up immediately.

"Had to pee, baby. What you sippin' on over there?" he smiles.

I shrug and extend the cup for him to try.

He takes the cup, gives it a sniff, and dramatically juts his face backwards, gritting his teeth, "Ohhhhh no. No, no, baby. Not the business. That's all you," he laughs.

I shrug again and down another chug.

"Kolton, you got a cig?" Aslyn bumps in.

"Nahhhh. Ooooooh, we should go get some," he looks at me expectantly.

"I'm not driving," I shake my head.

"Matt! Let's take a joy ride, Bruh. Ciggy time!" He smiles, places a pretend-cigarette to his mouth, giggles expectantly, and stares at Matt with wide eyes, like a small child.

"I like your thinking." Matt nods his head slowly, a stupid smile spread across his face.

We pile in Matt's car, headed for the liquor store around the corner. Aslyn and Kolton want cigarettes. Matt likes joy rides. I go because Kolton's going, and Britney joins because she wants a chaser that isn't carbonated. That girl will drink straight volumes of vodka—complete poison—but won't drink carbonated liquids? Beats me. I overthink a lot of things, but not my liquids.

Inside the liquor store, Britney starts busting up.

The world in slow motion with drunken stupor, I look at Britney, trying to figure out what's so funny. She keeps pointing at Kolton and laughing, not able to string any words together.

I look over at Kolton, who's wearing a pair of thick, cheap, black-framed sunglasses. I have no idea where he got them or when he put them on, but one of the lens is missing and he looks ridiculous. Nonetheless, he's all sipped up and feeling himself, lightly singing, "I wear my stunna glasses at night," and rowdily wrapping his arms around Matt's neck, strutting through the liquor store like he owns the place.

"Fool, get off me." Matt shoves Kolton off, laughing all the same.

Unfazed, Kolton keeps singing, this time raising both arms in front of him, palms up toward the ceiling like he's jeering a crowd to get rowdy, just like the first time he sat beside me on Aslyn's countertop a few months back.

"Hey, Stunnaman," Aslyn chirps. "You're missing a lens."

Kolton pauses, takes the sunglasses off his face, examines them in his hands, realizing for the first time that he is, indeed, missing one lens. He machine-gun chuckles, dons the stunna shades once more, ends the conversation: "Yeeeeee. I still look good though." He continues singing, "I wear my stunna glasses at night."

Nights like this, he's easy to love.

MAY 10, 2009,
Mother's Day & other sorts of flowers.

Kolton and I wake up slowly. He looks at his phone and says, "It's Mother's Day. I gotta get my mom flowers. Can you drive?"

"Sure."

Once back from Alberton's with flowers in hand, we walk through the back door, immediately greeted by the smell of bacon and crepes. James and Nancy are busy at work in the kitchen, and Neil Diamond's "Play Me" pours through the entire living room, spilling into the kitchen.

"Happy Mother's Day, Beans," Kolton says as he envelops Nancy in a hug from behind, swooping his arms in front of her to reveal the flowers.

James looks at me and smiles. I'm guessing his dad texted him this morning with these exact instructions, but nonetheless, Nancy is delighted.

"These are beautiful! Thanks, Bug."

"Happy Mother's Day, Nancy," I say and hug her after Kolton's released her from his embrace.

"Aww, thank you, honey. You guys hungry? Sit down, sit down. We're about ready to eat here."

"Always," Kolton answers for both of us, and discreetly grabs my butt as he passes behind me to sit at one of the barstools.

I shoot him a look, but he just smiles back innocently and giggles quietly.

Nancy and James continue flipping crepes and taking bacon strips off the oil, chatting away.

I sit beside Kolton and ask quietly, "Bug?"

"From when I was little. I guess I used to curl up like a little bug when I'd fall asleep. So, it stuck," he explains.

I laugh before digging into the next one. "And Beans?"

I don't hear his answer, though, because I'm distracted by James quietly pulling Nancy away from the stovetop, retrieving a little box out of his back pocket, handing it to her, and unfolding his hand to reveal three words scribbled in bold, black Sharpie with a period of certainty: *I love you.* I have never seen a more endearing Mother's Day card.

"Wait, what'd you say?" I turn back to Kolton.

"She farts a lot after she eats beans. She earned that one," he explains matter-of-factly.

Somehow, his plain delivery makes this even funnier, and I burst into a fit of laughter.

"What are you two trouble makers doing over there?" Nancy smiles into the conversation.

"Nothing, Beans. Just telling Jojo how hard you worked to earn your nickname," Kolton answers.

I slap Kolton's knee gently, anticipating Nancy's embarrassment, but she just laughs loudly, and says without the slightest hint of shame, "Oh, it's true, honey."

James chuckles softly at that and looks at Nancy with what can only be described as adoration and pride, and the four of us continue cracking up until it's time to eat.

Kolton eats quickly and excuses himself to go play *Call of Duty*. I hang back, continue chatting with Nancy and James, and help them wash the dishes after we're all done eating.

I soak up as much of their doting attention as possible, and an hour passes easily before I excuse myself back to Kolton's room, thanking them for breakfast.

I walk into Kolton's room, and he grants me a one-second glance. "Hey, baby."

"Hiiiii," I respond.

I sit on his bed behind him, wrap my arms around his waist, and gently kiss his neck. He immediately juts his right shoulder up to protect his neck from the tickling sensation, but I've got his attention.

He pauses his *Call of Duty* game and turns around with a smile.

I lean back, away from his face, matching his coy smile, knowing full well what's on his mind. "Play your game," I instruct coyly.

I slide off the bed and grab *The Thief Lord* from Kolton's bookshelf. I doubt he's read any of the books lining these shelves. I'm sure his parents put them up for display, and *The Thief Lord* is the only title I recognize. Any time Kolton chooses *Call of Duty* over me, I pick up where I left off.

So I'm about three-fourths into the book.

Kolton's watching me, his game still paused, and I can see his brain churning.

Call of Duty or Jordan?

That is the question.

I curl up with my back against one of his pillows, pretending I have no idea he's on the verge of paying undivided attention to me.

He un-pauses his game, and he, too, pretends like he was never on the verge of paying undivided attention to me.

"Kids, we're going to run some errands! We'll be back in a few hours!" Nancy shouts from the direction of the back door.

"'Kay, we're out of cran-grape, Beans! Can you guys get more?"

"Sure! Bye!"

About three minutes later, Kolton turns off his game, switches the screen to Spike TV, and nonchalantly comes to lie down on the bed right next to me.

I keep my eyes on the pages.

Another minute passes, and he suddenly rolls his body toward me, his face intently looking at me, patiently and expectantly. Undivided attention is always on his time.

I first shift my eyes down to the left to look at him, then turn my head slightly to follow my eyes, giving him a once over. I raise my eyebrows in question, "Yes?"

He doesn't say anything. He just takes *The Thief Lord* out of my hands, tosses it on the ground, and firmly pulls me down from my sitting position, and into his arms, shifting our bodies to run parallel.

"You lost the page I was reading!" I pout aimlessly.

He's not listening, and I'm not actually pouting.

I was merely filling the space.

He has the best lips, the sweetest taste, and he's giving me my favorite kisses—

> full, slow, controlled kisses on the mouth;
> gentle, light, almost ticklish kisses on my neck, all the way up to my ear;
> then runs just the tip of his tongue from my ear back down the side of my neck,
> so slow, it raises prickles on the entire left side of my body.

Then he pulls me into him even closer, his hands hugging the dipping curve where my lower back meets my butt. We continue as such, and like routine, he unbuttons my shorts, sliding both them and my underwear off simultaneously—so efficient. I pull his basketball shorts down his thighs with my hands until they're far enough down that I can link my feet into the waistband, pushing them down and off his body.

We don't even break our kisses.

Shirts are always a little trickier, so we just handle those ourselves. I break away, quickly pulling mine up and over my head, and he sits up to do the same.

Also routine, after about ten minutes of all this body-to-body, Kolton tries to poke the tip of himself inside me, and, as always, I thrust my butt backward, away from him. "No."

He continues to kiss me, pulling my body back toward his until I can feel the heat moving between us in tingling waves once more.

Kolton tries again.

I thrust my butt backward, away from him. "No…" I say, a little more dragged out this time, a little more like a "maybe" than a solid "no."

Two minutes later, Kolton tries again.

This time, I just don't stop him.

From day one, Kolton has always wanted sex. He's tried. Countless, countless times. And I've resisted. I've explained that I'm a virgin, but I get the feeling he doesn't believe that. I'm seventeen, and most of my friends have already had sex. I'm not holding out for any particular reason. My parents raised me as a Christian, and when I was eleven, my mom and I went away on a "special" weekend getaway, just the two of us. She explained the details of how it all goes down. She lit a match that quickly burned out, explaining how virginity is just like that flame—once it burns out, it's gone.

Whatever.

That's not why I've held out. I'm *terrified* of sex. Some big, scary penis inside my precious little vagina. I heard it's painful. I heard you don't even enjoy it the first time if you're the girl. I heard you *bleed*!

Despite all my past rejections, though, Kolton never stopped trying.

And today, it finally happened.

I know *exactly* how the "first time" is supposed to go down:
> She's hesitant (because it's her first time).
> He's warmly reassuring (because he's already slept with like ten girls; this isn't his first rodeo).
> She says, "I'm nervous," but looks into his face lovingly.

He says, "Don't be," and smiles back into hers.
Then they kiss.
It gets hotter and heavier.
And then it happens.
She's kind of in pain.
He's forcing himself to go slow.
It's so romantical (even though she bleeds, which is just weird and awkward).
They hold each other and kiss.
Yay.

Well. That's not how it was for us. After pausing to make him put a condom on, this is what actually happened:

She's hesitant (because it's her first time).
I wasn't exactly hesitant. He just stopped believing my "no" was genuinely a "no," and in all fairness, I stopped meaning it.
He's warmly reassuring (because he's already slept with like ten girls; this isn't his first rodeo).
Kolton's isn't reassuring with much, and sex happens to be no exception. And true, it wasn't his first rodeo. I have no idea how many girls Kolton's slept with before me, and I don't plan on asking.
She says, "I'm nervous," but looks into his face lovingly.
Actually, I just said, "No."
My body was clearly saying, "Yes. Maybe. Okay, yes."
And my face? Ha! Probably just looked into Kolton's face like, "I hope you know what you're doing, because I don't."
He says, "Don't be," and smiles back into her.
If he was smiling, I didn't notice. And it would have only been because he was finally getting what he wanted.
Then they kiss.
True.
It gets hotter and heavier.
I got hot because we were sweating against each other, and yeah, he's 180 pounds, so with him on top of me, he felt super heavy.
And then it happens.
Yep. It happened. We did it. Then he came. That's when it stopped happening.
She's kind of in pain.
Very much so.
He's forcing himself to go slow.

Sure, he went slow.

It's so romantical (even though she bleeds, which is just weird and awkward).

It was not romantical. Yes, I bled. Yes, I felt weird and awkward about that.

They hold each other and kiss.

After he flushed the bloody condom down the toilet and washed his hands, he did come and hold me. He kissed my forehead, my lips, and cuddled me underneath his arm. Undivided attention for giving it up. Fair trade, I guess.

Yay.

Yay?
I don't know.
Whatever.

JUNE 3, 2009,
high as high-school Prom.

High-school Prom.
Junior Prom, but nonetheless, Prom's Prom.
Here we go.
Hitting the golden hour, the lighting is perfect for pictures. We're all gathered around the man-made lake at Eisenhower Park. Our group consists of about thirty people, and little groups have split off here and there for a besties' pic, friends-since-elementary-school pic, and so forth.
I direct Kolton off to the side, where we take some couple pictures.
I walk without wait. I know Kolton likes to pause a beat before we parallel forward. He likes to watch the endless swish of my straightened hair, teasing to slap my butt in length, likes the thin dress-straps hanging from my shoulders, likes to notice the taut skin tug against my just-there calves, likes to hear the snappity-snap, clickity-clack of my heels kissing the concrete.
How do I know?
He told me.
In his own way, of course.
"Walk ahead, baby."
"Why?"
"So I can look at all *that*," he had explained as he circled his hands around in my direction.
All of this *taking-me-in* only requires a second or two, and then he presses to catch up with me. Together, we walk in stride. Our rhythm a mash-up of its own.

He walks with what appears to be a skip or a hop, like he's maneuvering his legs around a fire hydrant, like his dong's so big he won't allow his thighs to crush down upon it.

Slow and wide.

Gangsta walk.

    Face? Empty.

    Like a starless night.

I walk with hips like they're proving a point. Zigging to the left—quick, sharp, point, and zagging to the right, quick, sharp, point, and back to the left.

Brisk and acute.

Cat walk.

    Face? Inviting.

    Like a wink.

He placates me by allowing his mom to snap a few pictures of us, but he's getting restless, and when I go to look at the pictures his mom took, he bolts away to huddle up with Nick, Georgie, and Tobi.

Now that I've spent enough time with Kolton's friends, I've got their hierarchy down. Kolton leads, not because he actually possesses leadership qualities, but by measures of superficiality, he's the default. He has looks, mysterious charisma, natural athletic talent, and his family has money.

Tobi is Kolton's leading man. Like Kolton, Tobi also has family money and charisma, although his lure is more witty than mysterious. With white skin, black hair, brown eyes, and standing just under six feet tall, Tobi is attractive in a simple and almost familiar way. Tobi plays basketball too, although his skills don't compare to Kolton's abilities. Their mannerisms, sense of style, jokes, taste in music, hobbies, and attitude are almost identical, though.

One time, Kolton's friends and my friends were all drinking in Tobi's backyard while Tobi's parents were away. The guys were all drinking beer, and Tobi randomly started feeling nauseous. I started to tease him.

"You okay there, big guy? Two beers a lil' much for you, huh, Tobi?"

Kolton shocked me by protecting Tobi, shutting me right down. "Jordan, quiet," he had said in a clipped hush, followed by a firm shake of his head.

I knew then Tobi was the only one of their friends that Kolton saw as an equal.

Nick found his place in the group as the provocative clown. He constantly tests boundaries with his crude sense of humor.

Exhibit A: A group of five of us waited to place our orders at In-N-Out during the lunch rush, surrounded by at least twenty people eating or waiting for their food, and Nick shouted:

"*What!?* You had sex with your *cousin!?* Jordan, that's disgusting! Why would you tell me that?"

Subsequently, everyone inside the joint turned to stare at us, and I turned blazing red. I glared at Nick and punched him in the arm.

"Hilarious."

"Oh, come on. It's just a joke, Jordan. Lighten up."

And Georgie.

Georgie didn't have the same luck as Kolton and Tobi with his home life. I don't know much about his upbringing other than he was raised by and still lives with his aunt and uncle. Whenever a kid grows up with relatives, there's always a backstory. They live out in the canyon, a secluded area that feels like a small mountain town about twenty minutes away from Orange.

Georgie has straw-blonde hair, blue eyes, and white, almost pinkish skin. Even though all of our friends drink unhealthy amounts, it's clear Georgie has a real drinking problem. For the most part, he keeps up with Kolton and Tobi's cool-guy antics, but for anyone paying attention, Georgie's vulnerability is evident.

Georgie's number one is Tobi.

But Tobi's number one is Kolton.

Now that Kolton's already ditched me for his friends, I go find my own.

I make my way through the mass of people, plucking my girls away one by one, pulling them aside for our own bestie pic—Aslyn, Didi, Britney, and me.

We pose this way and that, the sun shining bright against our made-up faces and sequin dresses.

"Where'd Nick go?" Didi asks.

"With Kolton, Tobi, and Georgie. They went over the hill," I say, rearranging us for another photo, arms all propped on the side of our hips.

"Oh god—they couldn't wait? Jesus…" Didi scoffs, but the dramatic swoop of her hand and rolling of her eyes are accompanied by her big, perfect smile.

"I know," I say with exasperation.

Didi's amused. I'm actually annoyed.

You'd think the boys could at least wait until we poured back into the party bus, safely away from the parents, to start doing bumps of blow. Nope.

Britney got us our goodies for the night, some ecstasy. Two and a half pills for Didi and Aslyn, two for Britney, only one for me. I liked and didn't like ecstasy. I definitely couldn't take as much as the other girls. Even with just the one pill, I'd still get pretty bad anxiety. Makes sense.

Uppers heighten what already *is*.

And anxiety is always my *is*.

So, there's that.

But tonight's Prom, a special occasion. So, screw it.

In the party bus, the girls take their first pills. The thought of mixing school and partying stops my heart. Makes me nervous, and not in an excited way, so I wait until after the dance.

The venue for the dance is big, beautiful, and brightly colored. Kolton and a few of the other guys don't even come inside, so without dancing dates, the girls and I quickly grow bored. After thirty minutes, we're all back in the party bus.

Everyone accounted for, we head off to the canyon for the after-party.

Now, it's time.

Party time.

I take my pill and make myself a mixed drink. The girls' first pills have already kicked in and they're dancing around, hopping up and down the poll like idiots, Mac Dre's "Thizzle Dance" blasting throughout the party bus.

Kolton, Tobi, and Nick have been coked up for hours, but no matter. They each rotate between staying seated, high and satisfied, and getting up to do another bullet-bump in the bathroom.

Rotation in circles.
> Bullet bump in the bathroom.
> Sit back down, high and satisfied.
> Watch us girls, in our glitz and glam,
> our sequins and smiles, as satiating as the boys' high.
> Until it's not. Not enough. And they need more.
> And back up they go.
> Bullet bump in the bathroom.

Rotation in circles.

Thirty minutes in, and I'm definitely feeling it—that gush of serotonin, dopamine, norepinephrine. What a funny thing, the brain. Just release a few more chemicals up there, trap em' in the same area to ping around like kids piling into a jump-house, screaming with joy, happy as can be, faster, louder, more kids, more kids. More noise, more movement, more volume.

Jump. Jostle. Joy.

And uppers heighten what already *is*.

And anxiety is always my *is*.

But so is lovey-dovey affection.

That's my *is*, too.

I take turns dancing with the girls and stealing kisses from Kolton when he's seated in his sit-down, high and satisfied.

The tingle of my lips on his pricks his attention. He looks at me with a happy high. We lock loaded eyes for a second or two, the dopamine pouring out between blinks. It's only a second or two, just a second or two, but I'm so happy. I'm so fucking happy.

I break our contact and swirl back around to my friends, back to dancing. As I turn around, I take in the whole scene, as if in slow-motion. Everyone around me is so fucking happy. I'm so fucking happy.

We finally arrive in the canyon, and everyone shuffles around to jump out.

The girls take their second pill.

Kolton, Tobi, and Nick switch from bumps to lines around the coffee table.

A few hours go by, the night still going for those of us on uppers, leaving the drunkies to fall asleep one by one.

As people begin to drop and the vibrations of the party begin to mellow, I begin to feel my first

stroke of slight panic. This is the part I don't like. I don't like feeling up when the environment is going down. It feels misaligned to me, and when I can't force myself to match my environment, I feel out of control. And that's when the panic sneaks in.

I try not to think about the quieting party. Of the ten or so of us still awake, it's only the girls and me that are up-up, wanting to dance and move around. The boys' coke-bingeing has turned their *happy-high*, stale. Degraded it into a trance-like high, just numb. Barely there.

I nurse a mixed drink, but all I actually want is a little water and to keep dancing, keep moving.

With the panic creeping in, my anxiety ramps up, but so does my lovey-dovey affection. The lovey-dovey affection has taken on a different shape, though, fueled by an altered motive; it's not the *fucking-happy* of earlier, but rather something more elementary—a childlike impulse to be comforted, to be soothed, to be held. The impulse is now a living sensation in my body; pulsing like a heartbeat. It's excessive and feels like it's going to spill over. I need to dump it. I have to express and release this lovey-dovey need, and in turn be comforted, soothed, held.

Naturally, I seek out Kolton.

I'll lovey-dovey dump on him, and he'll comfort me, soothe me, hold me. And then it'll be fine. I'll be fine.

When I find him, he's sunken into a huge, brown La-Z Boy chair. His eyes are gazing straight ahead at absolutely nothing, his arms each glued separately to the puffed-up arm rests, his feet rooted firmly and squarely to the ground. Even with all four of his limbs planted down by gravity, he doesn't seem to be grounded, at least not here. Not in this living room, not in this house, not in the middle of the canyon on Prom night, not with me. He's not with me.

I try anyway.

"Koltooon," I gush, kind of kitten-like, as I crawl sideways into his lap, wrapping my arms around his neck. He doesn't say a word, doesn't move an inch of his body. He simply moves his eyes from inside their sockets to meet mine briefly, then shifts them back, continuing to look straight ahead into nothingness.

He's not comforting me, soothing me, or even holding me.

But he's not being mean, either.

He's not…doing anything.

Nothingness.

It's nothingness.

I'm sitting right on him, with the weight of me, but it's not enough.

Even with the weight of me, he's not grounded, he's not here.

    Not in this living room,
    not in this house,
    not in the middle of the canyon on Prom night,
    not with me.
    He's not with me.

Before a full-fledged panic attack strangles me from inside my mind and out, I jump off his lap and make my way toward the sound of Didi and Aslyn's laughter.

I find them outside in a bubbling Jacuzzi on the back porch.

I gulp up the distraction, instantly relieved in their company.

"When did this thing turn on?" I ask.

"I don't know, but it's hot. And feels amaze. Come in," Didi insists through a giggly smile.

"Jojo, I can see every single star. Every single one," Aslyn says with her head shot back at a ninety-degree angle, taking in the blanket of sky. Quite literally starry-eyed. I like Aslyn like this. Harmless, gentler, more loving. Granted, she's high, but I'll take what I can get. Aslyn wears her malice as thick as armor, but a few years of friendship have revealed her soft tenderness that sits close beneath the surface. I swear that's why we quarrel so much. She can't stand my sensitivity, can't understand why I'd wear it on my sleeve. I don't mean to, but all the same, I do. I think it reminds her of her own sensitivity, and she calls that weakness. I can hear her in my head sometimes: "Jordan, you can't dwell on things. You just have to get over it and move on." Depending on who her malice is directed at, it can be kind of funny, but I love her the most when her tender shows.

"I didn't bring a bathing suit," I say, startled.

"Who cares," Aslyn sings.

"Hmph." I shrug my shoulders and strip to my bra and underwear.

I climb in and think about how my strapless bra will be ruined by the chlorine water, but as the three of us girls begin to slowly swarm around the Jacuzzi in a slow, make-shift whirlpool, I echo Aslyn's words to myself. *Who cares...*

"Who cares," Didi says, as if reading my thoughts, supporting me, hearing my concerns about my bra.

"Whoooooooo cares," Aslyn sings again, this time drawing out the most beautiful *oooos* in who.

"Mmmm, who cares," I say again, comforting myself in the circular movement of our whirlpool, soothing myself in the repetition of the words on my tongue, and holding myself with the pressure of the surrounding water, warm and bubbling all around.

And who cares?

Who honestly cares?

Me.

Usually.

But not right now.

Not in this second.

Who. Honestly. Cares.

Who honestly cares?

It's 11:00 a.m. the next morning, and I care. That's who.

Shaded yellow rays of daylight tease through Kolton's bedroom blinds, mocking me, laughing at my *so-fucking-happy* and *who-honestly-cares* of last night.

I look over to check on Kolton, and, as expected, he's dead asleep.

We hitched a ride back from the canyon to Kolton's house around 4 a.m. Upon climbing into his bed, Kolton was out instantaneously, but I tossed and turned for a while, finally falling into an unpromising sleep.

And now it's 11 a.m., and I can't fall back asleep.

Of course, he's still sleeping like a baby.

His body like rubber.

Every poison, every emotion, every potential hang-up, every drug, every drip of alcohol—it all bounces right off of him. And he comes back from it all unfazed, unmoved, stunningly beautiful; charming and alluring as ever before.

Untouched.

He's untouchable.

As for me, I'm coming down quickly. The come-down always feels like this—a dull level of floating anxiety—anxiety that sits an inch off my skin, so if I'm not paying attention, I don't realize I'm anxious. But any movement causes me to bump into the suffocating bubble of floating peril.

I yearn for my depleted serotonin.

I yearn for more sleep.

Not happening.

I pull open my Statistics book and focus on finishing my homework assignment that's due tomorrow. I'm relieved of my floating doom for a bit. When I finish my homework, I glance at Kolton once more, and he's still sleeping. Peacefully. Absently.

I hear brief wafts of raspy laughter and exclamation coming from the vicinity of the backyard. I know the raspy laughter belongs to Nancy, but I can't tell who else is with her. Kolton's room doesn't feel comforting like it usually does. With his presence lost somewhere to his sleep, I feel alone and stifled in the room, the dull anxiety still floating around me. I'm craving interaction, so I wander out of his room, following Nancy's laughter.

The door leading to the backyard patio lies lazily half-open. I walk through it to find Nancy showcasing her new clothes to James and their son, Cyler. They all smile up at me, motioning for me to sit down with them around the patio table.

I've only met Cyler once before. He's a math major at UC Santa Cruz. He runs his hands through his hair, probably four inches long, the bright, bleach-blonde strands all hugged together, leaning and sticking up in whichever direction his hands lead. He reminds me of Andy Warhol, looks *and* mannerisms.

"Henry and I are in the middle of making a movie," Cyler explains as he clamps his hair between his hands, guiding it straight upward, leaving it to fall gently to the right like a wave.

"Oh. yeah? About what? And since when?" Nancy asks.

"Henry is Cyler's best friend," James quickly interjects for my benefit, answering the question I thought but didn't ask.

"Since last month, Mom. Duuuuuh," Cyler says in animated exaggeration, bursting into high-pitched giggles.

The high-pitched giggles and bizarre hair make me warm to Cyler in a safe, familiar way. Being around him feels easy and usual.

"*Right*, Cyler. Because you answer every one of our calls to keep us in the loop," Nancy pokes back, making a huge show of rolling her eyes, which makes James chuckle.

"Mom!" Cyler says coyly, in fake disbelief. "I answer *every* single one of your calls," he squeals before bursting into more high-pitched laughter.

Now the three of them are laughing, all in on the same inside joke. I can't help but laugh alongside them, quietly at first, not wanting to fully expose how desperately warm they're making me feel, not wanting to reveal just how much I wanted to be *right* here—outside on this backyard porch, cozied up in their company, the light breeze tickling our faces, and the rays of sunshine promising the nearness of summer.

I forget about Kolton for a bit.

Forget about Prom, drugs, anxiety bubbles, and depleted serotonin.

Lose track of who I'm actually with, and focus on the feeling instead.

The feeling of familiar, the feeling of easy, the feeling of usual.

Like home.

JUNE 12, 2009,
under the sun; wrestling restlessness.

Kolton texts me.
cum outside
Why?
just cum

It's fifth period. I'm in Yearbook class, and he's in the building directly across from me, in Computers. It's the second-to-last week of school. The yearbook has already been sent to print weeks ago, so the last few weeks of the year are a free-for-all.

There's a restless buzz in all the classrooms, kids itching to get out of class and into summer shenanigans. I've never liked the end of the school year. It makes me anxious, like I'm losing something. Is it the change I didn't like? Probably. Change typically means Disaster. And Disaster is something I learned I can't fix.

I've tried.

I've tried to fix Disaster.

Disaster takes many forms. Like, for instance, when my mom moved out. That was a disaster. And then the degradation of our dumpy house; that was another disaster.

    I tried to keep the dust bunnies out of corners.

               But they multiplied quicker than I could sweep them up. Between the dog hair, my hair, Justin's hair, Jason's hair, Jackson's hair, my dad's hair, our friends' hair, between all that hair, all that dust, all those particles shed behind, I just

couldn't keep up. Even when I was sweeping them up, the dust bunnies would somersault away airily as I continued to chase them with that black, hopeless, frayed, plastic broom. I swear I heard them giggling as they rolled away, mocking me.
I tried to keep the dishes out of the kitchen sink.

But with five of us left in the household, in addition to all my brothers' friends and my friends circling in and out, the dishes stacked up again rapidly. The rule was to at least rinse your dishes before putting them in the sink. The other rule was that each of us four kids had assigned days to do the dishes. Dad was barely home, so those rules weren't enforced. The boys frequently skipped their dish days, so the only time the dishes ended up getting done was when I grew so disgusted by them that I'd throw in some headphones and just have at it, the chunks of matted food seeming to grow larger by the week. Again, mocking me.

I tried to keep the dirty bathtub free from gunk.

But sure enough, again and again, it would grow grimy. Something was wrong with the drain, so by the time the water drained from a shower or a bath, the gunk grabbed the tub like that was its sole job. It grew so unmanageable, I eventually surrendered to keeping the shower curtain closed at all times, so I didn't have to see it. I moved my shampoo, conditioner, body wash, and razor to the blue bathroom by Justin and Jason's rooms.

My dad was a minimal presence in the house. In the past few years, he started going into the office again, but he didn't get home until late—eight, sometimes nine at night.

Dust bunnies, dishes, and dirty bathtubs fell to the bottom of the priority list.

I tried to keep the dust bunnies out of the corners.
I tried to keep the dishes out of the sink.
I tried to keep the dirty bathtub free from gunk.
I tried to *keep* the house.
I tried to be a house-*keeper*.
I sucked at it.

While my room was my sanctuary, everything in order, my bed neatly made every day, I admit I sucked at the house-keeping.

I was a room-keeper, but not a house-keeper.
I was a little, but not enough.

So yeah.

Change means Disaster.

And Disaster ate my house, so I'm not a fan.

Not a fan of change.

And yes, even though this end-of-the-school-year change also means summer, I'm not sure I'm a huge of fan of summer, either.

Summer is a big, wide-open runway of nothingness.

I don't know what to do with it.

Babysitting and my other part-time job will fill some of the free time, but not all of it.

I don't like all that time on my hands.

Don't know how to fill it with anything but parties.

Plus, it means more time stuck in our dumpy home.

??? Kolton texts me again, as I realize I haven't answered him.

I text him back:

Coming.

Everyone in class is gathered in little groups, chatting the time away, because there's nothing left to do for the yearbook. No one notices when I walk outside. The dry grass in the courtyard between buildings crunches beneath my sandals as I walk across to Kolton's classroom, blinking away the blinding sun.

"What are you fools doing in there?" he asks, as I wrap my arms around him.

"Nothing," I reply, still holding him in a hug. I don't typically hug him this long, especially at school.

"What's wrong?" He pulls back from me slightly to look at my face.

"Nothing," I reply again, looking back at him. I think he was expecting watery eyes, but my tear ducts are as dry as this summer heat. I don't cry. I imagine I just look blank.

"You're a bad liar," he teases, as I release him from the hug.

"It's hot out here," I say to take the attention off myself.

"What're you doing after school?" he asks.

"Nothing," I deliver my word-of-the-day once again.

"Gonna pick up later. You should drive us." He breaks into a manipulative smile. Kolton, Tobi *and* Matt all got DUIs this year.

"Oh, should I?" I ask with a drip of sarcasm.

"You said you're doing nothing!" he points out in false innocence.

"Which is still something," I respond, growing sloppy and apathetic in my argument. I don't have a good reason not to drive Kolton and his friends around to pick up weed. Besides the fact that I don't want to. But then I'd be doing nothing. And although nothing was something, it wasn't something I *liked*.

The bell rings, announcing the end of fifth period, and he looks at me once more, searching my face for a final answer.

"I'll call you after sixth period," I inform him neutrally.

Kids pour out of the classrooms, some calling it a day, some, like me, heading off to a sixth period, and others changing into their exercise clothes for after-school sports. The restlessness is alive and palpable—it's in the stomping of everyone's feet, the bumping of their backpacks, and the shrill yells of their comradery.

Even though Kolton and I are currently on good terms, the drama between us temporarily dried up, I still feel a heaviness I can't shake as I make my way against the swarm of people pouring out of class to get my backpack. It's weird. Nothing is wrong; nothing I can identify anyhow. I have no reason to feel the way I do. The sun is shining. Summer is just under two weeks away. People surround me. Kolton and I aren't even fighting. But I'm wrestling something. I'm wrestling something restless. Not the same as the surrounding restlessness of my peers, eagerly awaiting summer. Mine is different. Nothing, nowhere, and no one feels quite satisfying. I feel heavy with a dull, wide-open sadness and wiggly restlessness.

I don't want to sit still.
    But moving sounds exhausting.
I don't want to be at school.
    But being home is worse.
I don't want to be around Aslyn, Britney, Emily, or even Didi.
    But being with myself is unbearable.
I don't have anything to say to Kolton.
    But I don't want him to go away.
I don't want to talk to anyone.
    But silence is suffocating.

I don't feel like this all the time, but sometimes. And I hate when it happens. I can never quite put my finger on where it comes from, either. Almost like the feeling belongs to a long-lost phantom memory that dissolved as the years went on.

It feels like I'm missing something.
Or losing something.
I'm losing something.
The end of every school year.
Change.
Disaster.

Summer.

The school year is wrapping up, and that means change is near. I anticipate it with discomfort, not necessarily knowing what to do, what not to do. Not knowing if there *is* anything to do. Or if there is anything *not* to do.

I'm kind of just this little depressed ball of anxiety.

Feeling like I'm on the edge of losing something, threatening to pile on top of some phantom loss of the past, something I lost that I can't remember having in the first place.

When I feel like this, I cling closer to Kolton. Thank goodness we're getting along right now. Even though I don't want to drive him and his friends around to go pick up weed, I can't think of anything else to do. Plus, I want him near me. I never explain anything to him when I'm having one of my moods, but I'm sure he knows, because it's the only time I'm ever quiet. He knows I'm not the quiet type.

I text him after my sixth period.
I'll take you guys. Where are you?
awww, baby
...?
home. wen u cumin?
Now
bring ur bathing suit
Why?
I'm not in the mood for the pool.
jacuzzi after we blaze
That I can do.

I never smoke with them. Weed makes me feel slow, stupid, and sleepy. And hungry. The only setting it'd make sense for me to smoke and enjoy it is right before bed, with no pending responsibilities left to handle—definitely not in the early evening, while it's still light outside, and I'm tasked with driving people around.

Tobi, Nick, and Kolton are all taking turns passing around a joint in Matt's garage. I tolerate their hoots, hollers, and bad jokes by tuning them all out. When I think I'm going to burst from impatience, I catch Kolton's eye, giving him a flat stare to convey just how over this little rendezvous I am. He finally makes some moves to round up Tobi and Nick, so we can drop them off at home, and head back to his house by ourselves.

Driving home, Tobi and Nick yell just as loudly and obnoxiously as they did inside Matt's garage. They can't stop laughing at their own jokes, doubling over, and when Kolton notices my face going blank, he gently and quietly grabs my hand from the passenger seat. Tobi and Nick are so entrenched with each other, they don't even notice. Otherwise, I'm sure we would have been their new direction for banter.

I always want to hold Kolton's hand, but he's so finicky I tend to reserve the affectionate stuff for when no one's around, unless we're both unmistakably drunk. I keep my eyes on the road but steal a quick, sideways glance at him. I can still see him out of the corner of my eye as he looks at me calmly with hazy eyes. He's happily tucked away in some alternate state of mind; some happy, high place.

I don't mind that he's off somewhere else in his head, not all the way *with* me.

Holding my hand is enough.

Having him next to me in the passenger seat is enough.

Not being alone is enough.

We drop off the boys, and we're finally back at Kolton's house.

I follow him to the backyard as he turns a knob here and twists a lever there. The jacuzzi gently murmurs to life, bubbles jumping up at its perimeters.

We head back inside to wait while the jacuzzi warms up and change into our bathing suits. Kolton turns on the TV, and I cuddle up underneath his arm. He watches the TV. Piano streams through the TV as an NBA commercial proclaims *Where Amazing Happens*. Since it's a commercial, he focuses his attention down toward me as I look up at him. He places his hand on the small of my back and pulls me in ever so gently. I'm that much closer to him, and my heart quickens its pace. He expertly intertwines his lips with mine, and I become lost in all this, in all of him.

Half an hour goes by, and the jacuzzi awaits us.

We walk outside together, me carrying both our towels. Lights from inside the jacuzzi serve as the only source of light, save for a few stars tucked away in the night sky. The gurgling noises of the jets sound like a cheerful invitation to our own intimate party.

Bubbles are already caressing his body as I lower my own into the steaming water. He pulls me onto his lap, so that I'm straddling him, each of my legs separately tucked around his hips, leaving us head to head, faces inches away from one another. He holds my gaze.

"What?" I squint at him, "What're you thinkin' about?"

"You," he reports matter-of-factly.

"Such a sap," I tease dismissively as I playfully squeeze his cheeks together, because I don't know how else to react.

"My dad says you're a *catch*." He twists his tone around the delivery of the word *catch*. He's waiting to gauge my reaction. Kolton never says much, but he's always measuring. He listens, observes, learns, researches, and decides upon people. Constantly. He's constantly measuring.

"My dad says you're a *catch*." I think about his words and decide that his statement is premeditated. I'm guessing he's already leading me down a path. I love Kolton's dad. I melt in James' attention. Kolton relaying a compliment James spoke of me hits like a contact high—strong and potent enough to rock me, even delivered indirectly.

So, what does Kolton want in telling me this? What is he hoping I'll say? What is he hoping I'll do? Is he just trying to butter me up? If he wanted to butter me up, why wouldn't he just make up his own compliment? Why is he telling me about his dad's compliment? Is he that lazy?

He interrupts my runaway train-of-thoughts to elaborate.

"He says you're a catch because not only are you really pretty, but you're smart, too. And not all girls are both. *And* you're nice. Like, you're a *good girl*."

"Well, that was nice," I test neutrally.

"Well, I mean, yeah, but I already knew that," he immediately jumps in.

"Never said you didn't."

He doesn't answer again, and I wonder once more at his intentions in telling me this. It's as though he's contemplating the compliment himself—as though he's hearing it for the first time and realizing that I *am* pretty, smart, and nice—a *good* girl.

He begins looking me over in that measuring way of his, so I break eye contact because it feels too intense, too serious. But when I look back at him, his face is right where I left it, gazing directly at me. There's a layer of softness I didn't notice before.

In the softness of his eyes, I discover he could have offered up the compliment simply because he agrees. Both are possible. One never knows with Kolton.

I giggle again, softly place my hands on either side of his face, pull his head toward mine, and kiss him firmly. Our firm kiss turns hot and heavy, and when we finally take a breath, I wrap my arms around his neck, lying my head on my right forearm. He wraps his arms around my waist, and we sit there for a while, not saying anything, as I think about how I love him. I don't tell him, but I don't have to tell him. I know he knows.

Knows I love him for silly things, like being around when I'm in one of my moods, not asking me to explain those moods, holding my hand seconds before I'm about to lose all patience and tell his friends to shut up, understanding I'm a *good* girl, and wrapping his arms around me in a warm, bubbling jacuzzi.

Knows I'd probably love him for even less.

I know he knows.

He probably knew before I did.

For the minutes I'm loving him, the wide, dull sadness and wiggly restlessness quiet down a bit, making me forget about whatever it was I lost that I can't remember having in the first place.

Music picks up where words fall short:
["Summertime Sadness" by Lana Del Rey]

JULY 7, 2009,
home is where the beach is.

We pick up some pizza before finally arriving at Tobi's beach house in San Clemente. Whether I was invited along for company or the need for a driver who didn't have a DUI, I'm not sure. And I don't care. Any excuse to be near the beach, and I'm in.

Once inside, Tobi offers Kolton and me some beers and throws on a basketball game. A few minutes pass, and Kolton and Tobi begin hollering loudly at the TV as I sit in silence, quickly bored by the ball being passed rapidly back and forth between tall, sweaty boys. I stand up to let myself outside.

"Where you going?" Kolton pulls away from the game for a moment.

"The beach," I answer, closing the front door behind me.

I know Kolton won't follow, and I don't want him to. I want to explore the beach on my own. The sand is warm and exerts an evenly-distributed pressure along the bottoms of my feet, feeling almost like a massage. It never ceases to amaze me how different every beach feels. San Clemente is entirely new to me, even though it's still a west-coast, California beach, just thirty miles south of Newport Beach.

Newport Beach.

Even though I don't live there anymore, it's still my marker, my center, my hub; the point from which I measure other points.

I lived in Newport Beach until fourth grade, at which point my family moved to Orange. It was all rather exciting. The house we moved into was larger and sat on an acre of land.

Jason and Justin were fourteen and twelve at the time. For them, moving meant new schools to attend and new friends to impress with their big, new house.

Jackson was eight, and I was ten, so we zeroed in on the acre of land itself; our own personal playground. Trees to climb. Trails to trample. Rocks to unearth. The secret world of spiders and centipedes to reveal. There was so much adventure to be had quite literally in our own backyard.

My parents had their own ideas, hopes, and dreams invested in the move; becoming first-time homeowners, the promise of privacy with such a large piece of land, moving on up.

The potential.

I think that's what moving to Orange meant most to all of us: potential.

When my parents purchased the house, it was what my dad calls a "fixer-upper," meaning the house needed a lot of work. That was the plan.

What happened instead was a burst of progress when we first moved in, and then a slow, confusing nothing. I knew my life was changing little by little, but I mostly thought that's just how things were at that given age.

Not only did the rehab on the house putz-putz, then stall into nothingness, our family also stopped going to church on Sundays. Well, technically, my mom was the first to drop from the Sunday routine. I thought that was unfair. I never hated church, but I didn't necessarily like it. And if she didn't have to go, why did I?

I didn't know it then, but this was premonition of my life to come in the years that followed. A sneak peek. A preview. My mom missing from the picture entirely. Just me and the boys. My dad, Jason, Justin, Jackson, and me. The only girl. I had no idea what was coming.

That big, beautiful equestrian property in Orange. Long, curving driveway spilling into an acre of wide open land. No houses behinds ours—just a backyard with cacti, horse trails, and a dirt hill. A patch of nature, preserved despite the multitudes of nearby suburban tracks with uniform houses crowded close together.

Yes, all very exciting.

So much potential.

And yet, where everything crumbled apart.

Disaster ate our house in Orange, the plan to fix it never reaching fruition. When my mom moved out, I was twelve. Only two years after moving to Orange. I wouldn't discover, until about age fifteen, all the reasons why. Even when I found out, the details were scattered. Mismatched puzzle pieces. Some pieces missing altogether. There was never a firm, straight-forward conversation about what happened to our family.

An affair.

Drugs.

A restraining order.

All I know is we were one type of family when we lived in Newport Beach, and all the sudden, we were another type of family when we moved to Orange.

I was left disoriented.

I didn't know which way was up or down.

And my mom was gone.

In the same breath, I felt not enough for her, yet too much for my brothers and dad.

I was stunned.

I had always loved Newport, but when things fell short in Orange, the beach meant even more to me. It was the last place on our family map to feel safe, calm, and predictable. It beckoned to me like waves on the sand. Soothing in their reliably cyclical nature.

Come back, come back, come back.

Rise and crash, crash, crash.

Newport called to me the loudest, but it was other beaches, too. With sand that gives way to the pressure of your footprints, reassurance that you exist in every step, and the expansive, infinite view of the world beyond the water, the beach whispered of possibility, sanctuary, and peace.

Like this one right now. This San Clemente beach just beyond Tobi's house.

I feel my demeanor change in a subtle way as I dig my feet deeper in the warm sand and watch the waves crash on the shore again and again. It's times like this that I allow myself to love Kolton. I'm not on guard. I play out our future in my mind. We'd be together. We'd be happy. We're so different, but I don't think I'd ever want to be with someone just like me. I like how different he is. There are things I see in him that I want for myself, like the assurance that he's meant to be here. I used to feel like that, but not so much anymore. I admire his fearlessness, and dirty as it feels, I love his expression of anger. I'm angry at a lot of things, things I don't even know how to explain and worse, don't know how to express, say, let come out of my mouth.

I smile. He scowls.

School's my thing. Shenanigans are his.

I work part-time jobs in my free time. He works on getting high and enjoying his.

I push. He pulls.

But, put us together, and we actually make a little sense.

There's balance.

At least, that's what I tell myself in these moments of quiet calm, when I allow myself to love him. I tell myself we're working on balancing one another, and that it's a beautiful thing. Together, I make myself believe we can create an entirely new sound, something magnetic and unexpected.

A perfect paradox.

Like Eminem and Rihanna's "Love The Way You Lie."

Like Biggie Smalls and The XX's "Juicy vs. The Intro."

Like Mac Dre, Cutthroat Committee and Joni Mitchells' "Song For You."

JULY 9–12, 2009,
heatstroke strikes; again and again and again.

Britney squeaks out giggles in the passenger seat beside me as I blast down Imperial Highway, trying to figure out where we're going. I call Kolton back, asking for an actual address or something, but he doesn't answer. Of course. He said to pick him up at the Great Western off of Imperial, but I have no idea how far down the road it is.

Britney continues to giggle and changes the song on my iPod.

I eventually see the Great Western sign popping up on my right-hand side, and as I near closer, I pull into the driveway. The parking lot hugs the rows of hotel rooms with outside entries.

I call Kolton once more, and he finally answers.

"Hey, hey, baby." I can practically hear his drunken smile through the phone.

"I'm here. Which room are you guys in?"

"Just pull around the corner of the parking lot. I'm outside with Nick."

When I zoom around the corner to see Kolton and Nick smoking cigarettes, Kolton instructs me to park.

"Why? We're leaving," I say.

"Just a second, baby. Just park," he insists.

Reluctantly, I park. Britney and I get out of the car and make our way toward the hotel room.

Once inside, I see an additional five of Kolton's friends, and they're all passing around a bottle of Hennessey.

Kolton takes a swig, bums a cigarette from Tobi, and proclaims he's ready to go.

"You're not smoking that in my car," I warn.

"I know baby." He swoops me up from behind and spins me around as I squeal and insist he put me back down.

Britney gets in the front seat, and Kolton situates himself in the back-middle seat. As I begin driving again, he starts poking his head between Britney and me like a little kid.

Then he grabs the auxiliary cord, shoves in his iPhone and plays Mac Dre's "All I Want to Do."

Kolton's singing along, and he's on a good one tonight. He continues to sing, bobbing his head, and when I turn the music down just a tad so I can hear Britney's question—"Can you drop me off first?"—I can barely hear myself respond, "Yeah, that's what I was planning to do," because Kolton is reaching over the center counsel, turning the music back up and drowning out my answer.

"Kolton, knock it off! I'm trying to hear her!"

Not even the slightest bit fazed by my reprimands, he hits pause on his iPhone, silencing the car entirely. "Here you go, baby."

"Well, you can turn it back on now because we're done, but I couldn't hear her."

"Baby, you're not dropping me off," he abruptly redirects the conversation as he turns the music back on but at a slightly lower volume.

"Yes, I am. I'm taking you home after I drop Britney off. That's what you asked me to do…?"

"Nah, baby, you're stayin' with me."

"I can't. I have work in the morning."

"What the hell is going on?" Kolton says in the strangest, funniest way, hitting a high pitch with the last word "on," and delivered quickly, almost slammed together.

I know he's trying to be funny, and I hesitate to even respond as I try to prevent a smile from peeking its way through. I just shake my head slightly. Britney starts busting up.

"Whaaaaat?" she squeals in encouragement.

And like a child reeling from a parent's glorious attention, Kolton takes Britney's question as an encore request, repeating the question in his off-beat-cartoon-like tone, basking in the glory of his now entertained audience. "What the hell is going on?"

He continues, "Guys, seriously. What the hell is going on?"

Both Britney and I are cracking up as we pull in front of her house, forgetting momentarily how annoying and rude and selfish Kolton is.

Britney walks inside, laughing as Kolton pokes his head out the window to call after her: "Britney! What the hell is going on?"

"You are something else," I wonder out loud.

"That's why you *loooove* me," he informs me, drawing out the "love" as he pulls his head back inside the car.

It's true.

"Shut up," I respond instead.

"But for real, you have to stay with me, baby. My parents are making me go to a dinner party with them, and I need you to drive."

"What do you mean, you need me to drive?" I'm pulled from my thoughts.

"I mean I told my parents I could drive tonight, but I can't because I'm too drunk, so I need you to come, too."

"Kolton, I can't. I already told you I have work tomorrow. I would come with you if I didn't have to work tomorrow morning," I explain as we pull up to his gate.

"Fine. Fuck you," he spits as he slams the car door and makes his way around the front of my car to enter the gate code.

My car still idling in front of his opening gate, I sit dumbfounded, wondering how in the world the situation flipped so quickly.

Part of me wants to rewind two minutes and pause there—it's easy there. It's me. It's him. He's craving my attention and implementing the necessary ploys to grab it—*What the hell is going on?* I'm freely doling out my praise in full fits of laughter.

The other part of me wants to get out of the car, rip those ruthless words from his mouth, transform them into the crushing boulders they feel like, and dump them directly on his mean, stupid head.

Fine. Fuck you.
One. Two three.
Drop. Drop drop.

"In-N-Out! In-N-Out!" I drunkenly chant.

"Noooooo! Del Taco! I want the cheesecake bites," Britney whines back.

"Nah, In-N-Out," Kolton responds to all of us as he drives into the left-hand turning lane. That's the end of that discussion.

From the passenger seat, I turn around to throw a smirk at Britney because I won. Even though we're all piled in my Jetta, Kolton's driving. Between the five of us in the car—Britney, Aslyn, Didi, Kolton, and myself—Kolton is the least drunk, so he gets the honor of being DDD (Designated Drunk Driver) as well as FFD (Fast Food Dictator). If he was feeling the cheesecake bites, we would have gone to Del Taco.

"I have to pee soooooo bad," I say after we finish ordering our food. We're now sandwiched in the drive-through, and I look ahead dreadfully to see we are still three cars away from getting our food.

"Screw it. I'll be right back." I yell as I shut the door and run through the drive-through to the front door of In-N-Out.

When I'm done, I walk outside and don't see my car anywhere, so I figure everyone is still in the drive-through. I turn the corner and see my Jetta sitting at the pick-up window and run back toward the car laughing.

I stop laughing when I get back in the car and it's filled with cigarette smoke.

Everyone *knows* there is absolutely no smoking allowed in my car.

The girls don't fight me on it because they know that if they want to smoke, they're more than welcome to drive their own cars.

"Who's smoking in here?" I practically screech over the sound of the music and the girls' cackling chaos. Everyone has their window rolled down, and I'm drunk, so it's taking me longer than necessary to scan everyone's hands for the incriminating beholder.

I turn to my left and see Kolton staring back at me, unapologetically, the lit cigarette dangling from his outstretched hand.

I hit the music off.

"What do you think you're doing?" I ask Kolton in a quiet, tense tone.

"Smoking." He glares right into me, no humor in his eyes or smirk in his cheeks.

"You know you're not allowed to smoke in my car. Put it out. Now." I remain calmer than I think is possible, being as drunk as I am.

Britney, Aslyn, and Didi are silent.

I meet his eyes for what feels like five minutes. Neither of us blink.

"Okay, so that'll be five cheeseburgers, five fries, four pink lemonades, and one root-beer. Would you like any ketchup with that?" the cashier breaks in.

We hold our stance, neither of us flinching—Kolton doesn't even turn his head in response—this whole time, the cigarette still dangling between his fingers, accumulating a small pile of ash threatening to topple off the end.

He finally drops the cigarette and turns away from me to grab everyone's food from the cashier.

Kolton and I have been breaking up like crazy these past few weeks. On, off, off, on, on, on, OFF, ON, off, on, on, on, OFF.

He's been getting a little too close for comfort with other girls at parties, and I keep letting him have it, every single time. In front of everyone, too. Which never goes over well with him, so we end up having these big pissing matches party after party.

"You're fucking ridiculous," he yells at me as he turns to leave the party we're at.

"Where do you think you're going?" I yell after him, following him out.

"Answer me!" I shout again when he doesn't reply.

"We're pickin' up. You're not coming," he explains as he slips into the back of Georgie's car, Tobi already in the front seat.

"Yes, I am!" I slide in next to him.

"Get out of the car, Jordan," Kolton instructs, more firmly.

"No," I say defiantly.

Georgie starts driving, and Tobi turns around for comic relief. "It's all good guys. It's alllllll good, gonna' be all gravy." He laughs a little.

"Bro," Kolton says to Georgie.

"Bro. We'll be back in ten minutes. She's fine," Georgie responds.

I smirk at Kolton, who turns to look out the car window, avoiding me altogether. Georgie puts on some Mac Dre, and he and Tobi begin bantering back and forth, forgetting us in the back seat.

"Maybe if you didn't let stupid bitches sit on your lap, we wouldn't have these problems in the first place," I hiss at Kolton under my breath.

He doesn't respond, just keeps staring out the window.

"You're an idiot. You think I don't see these things? Think you can get away with shit like that? If you saw me sitting on someone's lap, you'd flip."

"Just shut the *fuck* up," Kolton mutters under his breath.

"Don't fucking talk to me like that!" I scream, punching his arm.

"Don't fucking touch me, Jordan." Kolton glares at me through black eyes.

I glare back at him, running through my options. I lay off for about thirty seconds, but that's all I can do before I start back up again.

"So fucking disgusting, Kolton. You're disgusting!"

He ignores me again, and I feel like I'm about to burst.

"Fucking look at me when I'm talking to you!" I scream as I shove him awkwardly with both hands from our seated positions next to each other.

"Are you fucking kidding me, bitch?! I said don't fucking touch me!" Kolton yells so fast, I can barely make out what he's saying.

"Get the fuck out of my face!" I slap him as hard as I can, and the slap he returns is so quick, so instantaneous, that I have trouble registering it at first. It's blurred. Did my slap ricochet from his face back to me? Wait. That doesn't make any sense. I'm drunk. And confused.

And *livid*.

When I register that he indeed slapped me back, I lunge at him, ready to kill him, but Georgie's stopped driving, and Tobi's already tearing us apart and pulling me out of the back of the car. Kolton comes around the front of the car, looking like he's ready to throw down himself. I yank to free myself of Tobi's hold, but I can't get free, and he's yelling at Kolton to get back in the car.

"Leave her, leave her, Bro. Calm down! Just get back in the car! Get in the fucking car!" Tobi yells.

Georgie tells him to do the same, and when Kolton finally gets back in the car, Tobi releases me from his hold, and I spin to the ground with the momentum that'd I'd tried to break free with. Tobi climbs in the car, and I can hear him yelling, "Georgie, go! Just go! Someone'll get her. Go!" They tear off into the night.

My face is streaked with tears, and I can't think of anything but killing Kolton. I think of how I'll do it, beating him senseless, ripping his skin to shreds with my nails, kicking him left and right to smash his balls. I can't stop seeing it play out in my mind. I'm gonna fucking kill him. This is it. He's a dead man. I'm gonna kill him.

I call Didi, but she's too drunk to make out what I'm saying between my gulps of fury and tears, so she hands the phone to Aslyn.

"What's going on?" she screams into the phone.

"Kolton hit me!" I'm bawling.

"What the fuck? Jordan, where are you?"

"I'm by your old house," I say between hiccups of tears.

"Stay there. We're coming to get you."

Sure enough, fifteen minutes later, I'm lying face down on the concrete of some street corner when I see the girls pull up. We drive off to a different party, and the girls pile out of the car, but I don't budge.

"Jordan, get out." Aslyn hangs back as Didi and Britney head into the house.

"I can't," I say stupidly, for no reason other than I'm drunk and pissy.

"Get out." Aslyn tugs on my arm.

My arms had been securely tucked across my chest, but when Aslyn tugs at the one, it shifts me slightly off balance, so I more or less begin to fall out of the car until I catch myself.

I glare at her, and go sit on the curb outside the house.

"You're fucking impossible," she says as she stomps past me.

My vision is spinning, and I want to be lying down. I refuse to go inside, so I go lie down on the grass outside the front of the house. I'm a heaping mess of tears, misery stinging every particle in my body, when I realize I'm wearing the black studs Kolton gave me for my birthday. I rip them hastily out of my ears and chuck them into the grass, nowhere to be found again. *That fucker.*

The next morning, I wake up inside the house on the floor of one of the bedrooms. I realize Didi, Aslyn, and Britney are nowhere to be found. They must have snuck out and gone back to the first party.

I hate them for leaving me.

I hate being alone.

I hate that Kolton and I are fighting.

I hate the fact that he slapped me. Less because of the slap itself, and more because it won't be so easy to kiss and make up this time.

My emotions aren't running correctly because the anger has completely evaporated, and I go back and forth between feeling desperately sad and feeling absolutely nothing, wondering which one is true. Something I know for a solid truth is how hungover I am, my head thumping.

I get a ride home, climb into my forgiving covers, and text Kolton.

Where are you?
Home
What happened?
u went crazy
You fucking slapped me!
u were hitting me and shoving me. i told u to stop
Doesn't mean you can slap me...
i dont think we shuld talk nemore
Why? Because YOU slapped ME?
u get too angry
This isn't my fault! That stupid bitch was sitting on your lap and you acted like nothing happened, and then you slapped me when I got mad.

we just dont get along
Look, I'm sorry I was giving you a hard time. We just need to talk it through and we'll be fine.
i dont think so
What do you mean you don't think so?
dont think its a good idea
Fuck you, Kolton. Fuck off then. Don't call me. Don't text me. I fucking hate you.
Why did I apologize?
I just want to be held.
Once I accept that I won't be held anytime soon, I realize I don't feel anything else.
My body and mind are depleted and drained.
I toss my phone to the ground and stare at my ceiling.

Tonight, there's absolutely nothing going on, so the girls and I drink at my house with a few of our guy friends. It's low-key, and around 10 p.m., the guys have meandered back to their own houses, and the girls have sought out one of my brothers to smoke them out.

With everyone dispersed, I take another shot by myself and go pee.

Sitting on the toilet, I stare blankly at a basket on the floor. It's full of dusty magazines with curled edges. My mom used to keep the monthly selection on a fresh rotation when she lived with us. I squint one eye closed at *Pottery Barn* in the front and try to read the date: *March 2007.*

After I finish up in the bathroom, I wander into the pantry because I don't feel like smoking with the girls. I peruse the shelves, and my eyes fall on the medicine bin. Another leftover piece of evidence that our house used to be thoughtfully organized with details tended to, such as an inventory of aspirin, Nyquil, Band-Aids, and the like.

In my drunken solitude, some thoughts float to mind:
    I miss Kolton.
    I miss my mom.
    I hate my house.
    I want a hug.

A few tears fall, and I don't want to feel sad, so I grab the bottle of Nyquil and figure I'll just call it an early night. I throw back a capful, wincing at the taste. I figure it's expired, so I take another capful to make sure I get enough of whatever ingredient causes me to get sleepy.

I lean against the wall, waiting for the taste on my tongue to mellow, and it occurs to me if I take even more sleep medicine, I could probably knock out for even longer. Maybe even tomorrow afternoon. Just skip right on through.

I rummage through the medicine bin, find some nighttime flu pills, and start popping them out of their pockets.

It then occurs to me mixing any medication with alcohol could be fatal because of certain chemical reactions.

Fatal like death.

Huh.

Would I care?

I grab a plastic water bottle from the case sitting on the bottom shelf, unscrew the cap, and chase down the five pills I just extracted from their packaging.

I wouldn't have to feel sad, or anxious, or heavy, or angry, or anything—if I just wasn't here.

I grab the aspirin bottle, pop the cap, and decide to top off the whole sleepy medley with a handful.

Screw it.

Worst case. It's all fatal.

Best case. I sleep an exceptionally long time.

I wake up, and my throat feels sore.

I need water.

I sit up and simultaneously, my head thumps viciously while a putrid smell clogs my nose.

Oh my god.

My floor.

It's covered.

With an impossible amount of puke. I cannot even fathom how much vomit is covering the square footage of my floor, chunks splashed randomly throughout the semi-dried liquid.

Good god.

I need to clean this up.

I grab for my phone to check the time. My dad usually leaves for work around 7:30 a.m.

It's 8:03 a.m.

I strategically tip-toe around the liquid mess, open my bedroom door, and head across to the bathroom for some towels. Thank god none of my friends are in sight. The girls must have gone home shortly after the guys left.

"Jordan." A stern voice interrupts my gratitude.

I jump as my heart starts beating uncontrollably fast from being startled so unexpectedly.

"Dad. I thought you were at work."

He pauses, and an ambiguously distraught look settles across his face. I can't decide which emotion leads—anger, disappointment, or disgust.

"You're gonna need to do some serious soul-searching."

We lock eyes. He looks like he's going to say something else, but clamps his mouth shut. My face burns as my head thumps, and my brain isn't working at all. *Did I make a bunch of noise last night? Did he just see the floor walking by right now? I'm such an idiot.* A few tears escape. Stupid tears. Weak. Weak. Weak. I clench my fist to stop crying.

"Yeah," I say.

He subtly nods his head, and that's that.

He leaves for work, and I'm left to clean up the mess I made.

JULY 14, 2009,
happy pills.

"I hate this song."

"Jordan, shut up," Didi dismisses me through a smirk. I roll my eyes at her before I lay back down on the pillow, placing the cool washcloth against my forehead once more. We don't say anything for a few minutes, and "Get Shaky" by Ian Carey Project continues to bounce around in the background.

This song was one of many played the night of my birthday, when we all rolled. It gives me anxiety. Ha. At this point, what doesn't give me anxiety?

Whack!

"What the—*fuck*, dude!"

"Jordan, get up. You're not staying in tonight," Aslyn snips after chucking her mascara tube at me.

"You idiot, you hit me in the *eye!*" I protest.

"Start getting ready. You always take forever to do your hair."

I scowl back at Aslyn and quickly turn my glance to Didi's face, reflected back to me in the mirror. She gives me another smirk, and I try to hold my scowl, but Didi giggles into one of her full-lipped, soft smiles.

Didi's not laughing at me. She's laughing with me. Aslyn's a bitch, and we both know it. Tolerate it. And she's not about to let me get away with staying in tonight when I'm the one who secured our ride with Wyatt.

Wyatt's an old, flip-floppy fling. I was into him for years and he let me chase him around. Then, one day, the dynamics flip-flopped. The second he wanted me back I didn't want him anymore. Not on purpose. The feelings just died. But he comes in handy for rides, so I let him linger close by in the background.

I allow myself a small laugh through my scowl, throw my head back with a heavy sigh, and then bring my head back to normal, looking forward at Didi's reflection once more. She pauses in applying her mascara, meets my eyes in the mirror, and raises her eyebrows, waiting for me.

"I *do* have a headache," I insist.

"No, you don't." She drops my eyes and continues with her mascara.

"I do," I whine.

"Jojo, you don't have to lie to *me*," she singsongs as she glances to meet my eyes in the mirror once more.

I know why I don't want to go out. Didi knows, too.

Kolton and I aren't together right now.

I haven't heard from him in three days—two whole days longer than our usual breakups. I know exactly what kind of night this will be if I go out and drink. I'll be in fight mode.

When I don't respond, Didi probes, "Seriously, you'll be fine. Do you want one of my happy pills?"

Didi's dad passed away our sophomore year of high school. He was an alcoholic, and their relationship was strained when he was alive. I only remember Didi crying at school once—that was it.

It was one day during Nutrition break. Our group of friends and acquaintances huddled in the same spot every day, all thirty or so of us. I just remember Didi suddenly snapping forward as she burst into tears, her body at almost a ninety-degree right-angle as she bent at the hips, like her pain had physically collapsed her in half. It was as though the laughter she always threw her head back with caused an inverse, 180-degree reaction, contracting her body forward instead. I wondered if all the times she threw her head back in open laughter she was simply trying to counteract the energy inside her; the inward pull to close, to collapse, to crack.

This was around the same time Aslyn's mom had moved to Georgia. Guilty as charged for leaving, Aslyn's mom left her checkbook and never questioned the $600 checks Aslyn forged every month for "groceries" and "household bullshit." Aslyn moved in with Didi for three months, and they spent those checks on Xanax. Each morning, they'd pop a Xanax, chase it down with milk, show up at school, and spend every Nutrition and lunch period lying in the grass. If they felt so inclined, they'd prolong the lunchtime lounging and skip fifth period, too.

Both girls decided to climb inside themselves. For three months. They didn't talk much. They didn't have anything to say. They also don't remember much. Didi later explained what those three months felt like. "Once the calm sets in, everything slows down, and things you'd normally feel just fall away. Almost like being drunk and high, but without the sloppy shenanigans of being drunk, and without the paranoia of being high. You're just numb. Not a care in the world. Just high above everything, and you don't remember much else."

Aslyn's mom eventually came to her senses and moved back to California, reclaiming her checkbook, so I'm pretty sure the lack of funding cut the girls' habit.

A full-time nurse with a trio of daughters packed tightly into their trailer-park home, Didi's mom was absolutely determined to ensure her daughters had different opportunities; and that included college. Didi's mom pushed both of Didi's older sisters through high school sports, which allowed both of them to attend college on full-ride scholarships. Didi's mom had the same plan for Didi's future: kick ass at soccer and earn a full-ride scholarship right out of the trailer park.

The fact that Didi lost her dad didn't change any of that. So, the plan remained, and Didi was put into therapy. Didi's been back on Xanax ever since, this time properly prescribed and monitored; she calls 'em her *happy pills*.

Nyquil and some aspirin with alcohol was one thing, but I *definitely* know you're not supposed to mix xannies with alcohol because every time we get ready at Didi's place, her mom always wishes us off shamelessly. "Be safe girls. Please use protection. Didi, did you take your pill? Don't drink with it. You'll die."

Pulled back to the moment, I respond to Didi's kind offer. "Don't they say you're *not* 'sposed to share your 'scripts?" I say, just to say, because I'm already reaching toward her outstretched hand for the little white pill.

"Who's *they*?" Didi answers me with a question as she turns back to the mirror to finish her makeup.

"I dunno. Your mom. Doctors. People who know things." I toss back a gulp of water to wash down the pill.

"Worst case scenario"—she pauses dramatically—"you die," she finishes with a low chuckle.

Oh my god, I thought the same thing! I want to say, but then remember I haven't told anyone about my sleepy medicine medley the other night. I also haven't had the chance to do any soul searching yet.

I chuckle back darkly instead, which makes Didi laugh harder, which makes me laugh harder, and then we're both cracking up.

Aslyn snips in the room in her snippy, clippy way, hating the fact the Didi and I are laughing at something she's not in on. "Are you bitches ready yet? Britney and I are already pre-gaming."

"Yeah, yeah, yeah. Ready in ten," I respond calmly, blowing her off. As she turns to stomp out of the room, I chuck her mascara tube at the back of her head.

She whips her hair around, gives me a dirty look, picks up the mascara, and retreats back to the kitchen.

When Aslyn's out of earshot, Didi and I lock glances in the mirror once more and start laughing all over again.

JULY 15, 2009,
These Days. This Day.

If blocking out your memories is the goal, then happy pills absolutely work. Also, I didn't die again. So, there's that.

After popping Didi's little white pill last night, my memory of the evening hit a dead end. I suppose that's a degree of happiness: the absence of sadness. Was I truly sad if I can't remember anything? The pill may have erased my memory, but no such luck with my hangover.

This morning I get a ride back to my house so I can nurse my headache. I try to decide which movie to watch and remember one of Didi's suggestions, *The Royal Tenebaums*. She said it was funny. I watch broken clips for free on YouTube, but they take forever to stream, and the whole ordeal makes my headache feel louder.

There's a song from the movie that makes me feel weird. I like the way the song begins; it's soothing and disarming. But then the singer starts in, and her voice is the epitome of nostalgia. The instruments quiet down, fading to background music, allowing for more lyrics. My curiosity is piqued. I have to find out the name of this song. I shut down YouTube and start Googling *The Royal Tenebaums* soundtrack until I find what I'm looking for.

♪
Music picks up where words fall short:
["These Days" by Nico]
♪

The song makes me feel suffocated, like summer itself. I can feel the heaviness creeping back in. I can feel the wide-open sadness wrapping me up in its sweltering blanket, the wiggly restlessness circling above. Suddenly, my phone buzzes. It's a text from Didi.

Jojo, come pick me up. We're doing something fun.

Kk, on my way. I don't even question her because I don't care what we're doing. I just want to be doing something. I don't want to be alone.

"We're going to Wyatt's," she instructs as she climbs in my car.

"Wyatt's? Blehhhh, for what?" I say, unimpressed by the plan.

"Rhory's over there, and they invited us to come have a few beers with them until later tonight. Then Alex is having a party, so we can just hang until then," she explains quickly.

"Ugh, but Wyatt…" I trail off.

"Just let him give you drinks, but don't make out with him," she offers.

"Well, duh. But still. He's just so mushy sometimes. It's annoying and freaks me out," I respond, but no matter, because I'm already getting on the 55 South freeway, on our way to Wyatt's.

"Can't blame the kid for bein' in love with you, Jojo," Didi giggles, trying to appease me.

"Well, duh," I indulge, not because I agree, but to let her feel like she was helping.

"Didi, serious talk. You have to listen to this song. It's the happiest thing I've ever heard," I proclaim as I plug in my iPod.

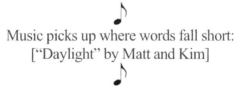

Music picks up where words fall short:
["Daylight" by Matt and Kim]

The song ends, and I play it again. We roll down our windows and tuck our hair into messy buns. I blast the song at full volume, and with the sound of the dry summer breeze ripping through the car, I begin singing along, my voice lost in the wind. Didi quickly catches on and starts singing along too.

When the song ends again, it's Didi who replays it.

And so it goes.

Just the two of us, blasting "Daylight" over and over again at full volume, like it's enough to scare away the wide-open sadness and wiggly restlessness.

But it is.

In these seventeen minutes, with Didi at my side and "Daylight" blaring happiness through my speakers, I swear the summer air promises me something better, something sweeter than its usual sentencing of suffocation and loss. Summer winks at me, tells me how much fun we can have. As the freeway ends in Newport Beach, I feel the smallest inkling of hope that there's happiness to be had, somewhere, somehow, in some way, someday. Like maybe today.

As we pull up to Wyatt's house, I force myself to remain optimistic. Maybe this will be fun. Maybe I'm better off without Kolton. Maybe I can feel happy today. Maybe I can love Wyatt. Why not? Maybe.

Wyatt greets Didi and me at the door, steering us inside and to the backyard, where we find Rhory sitting in a lawn chair, nursing a beer, basking in the sunshine. As advertised, Wyatt offers Didi and me beers. Didi sits on Rhory's lap, her latest love interest of the month. As they canoodle and giggle, Wyatt turns his attention to me.

"What chu ladies been doin' all day?" he asks with a sincere smile.

I hold his eyes for a moment, pausing before I answer, reminding myself to be patient, nice, optimistic. I repeat my earlier thoughts like a mantra: *Maybe this will be fun. Maybe I'm better off without Kolton. Maybe I can feel happy today. Maybe I can love Wyatt.*

"Nothin' much. Hungover from last night," I offer with a forced smile. Wyatt smells like some form of salami and shaving cream, and I hate it.

The beer helps though. Makes the mantras a bit more plausible. Alleviates some of my resistance toward Wyatt. Encourages me to even sit on his lap, as canoodley and giggly as Didi on Rhory. The beer even coaxes me into a nap.

When I wake up, it's dark outside, and it's time to head to Alex's party. Aslyn and Britney will be driving down to meet us after Aslyn gets off work.

I'm not hungover, but I'm not buzzing either. I'm a weird, dried out in-between.

We arrive at Alex's parents' house and head toward the backhouse. Alex greets us with excessive animation. He's probably been doing blow for hours. I don't understand how the kid keeps up with himself. I'm highly suspicious he isn't capable of returning to any level of normalcy, his brain probably perma-fried from too many drugs and the constant drinking.

The backhouse has daunting hues of a yellow so pale, it's closer to eggshell and beige, but with an overlay of dulled gray, like the walls themselves are sickly. The living room is a mess of sunken, mismatched couches. A coffee table sits at the center of it all, littered with smoking contraptions of all shapes and sizes, bongs of different heights, all with murky bong water floating around at the base, empty coke bags, and half-eaten bags of stale Doritos and cheddar-flavored Ruffles. "She Wants Me" by Living Legends beats through the speakers, sounding sinister considering the setting.

Didi heads straight to the kitchenette to make us mixed drinks. The additional alcohol doesn't significantly move me in one direction or another. I still feel caught in some lukewarm version of drunkenness, where I can't escape myself or my feelings. I decide to drink more.

The next thing I know, I'm waking up on a bare mattress in one of the rooms. I check my phone. It's 2:33 a.m. I blink my eyes at the darkness and see Wyatt asleep on the floor. Good. I don't think I could stomach him sleeping next to me.

I stumble out of the room as quietly as I can to see if any of the girls are still there. Didi's gone, probably at Rhory's, but I find Aslyn and Britney asleep on the couch. I gently try to wake them so I can drive us all home, but they won't budge. My anxiety feels like it's swallowed me whole, and I accept the fact that I have to wait it out a few hours before bailing out of this dirty, aimless backhouse. A few tears spill out, and I'm shaking a little. Aslyn is sleeping on the larger of the two couches. She's curled up under a blanket, so there's a little bit of room at her feet. Instead of making my way back to the room I woke up in, I quietly fit myself into the small space between her feet and the end of the couch. She shifts with irritation, although I can tell she's still asleep. I stay perfectly still to let her settle again before I lie my head down behind her feet, curled impossibly and uncomfortably into a ball. But I just can't go back to that empty room with its stripped mattress, where Wyatt lies on the floor, waiting for me to give him a chance, love him like he loves me, save me from myself and my misery. I don't want any of that. If I go back in there, I feel like I'll truly just fall apart. It's too much.

That dull, wide-open sadness has crawled back in its entirety, along with the wiggly restlessness. And something else, too.

Disgust.

I'm disgusted with myself for thinking this could be fun. Entertaining the idea that I could pull a quick-switch out of my heart and pour into Wyatt instead. He can't replace Kolton, and I feel dirty for wanting to use him in that way.

Summer is such a lie. I can't believe it winked at me on the drive down yesterday, whispering promises of a different narrative, planting infectious mantras in my mind: *Maybe this will be fun. Maybe I'm better off without Kolton. Maybe I can feel happy today. Maybe I can love Wyatt.* What a delusion.

As I lie next to Aslyn's body, tucked away to sleep somewhere, I try to fall asleep, too.

Suddenly I'm on the floor in that empty room, where I'd first passed out. Wyatt's gone. And there's a gaping, fiery hole burning through the floor on which I lie. I'm trapped flat on my back. I can't move, can't skirt my body away from the yapping flames that singe the splintering perimeters of a hole that drops straight down to hell. The fire rages on, eating more and more of the wood, disintegrating the floor beneath me, tearing the hole open larger and wider. I'm losing surface area by the second. My thighs remain on the ground, but with less and less of the floor intact, my legs give way at the knees, my feet and lower legs dangling into the flames below.

Unable to move, I lay helplessly as the Devil's serpents lick my toes, slither themselves securely around my ankles, yanking me down, down, down, while God's angels cup their arms beneath each of my shoulders, imploring me to *just hold on*, holstering me back up, up, up—my body the center of the conflict.

But I'm physically frozen, so there's nothing left to do, nowhere left to go. I can't see beyond this war, this day. And worse, this day on repeat. It feels like most days have been crumbling into This Day. This Day, where the war wages tirelessly, my body held captive between God's angels and the Devil's serpents.

I wake in a panic, realizing I was having a nightmare. I need to get as far away from this backhouse as possible. It's 5:57 a.m., so I wake the girls with more force this time, telling them I'm leaving their asses if they don't get in the car. They bitch groggily, but I ignore their woes, pick up my purse, and get in my car.

I think about my nightmare.
The whole drive home.
I can't shake the images, alive in my mind, but more than that, alive in me.
Love got me here.
Love brought me to This Day.
This Day, on repeat.
Love, a tricky, slippery lie.
I think of my mom: the trickiest, most slippery lie of love ever promised.
I think of her slow, confusing disappearance.
I think of how she was everything until she was nothing.

I think of me: gullible, romantic, trusting.
I think of me falling for her, believing in her love.
I think of Kolton: the highest high, kissing my wounds, only to slice open new ones.
I think of his constant, pressing attention, another whisper of love, another lie.
I think of how he feeds me until he finds fault, and then starves me.
I think of love promised and then withdrawn, so often without notice.
    Tricky, slippery love.
    Love as a lie.
    Love as a trap.
    Love as an inevitable path to war.
I think of giving up altogether, letting the angels and the serpents fight their fight. Angels that hold. Serpents that sting. War that wages tirelessly, and all for what?
All in the name of love?
Count me out.
Love is a ticking time bomb of heartbreak waiting to explode, blow your life to smithereens, leave you frantic.

JULY 16, 2009,
*let's break it down;
she broke down.*

No Kolton tonight.

Just friends. Twenty of us, give or take. My brothers, too. My dad's visiting his girlfriend in Palm Springs, so the party's at my house. I'm wearing a lime-green pullover sweater and checkered shorts.

It's just another night. Nothing in particular that feels sadder or more depressing than any other day this summer, I suppose. Except every day that passes marks another day that Kolton hasn't called, texted, missed me, loved me, asked for me back. Why? I can't fathom a *me* without a *him*. That's not the way this is supposed to work. That's not how this ends.

I'm already drunk but I pick up the bottle of Crystal Palace vodka, a degree shy of rubbing alcohol, and take an enormous chug. I don't even use a chaser.

I have a living and breathing *need* for love. To be loved. To feel love. To give love. To receive love. To be taken care of by love. To be tightly held and swaddled by love.

I've been fighting for this love too long. Fighting for this breath of life, like the first choking-gurgling-spitting breaths of a newborn entering the world. But I can't feel it. I don't feel the love. I'm not getting the oxygen I need. Every day that passes as This Day, my world shrinks, narrows, constricts, darkens around me.

I can't do This Day anymore. This Day is on repeat, no end in sight. There's no fucking way. I don't know what else to do. I can't feel like this anymore. I can't think beyond this moment.

People surround me, but I'm not entirely here.

I remember the assortment of sharp objects in the kitchen tool drawer. I surprise myself a bit as I turn the solution over in my mind—all this pain finally coming to an end.

All gone.

All done.

What surprises me even more is the substantial relief that follows these thoughts, settling over me like a blanket. Making me feel soothed. Assured. Calm.

Just like that.

The decision is made.

I make my way past nameless faces sitting on my countertops. I open the drawer, sift past a stapler, pair of scissors, and loose rubber bands, until I find something suitable. I grab a bare, rectangular box-cutting blade, and among all the banter, the music, and the drunkenness, no one notices.

With a horrible taste in my mouth, a lot of guts, and the razor blade, I walk into my room, lock the door behind me, plop down on the floor by the side of my bed, unpack my tears, and start slicing.

I'm not stupid. I'm not going to mess this up. I don't want the attention. I want to leave. I am never going to deal with This Day or any of it ever again. I'm going now. I'm leaving and never coming back.

I slice straight up and down.

A request for death.

With each new slice, I start high, where my wrist meets my hand, gently placing the point of the blade, and slice down; hard, steady, and fast. Every time.

Again and again.

I don't even know if it hurts. All I know is I feel open and sickly. Moonlight peaks its pity through my blinds, the only source of light in the room.

All I see is white. Right in the thick of each slice. Right in the middle of each vertical slash, at the deepest point, I see white. The blood comes eventually, though.

I lie down on my back, turning my cheek to the cool grain of the wooden floor beneath me, my left arm splayed out in front of me, the perfectly straight vertical separations screaming towards God, screaming and crying and giving up.

I start to drift toward sleep, and I know I will die like this.

I feel a surge of peace. I match. I finally match myself. My exterior finally matching and reflecting how my heart feels inside of my body. Lethally sliced. Bleeding with a hope for death.

I hear the click-slip of a credit card, pushing the tab on the door handle open, unlocking it. Most of my friends know the trick. Someone turns on the light, skirts around my bed, and comes upon me lying on the ground.

"Oh my god, Jordan, what the fuck!?" Didi rushes down to the side of the bed.

"What are you doing in here?" I ask through slow tears.

"What are *you*—oh my gaaaaahd. Jojo!"

"It's fine," I say flatly.

"It's not fine."

"It's fine."

"No, it's not. I'm gonna go get someone."

"Didi, don't!"

But I don't move.

And she leaves the room.

I lie on my bedroom floor, vaguely aware that I am insane.

Jason, my oldest brother, comes into the room.

"Come on." He instructs flatly, him and Didi helping me to my feet with my good arm.

Once upright, he gently places a towel in my hands.

"Use this to cover them while we walk to the bathroom."

The three of us walk to the bathroom, and once inside, Didi locks the door behind us. Jason begins rummaging through the drawers. He pulls out some large Band-Aids, gauze, and Neosporin.

"Here, start putting this on them," Jason instructs Didi as he passes her the Neosporin.

He gets the gauze situated and opens the Band-Aids.

I extend my arm until my hand falls into Didi's, my forearm positioned upward. She slowly begins to apply the Neosporin thickly onto the open cuts.

After just two, she pulls back, and when I look at her face, she's completely fallen apart. I have to close one eye to see her clearly, but she's crying.

"Uhhh, Jordan. Why?"

Jason takes the Neosporin from her hands and continues where she left off.

"I got it. You can go back out there. Don't tell anyone."

"Sorry," I say as Didi looks at me once more before leaving the bathroom.

I look up at Jason as he begins covering my cuts with the gauze and Band-Aids. The middle of some of my slices are white again, empty. I don't say anything. He won't look at my face, just continues to bandage, gently.

I think he's confused. I mean, pragmatically confused—there's so much open flesh that it's probably hard to decide where to even apply the bandages. The silence continues, and when he's done, he gently and carefully pulls my sleeves down over the bandages.

"Jesus, Jordan."

And he leaves. We've never been super close, and he isn't one for heart-to-hearts. I don't mind. I don't feel like talking much tonight anyway.

Alone in the bathroom, I stare at my reflection in the mirror, and there's two of me. I close one eye and that helps.

Why am I still here?

I have no answers.

After a minute, I rejoin the party like nothing happened. No one to be the wiser. I somehow manage to find the Crystal Palace bottle when Jason and Didi aren't looking and take another chug. And when I finally retreat to my bed for the night, I hope with everything in me that I never wake up.

JULY 18, 2009,
show & tell.

Ring, ring, ring. I look at my phone and recognize his number blaring across the screen. It's pointless to even delete his number since I know it by heart, anyway.

I push down on the side of my phone to ignore the call. A small but festering ball of power and pride begins to swell from within.

Predictably, he calls again.

I hit ignore once more, the ball of power and pride within swelling larger.

As I knew he would, he calls a third time.

I ignore it again. *Ha! You douche! Who's ignoring who now!?* I think to myself.

A text shoots through my phone. *Jojo…*

I finally concede and respond. *What?* I knew I was going to respond all along.

Kolton answers. *we need to talk*

K.

Kolton calls me once more, and this time I answer, slowly thawing out my feigned indifference as he begs and pleads for a few minutes, asking me to come over and see him. I agree, and my tone implies I'm doing him a favor, but the truth is I need to see him.

And I'm off to his house.

"Nice haircut," I offer as I walk into his room. The familiar scent overwhelms me, and it's all I can do to nonchalantly toss my purse on the floor and gently set my cellphone down on his dresser. I sit safely across the bed from him, with one knee bent into a flat triangle, the other leg still dangling, foot planted to the floor. Half in, half out.

"So, why did it take you four days?"

I look him straight in the eye. Four days is our longest break. Long enough to make me believe the break may have been real this time, may have truly been the end.

I wait for Kolton to provide an answer that makes sense, something well thought out so this can be an easy make-up and I can buy into his bullshit at the right price. Something to contradict what I already know and feel: He's been with Jackie.

He doesn't deliver. "You said you wanted nothing to do with me."

As expected, I feel cheap and easy. I just want to make up already. I want to close the distance on the bed between us. I want to cradle myself into him. I need to be held.

No matter the cost.

I swallow his sleazy excuse and close the distance to lie by his side, offering my treaty. Kolton slips his one hand beneath my sweatshirt to pull me in closer, simultaneously pulling at the hem of my sweatshirt with his other hand.

Slightly alarmed, I try to pull away from him slowly, disengaging from what will inevitably turn into sex. I can't be without this sweatshirt. I can't be naked.

Unfazed, Kolton instead takes off my shorts and then his own, pulling us closer once more, until I can feel the whole of him inside me. I distract him as well as I can with kisses, trying to pull his attention away from my still-clothed upper body. Eventually, he grows tired of me pulling away every time he tries to take off my sweatshirt, and his frustration quickly turns to angry suspicion.

"Why won't you take off your sweatshirt?" he finally probes.

"Why does it matter? I'm comfortable."

"What are you hiding? You have a hickey or something?"

"Nothing, no," I spit back. "You're being crazy."

"Well, why won't you just take off your sweatshirt then?"

Kolton has disentangled himself from me entirely and our sex is dead.

    I can lie,
    I can leave,
    or I can confess.

But I'm not a good liar. And if I leave, it'll just postpone the inevitable.

"Okay. Okay. I've just. Look. I've been sad—," I start, "—really, really sad these last few days. I thought we were done for good, and, I don't know…I just. I don't know. I was really sad."

Kolton's expression turns from suspicious to apprehensive—no less angry, though. His eyebrows are furrowed down and he inches himself away from me.

"I don't know what I was thinking. I was really drunk. I just—," I try, but another glance at Kolton's face and yet another inch between us tells me he already knows. I'm still raw and confused myself. I have no idea how to explain this to someone else…out loud. Specifically when that someone else is Kolton, staring back at me like I'm a disgusting, slimy, mutant spider.

Raw, confused, and now ablaze with shame, I challenge Kolton in the eye, daring him to speak. I raise my eyebrows at him and stay silent.

"People did that shit in rehab, too. It's stupid."

His curt answer confirms everything I read in his face, but, somehow, out in the open like that, it stings hotter and colder all at the same time. I fight back tears and try to remain concrete, unmoved.

"Fuck you, Kolton," I seethe before storming out of his room.

Before this moment, I didn't know there was anywhere lower to go than where I already was.

Now I know.

Later that night, I'm drinking at Aslyn's mom's house with a bunch of friends. Abruptly, Didi comes into the kitchen to tell me Kolton is outside with a car full of people. Aslyn overhears and starts to scold me. "Jordan, you know I can't have that many people over."

I answer in my defense, "I swear I didn't invite them. I'll make them leave." Aslyn and Didi both trail me out the door.

I approach the car. There are six of them in there: Kolton, Tobi, and a few others. I don't know how they all squished into the car.

I rip after Kolton. "You guys can't be here. You need to leave. Now. You weren't even invited. What the fuck is your problem?"

"Okay, Jordan." No movement…

"What about that did you not understand?" I exclaim as I jerk my head from left to right.

"Whatever." He looks at the guys, a bit uneasily.

They all mill around awkwardly, all outside the tiny confinement of the car. They're all aware they need to leave, but no one wants to give in and be the first to make the move back into the car. At this point, Aslyn and Didi have made their way outside as well.

I'm heated. "Get. The. Fuck. Out of here, Kolton! You're not allowed to be here!"

"I said *oh-fucking-kay*, Jordan. Why don't you go fucking kill yourself, you crazy lil' bitch?"

Normally, I would lunge for him, grab his throat, twist it, cut off his breathing.

But I can't.

I can't move, and I can't breathe.

I can't even cry.

I'm stunned.

No one even knows—except for Didi.

Didi is the only one that knows.

Aslyn doesn't know.

And now all these guys?

I don't even have to do anything. Didi loses it for me. "Get the *fuck* out of here, Kolton, you lowlife piece of shit! You stupid fucker! All of you! Get the fuck out of here. Leave, *now!*"

I just stupidly, unsteadily back step as Aslyn alternates her perplexed gaze between Didi and me. She's puzzled, and the anxious confusion drips from her pinched features, her mouth half-open as if grasping something but still not fully understanding.

"Wait, what? What is he talking about?" she stumbles.

I snap back to reality and walk back into the house, ignoring Aslyn's questioning face, forcing my heavy legs up the stairs to Aslyn's room, and shut the door behind me.

The tears explode, and I'm breathing again—all at once. I'm spitting and choking and gasping and clenching my fists.

That. Fucker! That fucker!

I'm going to *kill* him!

I'm going to rip him apart. I am never speaking to that fucker ever again. *Oh, my*—Aslyn bursts through the door with Didi right behind her. "Jordan, what was Kolton talking about?"

I'm mid-meltdown. Before I can satisfy her nervous questioning, I focus on regulating oxygen through my lungs. I shoot a pleading look at Didi. She brings Aslyn up to speed as I try to calm down.

"Let's just go back downstairs and drink." And just like that, I relieve us from the weight of a conversation no one wanted to have. I know Aslyn and Didi both care. But I don't have any answers for them.

The night goes on, and Kolton and I are shooting nastier and nastier texts to each other.

Then he shows back up.

Comes back to Aslyn's.

He's by himself this time.

I cannot believe his audacity.

I stomp down Aslyn's front porch steps to meet him.

And the anger is too much—it's buzzing to a burst.

As the first sting of my slap surprises his face, I know I've called to rally all the other wasps buzzing within my body, signaling them to attack. There is no coming back from this.

I shove him with impeccable strength that surprises even me, nullifying his eight-inch and sixty-pound advantages over me. The burning wasps unleash, and no dimension of physicality, no height, no weight stands a chance of rivaling their fury.

I rapidly close the distance that I had just thrust between us until I'm close enough to slam contact against his face, my thumb curled around the outside of my bare knuckles, precisely how I'd seen him deliver blows to others.

He reads me a second sooner and side jumps to the left. As my fist drives through the air into missed opportunity, he juts over to me, and with his front to my back, he jaggedly wraps his arms around me, one at a time, trying to contain me.

I thrash violently against him. The wasps inside me are swarming, fuming, screaming against his hold. The throbbing pressure within exceeds anything I've ever held inside my body. I turn my head to the side, and every ounce of hurt and anger and pure rancor seethes into the force of my clamping molars as I bite down, overwhelming the soft-yet-taut skin of his forearm.

He releases me like a scalding-hot iron with a tormented, "What the *fuck*!?"

"Get the *fuck* out of here, and don't *ever* fucking speak to me again," I drunkenly hiss back at him.

Before he has a chance to gather himself, I make my way back into Aslyn's house, slamming my feet up the porch steps, sledgehammers against the concrete. I'm sure the cops have been called by now.

AUGUST 7, 2009,
like boyfriend, like girlfriend.

Things are getting bad.
Obviously.
But Kolton and I can't stop.
An endless circle: We keep going back to each other.
The fights are constant, accelerating from weekly to daily.
So, yep, we're fighting.
What's new.
    Nothing new. Just knew I had to get to him.
    Determined in that drunken way of mine.
    It's simple. I'm going to see him.
    Drunk or not.
    No matter.
    I'm going to see him.
    Convince a friend to take me back to my car.
    Make up a lie: "I have to be home or my dad'll kill me."
    Lol, when have I ever had a curfew?
    Back at my car, time to focus.
        Gotta drive to him.
        Gotta get to him.
        I need to see him.
        I'm going to see him.
            Tricky, tricky, this car.

Somewhere in between needing to see him and
Blank—blank—blank—
I turn the car around to steer it out of Aslyn's community.
Blank—blank—blank—
fifty feet stretch of black asphalt ahead.
Blank—blank—blank—
I don't remember turning the car around to steer it out of Aslyn's community.
Blank—blank—blank—
I don't remember driving fifty feet with a stretch of black asphalt ahead.

and then I come to.
Crash—crush—thud—smoke—rubber
Burnt rubber—smoke—oh no.
Oh no. Burnt rubber. Airbag. Smoke.
stumble out of my car. crawl back into my mind. trying to make it back out, of my blackout.

barely here, but i'm here. i've never seen an airbag deployed before. the smell of smoke & burnt rubber stings my nostrils. the front of my car is totaled. i have driven straight into a parked car.

Oh no, okay, time to fix things. Neighbors are coming out of their condos. "It's okay. It's fine. I'll pay for all of it. It's no big deal. It's fine. It's fine."

Sirens scream. Lights blare. Red, blue.
Flash, flash, flash—
"Ma'am, you have the right to remain silent. Anything you say can and will be—"

[Misdemeanor #1:
Driving under the influence.]

oh & here it comes.

"Fuck you! Shut the fuck up!"

        "Ma'am, we need to read your Miranda rights."

"Fuck off! Fuck my Miranda rights! You don't need to read me jack shit."

        "Alright, put the handcuffs on her."

"You're not putting shit on me! Don't you fucking touch me! Don't fucking touch me! Nooooooo!"

        "Thompson, I need backup."

"Don't fucking touch me!"

        & I rip back and forth,
        back & forth.
        Screaming like this is rape.
        Screaming all the screams
        I'd been holding in.
        I'm screaming at Kolton.
        I'm screaming at my parents.
        I'm screaming at my life.
        Why am I still here?
        I scream for questions
        unanswered.
        I scream for anger.
        I scream for sadness.
        I scream for injustice.
        I scream for hate.
        I scream for death.
        I scream for me.
        I scream because I tried to
        give up & the world kept
        bringing me back.
        I scream & I scream
        & I yell obscenities.
        Fuck streaks every sentence.

"Hold her down, she won't stop moving."

      The police shove me down
      hard & cheek to concrete
      I cry.
      I don't let it just be sadness.
      I make sure anger claws
      through, too.

First cop.

      I kick up fiercely,
      straight for the balls.

      [Misdemeanor #2:
      Assault & battery
      on a police officer.]

Second cop.

      The kicking isn't over.
      Harder than kick one,
      straight for the balls.

      [Misdemeanor #3:
      Assault & battery
      on a police offer.]

"Fuck you guys! Let me go! Don't fucking touch me! Let me go!"

    "She's over here. Are you the mother?"
    "Yes, I'm her mother. What happened?"

      I see her.
      And I wouldn't have known
      I'd had anything left to
      scream.
      Sorely, sorely mistaken.
      Screams are a plenty.

"Get. Her. The. Fuck. Away. From. Meeeeeeee! Get her the fuck away! Get her out of here! I fucking hate her! Get that fucking bitch away from meeeeeeee!"

"Ma'am, we're going to need to escort you away from the scene. We can talk with you over here. Thompson, calm her down, will ya?"

"Miss, you're going to need to calm down."

"Don't tell me to fucking calm down! You don't know shit about shit! You don't know anything! Nothing! You don't know anything about me! Don't fucking tell me to calm down, you piece of shit! Go fuck yourself. And where the fuck's my dad? Get me my dad. Now! Get me my dad!"

"Your dad's not coming. Said he didn't want to come down for this."

And the screams subside.
The tears flow heavy.
But the screams go silent.
The police take my mom
away from the scene &
my dad isn't coming.
What now?

"Can't admit her at that level of intoxication."

Back of the cop car.
Hospital. Detox. Drip. Drop. Detox.
Back into the car.

Why didn't my dad come?

Orange County Juvenile Hall.
Brought in through some side entrance.

Shooting everyone in

sight a look of scorching hatred, my rage turning toward insanity.

Not for much longer, though.

"Look, little missy, we've heard all about you, all night. You're gonna lose the fucking attitude. And you better wipe that fucking look off your face or there's going to be trouble."

He jams me against a wall, my face spewing black tears, my hands still handcuffed behind me, & he thrusts my arms further up my back, driving home his point with a twist of pain.

He releases my arms, walks away, and I slump down to the floor to sit on my butt, shooting my legs out before me. He must have heard the jingle of my sandals as I slide to the floor because he turns around.

"Get her off the ground,"

he instructs the police officer next to me—a third cop that I didn't happen to assault at the scene of the crime.

"She's fine,"

my third cop challenges the

dick-off juvie intake officer.
Why he offers up
even an ounce of mercy in my
favor, I don't know.

I smirk at the dick-off.
Exactly, leave me alone,
fucker. I'm sad. And suicidal.
So leave me alone.
    I think,
but don't say.
My arms still burn
from his thrusting
twist-up. Not looking
for round two.

I have no idea what time it is.

How many hours have passed?

I'm curled up against the wooden bench inside the holding tank when I finally hear my name being called, and the door clicks open to the intake desk.

"One call." A fat policeman with a mustache points to a phone hanging from the wall.

I hesitantly walk to the phone, my eyes on the policeman the whole time, apprehensive he'll yell at me for one wrong move. When no objections are made, I take the phone off the receiver and dial my dad's cellphone number by heart. He answers on the second ring.

"Dad? It's me," I greet him through tears welling up in my eyes, my throat closing. "I'm in juvie," I explain.

"I know," he says with surprising calm.

"How?" I try to regulate my breathing to avoid hyperventilating.

"I was there last night," he continues.

"They told me that you weren't coming. They said you said you didn't want to." I almost fall apart with my last words.

"What? Jordan, I was there. They wouldn't let you see me. You were very upset when you saw Mom, so they didn't want that happening again if you saw me," he rushes.

"Can you just please come get me?" I beg.

"I'll do what I can," he reassures me.

"Time, young lady!" the fatty barks from his chair.
"I've got to go. Please come get me. Please," I whisper.
"I'll see what I can do," he says.
The line dies.

After I hang up the phone, the bulky intake officer redirects me to the holding cell, where I wait again. My anxiety is so sprung out of control at this point, I'm not even sure it can be considered anxiety. My mouth feels like sandpaper, and that ever-familiar headache is hugging my brain, slowly suffocating the blood-flow into a pattern of deep and steady thumping.

I think about everything.

And I mean *everything*.

Pieces are coming back to me.

Or maybe not even coming back to me, but simply being comprehended through a new lens. A less inebriated lens; just as angry, just as spiteful, just as mutilated and sad, but mostly just less inebriated.

The details grow more horrifying as I sort through them in my head.

Burnt rubber.

Smoke.

Screaming sirens.

Don't fucking touch me.

Drip. Drop. Detox. Hospital.

I don't want to remember any more right now. I just want to go home and sleep off this hangover. It's excruciating, and I can't be in a foreign place when I'm this sick. I need to be in my bed with my pillow over my head. I try to stop thinking, but it's impossible. My thoughts become singular and spinning.

Spinning over being physically separated from Kolton.

I gotta get out, get to Kolton.

Get out of here, go to Kolton.

Deal with the rest later.

Oh *no*, the DUI.

That's bad.

That's remarkably bad.

Screams, so many screams.

My screams.

Siren screams.

Singular. Spinning.

Kolton.
Just need to nuzzle into him; I'll deal with the rest later.
I just need him to hold me.
I just need to be wrapped up in his arms.
I just need a reprieve of cocoon.
    I won't be greedy. I won't take long. I just need enough to get to *okay* again.
Just touch me, hold me, love me back to baseline.
Just enough so I can take care of all the other stuff.
    Oh *no*, the DUI.
    I am such an idiot.

After fingerprints and my mug shot, I'm lined up in an enclosed room with four other girls.

My shorts are army-green, three large pleats on the front, rolled cuffs on the bottom, and loose on my hips.

My belt is thick and brown, wrapped solidly around my waist.

My cotton underwear is lavender with off-white polka-dots and the tiniest lime green bow sewed on the front-and-center seam.

My shirt is thin, white, almost see-through, but not quite, and tucked into the looseness of my shorts. The lining of the V-neck dives down to reveal just the tops of my subtle breasts. The sleeves are capped.

My bra is nude in color, just nude.

My sandals are brown, strappy, and decorated with bronze, diamond-shaped studs.

And it all has to go.

"You want me to strip all the way?" I ask.

"Yep. Now. We don't have all day," the correctional officer barks back.

I scowl as I slowly crisscross my arms over my waist, pulling for the hem of my shirt, hesitantly lifting it up and over my head.

I shiver a bit as I unbuckle my belt and pull it gently through the loops of my shorts.

I barely have to tug down at my shorts, the absent belt releasing their looseness, threatening to slip down entirely past the circumference of my hips, with or without the help of my hands.

I redirect my scowl to the ground as I reach behind my back to unclasp my bra. It falls forward slightly, and I shiver once again as I un-hug it from my body.

I slip my thumbs in between my goose-bump-prickled skin and the elastic of my underwear from each side, bending down to pull them all the way off.

All of it, once protecting my nudeness from the world, is now mercilessly lying on the ground. All of it. On the ground.

The correctional officer thumbs through my clothes in search of illegal knickknacks like weapons or drugs. Upon finding nothing, she bags it all up and offers me a stack of clothing in exchange. The stack includes a white, stretched-out sports-bra, an enormous, plain gray T-shirt, a worn, muted, cough-of-paled-yellow pullover sweatshirt, a pair of rough, loose blue sweatpants, chunky white socks, and the most heinous pair of dirty, cracked, white slip-on shoes with Velcro clasps.

Once dressed, I'm escorted into a larger, wide-open day room, where there are tons of girls stationed around. I'm dropped off next to a girl unwrapping toilet paper from the cardboard roll, rewrapping it into bundles of equal length.

"You just have to unwrap the toilet paper and then rip it into pieces with about ten squares," the girl explains quietly.

"Okay," I say warily, as I seat myself on the other side of the table, facing her directly, the mounds of toilet paper between us.

"I'm Tabitha, but people call me Tabby. Like tabby cat."

"Jordan," I offer, just above a whisper.

"What happened to your head?" she asks.

I touch my hand to my head, and sure enough, I feel a large, circular lump the size of the bottom of a coffee cup rising on my forehead where my head must have slammed against my steering wheel only twelve hours ago.

"Car accident," I explain.

"Were you driving?"

"Yeah."

"Did you hit anyone?" she presses, asking quieter than any of her other questions.

"No one died, if that's what you're getting at," I snip back.

I see Tabby's face catch slightly, like she might cry. She looks fragile, and I immediately feel bad for responding defensively.

"I crashed into a parked car," I say with the slightest bow of my head, both in shame for myself and apology for her.

She shakes her head up and down, as if to soothe, comfort, and accept my apology. I don't mention that I'd been drunk when I crashed. She either assumes or doesn't think to ask.

"So, why are you here?" I ask her gently.

"Drugs. I was rolling at the OC fair and some cops came up on my group. We all got questioned, plus I had a bunch of extra pills on me because I sell a few here and there, to friends," she concludes matter-of-factly, neither with angst or shame.

"Not so bad," I answer.

"Nah, I'll probably get to leave today."

"Me too. Hopefully…"

She looks at me skeptically with pause in her mouth and pity in her eyes.

After rolling endless bundles of toilet paper, we eat lunch. Meals are different than chores, though. No one's allowed to talk to each other during meals, or to even look at each other. Each square table accommodates four girls. The correctional officers assign Tabby and me to different ones.

One of the girls at my table, a chubby Latina chick, seated directly across from me, glares at me with a smirk. I look back at her with a small scowl between my eyebrows, a question. *What was her problem?*

"Eyes down, children. Stop looking at each other," a nearby correctional officer barks at us.

Stupid bitch, getting me in trouble.

As soon as the correctional officer meanders far enough away, I look up at the chubby chick once again, this time with narrow eyes and a sharper, deeper scowl. But she breaks into a quiet giggle that jostles her thick shoulders up and down. My scowl melts to confusion. *Seriously, what's her issue?*

"What's wrong with your head?" she whispers so quietly, I'm not sure if I even heard her or read her lips and gestures.

I touch my hand to my forehead again, feeling the lump in its full form. With three fingers, I tenderly push into the lump, testing my level of anguish. It hurts. But not as badly as my wrists. The handcuffs bruised my wrists so badly that even the slightest amount of pressure, the hem of my ratty pullover sweatshirt, makes me wince.

Chubby Chick stares at me expectantly.

"Nothing," I whisper back, slightly shaking my head left to right.

After lunch, everyone is dismissed to their cells.

Back in our cell, Tabby and I both fall asleep, although my sleep is fitful. I wake up a few times, my body shivering with cold. Each time, I check behind to make sure Tabby was still with me. Each time, she's still there, wrapped under her tattered, off-white knit blanket. I turn away so I'm staring at the divots of the dull, white concrete walls. I trace their rectangular paths with my pointer finger.

I startle to the buzz of all the cell doors clicking open simultaneously.

Dinner time.

Same tables.

Same smirky glares from Chubby Chick.

And then dinner's over, and it's back to our cell.

"What do you like most about being high?" I ask Tabby once the door clicks and locks behind us.

"Oh my god! That's hard! It's all so good," she gushes and laughs, like I just asked her about her first love.

"It makes me super anxious," I respond, thinking, not for the first time, that I had to be doing it wrong if everyone else enjoyed it so much more than me.

"Ecstasy is just…it's better than everything. Better than sex, better than funnel cakes, better than friends…" she drifts off in her own ecstasy fantasy bubble.

"I guess I get that part. But what about the comedown?" I'm trying to understand.

"Oh, the comedown's the worst. That's why you pop a xanny after. Sleep it off. Wake up, and you're good as new," she explains so simply.

"Never thought of that," I respond. Tabby had to be all of a hundred pounds, maybe five feet tall. I wonder how her little, baby frame handles her acting like she's some body chemist, thrusting her mind and body into a high frenzy, up, up, up, only to drown it into oblivion, down, down, down.

The cell door clicks open, and a correctional officer summons Tabby out.

"Bring your things," the correctional officer instructs her.

Tabby smiles briefly at me, gathers her things in a rush, and practically skips out of the room, entirely unperturbed like this whole thing was a stay in time-out. No big deal.

Just like that, she's gone.

I'm completely alone.

I slowly open my eyes to see the pale grays and whites of the room, the cold silver of the bare toilet jutting out from the wall offensively.

I remember why I'm here, but I can still hardly believe it.

I sincerely believed I would go home yesterday, but all my extracurriculars the night of the arrest earned me a few extra days. Today is Sunday, and my court date is Tuesday.

With Tabby gone, I'm in complete isolation.

I fight the panic swelling up in my chest.

I shouldn't be here.

I deserve to be here, but this isn't me.

I don't understand myself.

I feel the war begin to take form in my mind once again, like my nightmare just weeks ago.

> Angels and serpents.
> The angels whispering to *just hold on.*
> The serpents hissing to *just give up.*

I can hardly comprehend the actions that landed me here.

I can't stomach all that *bad* belonging to me.

It frightens me.

I've created my own worst nightmare, in real life.

My wide-open sadness, my wiggly restlessness. This is it. Being stuck here is just that. Being completely cut off from the world, from all touch, all contact, all communication, wholly alone. I brought this to life.

I scare myself.

The destruction. The hate. The anger.

I've manifested my own, real-life trap.

I want to hate Kolton for this. I want to hate my mom, even my dad. But mostly, I just hate this purely demonic version of myself.

And the angels and serpents chime in simultaneously.

> The angels sing, loud and clear, "*Version* of yourself. Not you. This *isn't* you."
> The serpents hiss with sticky lure, "Purely demonic. Rage. Power. This *is* you."

I don't realize I've been slowly crying until the new coldness on my cheek stings my consciousness. My tears should be warm, but the second they hit the air, they're cold. Everything is cold. My feet, my fingers, my body, this room. I gently pull the blanket toward my face, maneuvering carefully to avoid banging my tender wrists. I wipe the wetness away from my left cheek, but the cold remains.

I cannot escape this chill; it's progressed to my core.

Cold and alone.

Punishment from me, to me.

I had wanted to die before, but this is it. This is the worst of all. If I make it out of here, I can never come back. I can't handle this. I can't do this again. I tuck my head under the blanket, praying for more sleep, hoping for escape.

A few days later, a correctional officer buzzes my cell door open and tells me to gather my things. I think this is it—I get to go home.

I gather my short pencil, which lacks an eraser, and my manila folder, boasting a few legal documents and stray pieces of paper, and follow the correctional officer out of the cell, hugging my personal items to my chest like I'm off to my first day of school.

I follow the correctional officer up a stairwell, branching off into the second-floor cells, and she turns back to me. "You're getting a roommate," she says plainly.

Oh.

Another cell door clicks open in front of me, and I walk inside.

"Child!" she barks.

I turn around with surprise.

"Leave your shoes," she instructs.

"Right." I remember the rule, remove them with hurry, and walk back inside the cell, placing my personal items on the empty bed.

The door clicks behind me, and the girl on the other bed wastes no time.

"I'm Gina!" she nervously giggles. "Okay, hope you don't mind, but I have to shit so bad. I was holding it because after breakfast, they told me I was getting a roommate. I didn't want to be mid-shit when they walked in with someone, so I've been holding it. Hope you don't mind." She giggles and plops down on the menacing, silver toilet.

I've never been so grateful to have someone shamelessly toot and poop in front of me. My body noticeably relaxes. This is the first human contact I've had in days, aside from the barking correctional officers and smirky glares from across tables during muted meals. Relief immediately floods my veins and warms my blood.

Over the next week, I grow to know Gina intimately. She asks me to read her plea letters that she's scribbled to the judge, three pages long, with scratched out phrases and words. I rework the letter so it sounds sincere and smart, telling her to rewrite it so it doesn't look so sloppy. She shares stories of her childhood, endearing snippets like how her dad cooked meth in her plastic playhouse in their backyard. She explains how she landed herself back in juvie—breaking probation. Her original crime? Intentionally driving her brother's car (stolen for the deliberate hate act) through her ex-boyfriend's front living-room window while she was coked out of her mind. He had cheated on her. Say no more, girl. I understand the venom.

Tabby's crimes were petty compared to mine, but mine are petty compared to Gina's.

Gina is five-foot-nine, with medium-length brown hair and a chop of middle school side bangs, bouncy C-cup boobs, and a huge ass that she adores. She constantly asks me to check it out, tell her how it looks in our ugly, washed-out blue sweatpants. Sure enough, though, her ass is so bodacious, it *still* looked good in our hideous attire.

She attempts to thread her eyebrows with a makeshift rubber-band twisted into a threading tool, using the scratchy, blurry reflection of the metal mirror above our sink. It's a wonder that she can even remove a few stray hairs. She also attempts to fill in her brows with the dull charcoal of our half-sized pencils.

"How do they look?"

"Good," I'd say, even if her skin was temporarily rubbed raw and red from the pokey circumference of the wooden pencil where the charcoal sank below.

"How's my ass?"

"Great," I'd say, meaning it.

"Junior's in one of my classes. I have to look hot!" she'd squeal, jumping up on the mat of her bed, excitedly jumping back down to the cold, concrete that remained perfectly still, even under the weight of her exclamatory jump.

"I just want to sit on his face! Ahhhhh!" she'd squeal more.

"Then sneak in his cell and do it!" I'd deliver some nonsense on top of her nonsense, just happy she was happy.

Gina's been in for a month already, and is enrolled in school here. It's a continuation school, a way to stay on top of credits.

I hate when she leaves for class, not arriving back in our cell until after lunch. I read during the hours she's away. After my first court date came and went, I'd asked my dad to bring my summer reading. My AP Literature class requires us to finish reading *The Stranger*, *The Outsider*, and some Greek mythology book *before* senior year starts. I have no idea when I'll be released. I have no idea if finishing my summer reading will prove pointless, if I'll get out before my last year of high school begins. I have no clue.

The not knowing is the hardest part, boundless and suffocating.

Gina is loud and obnoxious, someone I'd never hang with outside these walls, but in here, she's my saving grace.

Her, my books, and sleep.

These three things offer me small reprieves of escape, short opportunities to forget where I am and how I got here.

One night, I think I'm going to lose it, though. And even Gina isn't doing it for me.

There are fireworks—the Disneyland fireworks.

I stand up on my bed, which is essentially just a slab of yellow-white concrete topped off by a thin, flat mat. It provides just enough of a boost to peer outside our barred window into the night sky.

Gina comes to stand on my bed, so she can see, too.

"Look!" she squeals.

"I'm looking," I respond, not with the slap of obviousness, but gently.

"I'm looking," I say again after a pause, even gentler, quieter.

"I love fireworks. Reminds me of sex," Gina says longingly.

Normally, I'd press into her bizarre statement, eager to know why, but tonight, I'm not interested.

Tears fall silently instead. Damn, stupid tears.

"Why are we here?" I ask, waiting upon an answer from God, not Gina. "What the hell," I whine quietly, sinking cross-legged down to the mat.

"It's okay. We won't be here forever." Gina plops down next to me and hugs me quickly.

"I know, I'm just tired," I dismiss.

I wasn't talking about juvie, though.

I wrap the tattered, knitted blanket around me, laying my head gently on the pillow, listening to the muted gunshots of the remaining fireworks.

"It won't be long," Gina reassures.

"I know."

"Dude, when I get out of here, the first thing I want to do is get Taco Bell," Gina informs me excitedly, unfazed by my tears and soliloquy of sadness.

"Why?" I chuckle into the wall, letting the laughter spill out like a machine-gun, a few seconds of relief as I contemplate Taco Bell's most alluring offerings. In between images of Cheesy Potato Burritos and Crunchwrap Supremes, she explains, "'Cause the food here is shit. And Taco Bell is bomb."

"Taco Bell *is* bomb," I laugh again, softer this time.

I drift into a fitful sleep.

All of my sleep here is fitful.

But it's also one of the few ways I get to be away from where I am.
Through a little sleep.
Or my books.
With Gina.
And so it goes.

Laughter. I can hear a steady stream of giggles coming from the corner of the house. I have a panoramic view of the entire, long house, basking in sunshine, left to right, window after window of room after room, the front door situated toward the right side of the house, and one last, long window into the living room. The enormous house made up of light blue wooden panels and surrounded by bright green bursts of grass, only interrupted by the slithering s-curve of the paved driveway.

A monster of a property.

Only takes me a second to understand it's in Orange Park Acres.

Where monstrous properties are aplenty; monstrous people, too,
                                        (myself included).

But this is no house of mine.

Or Kolton's, for that matter.

I recognize the house slowly.

    Megan's.

The laughter continues, and now that I know it's Megan's house, I know the laughter is coming from her room. I remember where her room is situated because we all went to her house after Winter Formal.

Winter Formal, last November.

Seems like forever ago.

By that point, I'd met Kolton, but he hadn't set my life on fire yet.

I'm suddenly no longer outside the house, but inside, walking toward Megan's bedroom door. I walk inside, and they both look up at me. She's underneath him, her boobs falling to either side like lop-sided water balloons. She looks all wrong underneath him like that, strained, too short, too much surface area of body and flesh squeezed underneath him.

Megan has a beautiful face—wide, sparkly smile, which always spreads to her eyes, darling dimples, cute button-nose. She's short, maybe five-one. She's a year older than me, and I've been loosely acquainted with her since fourth grade. In elementary school, we were in after-school plays together. In middle school, we were AIM friends. Nowadays, Didi plays soccer with her, and we all frequent many of the same parties. Two years ago, she also happened to be Kolton's girlfriend. Although they've been broken up for a while and she's now dating one of his friends, I still get the uneasy feeling she'd sleep with him given the chance.

"What are you doing!?" I scream.

I go straight for Megan's throat to choke the width of it.

Before I can make contact, someone's yelling, "Alright, 6:00 a.m., children, time to get up! If you want to take a shower, let your correctional officer know as they stop by your room."

I'm awake.

It was a dream.

Anxiety punches me in the stomach as I ache to escape these yellow-white cells, away from this place, back to my life.

> Which was what?
>
> I don't even know now.

The lack of control spins me out of my absolute mind.

If Kolton wanted to sleep with Megan, he could and would. And there'd be nothing I could do about it. I ached to talk with him, find out the rest of the details from the night of my arrest. Where had I been going? I know it was to see him, but where? Where had he been? Did he know I was coming? Did he tell me to stay put? Did he know I was in here? Did he try to call me? I had no idea where my cell phone was. I didn't have it with me during intake. Was it confiscated at the scene?

I shake myself from the dream, stall the questions, watch the small, square window on the door, and wait for the correctional officer to peek her head in and summon Gina and me for the showers.

Day nine, here we go.

Today's the day.

Day eleven.

My second court date.

They have to release me, I think blindly, not seeing any other possibility.

> This is a dangerous thought; most blind thoughts are.
>
> The last time I thought this dangerous, blind thought was the day of my *first* court date.
>
> *They have to release me.*
>
> The memory takes form.
>
> > It was a Tuesday, day four.
> >
> > My court date had finally arrived.

I was summoned into a blank room, where I waited.

I was assigned a public defender, who I spoke with for only a minute.

I had never witnessed someone jam-pack so many words into one minute. The words like sardines, packed together with no breathing room to spare.

Words like:

"Courtroom. Call your case. Confirm your name. Nothing more."

"Three misdemeanors. DUI. Assault and battery. Two different cops."

"First-time offender. Clean track record."

"Requesting early release until final sentencing reached."

Jasmine. My public defender's name was Jasmine.

My stomach wasn't just somersaulting. It was a goddamn circus in there.

Back in the blank room, I waited, and stared at the clock on the wall.

Waited, waited, waited.

One hour.

Two hours.

Three hours.

Three hours and forty-five minutes later, I was handcuffed and ushered into a larger room, a courtroom. The correctional officer steered me from behind, motioned for me to sit on a bench.

Within one minute, all the following managed to happen:

My case was called, a series of letters and numbers.

Like springing from a sling-shot, Jasmine jutted up from a bench situated close to the judge, jam-packed her words in more sardine-like-fashion. I recognized some of the same words she briefed me on hours prior—

"First-time offender."

"Requesting early release."

The judge had responded with words of his own, a string of sentences taking up about twelve seconds. The only word I recalled hearing was his conclusion—

"Denied."

I went blank.

I was brought to another bench, this time in a hallway.

I was melting.

Jasmine came and briefed me again. Can't tell you what she said. All I knew was I wasn't going home. I was stuck here. Trapped. No control.

"You have the right to a ten-minute visitation with your parents. They came to the trial. Do you want to see them?"

"Just my dad."

"Are you sure?"

"Yes."

My dad sat beside me on the bench, and I hadn't even pretended to be strong.

I melted into him, my tear-stained face in the nook of his arm, his arm wrapped around me,

"Dad…"

"It's okay Jordan. It's going to be okay. You know Mom came, too?"

"I can't see her."

"I understand."

"Can you bring my books? I start school in a week and a half. My English teacher assigned three as summer reading. They're on my desk in my room."

"I'll get them for you."

Ten minutes came and went.

Jasmine told us time was up, but I wasn't done melting into him.

"It'll be okay, Sweetie. Hang in there."

I didn't speak the rest of that day.

That was day four, though.

Today is day eleven.

Today's the day.

Day eleven.

My second court date.

They have to release me, I think blindly, not seeing any other possibility.

Another panel comes to visit us. Alcoholics Anonymous today. We're all huddled cross-legged on the floor, listening to the stories of five different women, when a correctional officer calls my last name: "Luther, court time. Let's go."

My stomach flips in excited anticipation and I jump to my feet. Safe in numbers from being singled out by the correctional officers, the girls begin to taunt—

"Ooooooooohhhhh—"

"See ya in a few days, girl!"

"You'll be back!"

"Never say never!"

I don't speak. I'm tempted to steal a quick goodbye glance at Gina, but I'm not willing to compromise my chances in the slightest. No talking. No eye contact. Hands behind my back. I know the drill.

We've already said our goodbyes, anyway. Gina loaded me up with a list of people she wants me to connect with on Facebook, on her behalf. We exchanged numbers, too. We prepared for this.

Ladies, I'll never be back. Don't wait for me.

And release me they did. Consequences in tow. A year of probation. License revoked. DUI classes. Yada yada yada.

No matter.

I was going *home*.

A correctional officer hands me a sealed bag with the clothes I wore the night of the arrest. She shows me into a room to change, and I've never been so eager to put on a crumpled pair of underwear.

I am released to my dad's custody, and we walk away from the facility side by side, half of me afraid someone's going to run after us, yelling, "Just kidding! Get your ass back here. You're never gettin' out!"

But no one comes running after us, and we make it all the way back to the truck.

Safely inside, I cry tears of sweet relief.

"I'm so sorry, Dad," I gush.

"I know."

"Are you mad at me?" I ask weakly, childlike.

"No, I'm not mad at you," he assures.

"You don't hate me?" I voice my fear aloud, feeling like I'll just fall apart if he answers yes, but I need to know one way or another.

"Jordan, I'm never going to hate you."

"You can tell me if you do. I can handle it."

"I don't hate you."

"I can't believe all of it."

"You just can't drink. You don't make good choices when you do. It's dangerous. We've talked about this."

Part of me thinks he's right, but part of me feels it's not that simple. I know we'd both like for it to be that simple. Just don't drink and you'll be fine, normal, happy. But I know it's more than that. It's all the gunky muck that oozes out *when* I drink.

"I know," I respond simply instead.

"We'll figure it out, Sweetie. You're gonna be okay. Are you hungry?" he changes the subject.

"Yeah. Can we get Taco Bell?"

Now that I'm home, I'm practically itching out of my skin to call Kolton.

As much as I want to talk to him, I'm nervous nonetheless, and I wait it out until night falls and everyone at my house is in bed.

I call him, and he answers.

It's not the rejoice I was anticipating.

"Hello?" he answers.

"Hi," I say, stealing his bare line.

When he doesn't say anything, I press on. "What are you doing?"

"Watching basketball."

"Do you know where I've been?"

"Yeah."

"Don't you want to see me?"

"You broke up with me."

Just like that, all my patience shatters, "Oh, fuck off, Kolton. I was driving to see *you* that night. I left to see *you*."

"I told you not to."

"Well, I did."

"You shouldn't have been drinking and driving."

"Oh, fucking please. You're one to talk."

"I know. That's why I'm sayin' you should know better."

"Are you going to keep lecturing me or are you going to see me?"

"Well, it's 12 a.m. and neither of us can drive."

"I know. Still…"

Two hours pass, and Kolton's finally warmed back up to me.

Just like any other fight, right back to good.

Ablaze.

Back to fire.

We're giggling the night away as I fill him in on how ridiculous the past two weeks of my life have been. I tell him all about Gina, and how quickly she broke the ice with her farts and pooping. We laugh at the wild girls banging on the walls and screaming out "ciaaaaaoooooooooo" in the middle of the night. What is that about, anyway?

Kolton fills me in on more stories from his own stay in juvenile hall, although his stories aren't as funny since he was isolated the whole time.

Even though we're right back on track, something is still poking sharply at the back of my mind. Normally, I'd only bring this up if I were gearing up for a fight, but we'd created something calm and safe in our conversation.

Something protective about a black night at 2 a.m., just him and me, no audience to be cool for.

Enough distance for breathing room—him tucked in his own bed, me tucked in mine.

Something whimsical in our giggles, building upon the commonality in our consequences—DUIs and stints in juvie—things of romance.

If I'm ever going to get some honesty from him, now is the time.

So, I go for it.

"I have a question I want to ask you."

"Okay, shoot."

"It's a random question. But I want you to answer honestly. And I promise you, I won't get mad. I just want you to tell the truth."

"Okay, what is it?"

"Did you have sex with Megan while I was in juvie?"

"What? Why would you ask that?"

"I just want to know. I promise I won't get mad."

He answers with what I somehow already know.

"Yeah, I did."

"Okay," I say calmly, as promised.

"How did you know? Did she tell you?" he asks in bewilderment.

"No," I respond, still calm. "I dreamt about it while I was in there."

―

The next morning, I get a ride to Kolton's house.

We're apprehensive of each other all over again.

He slept with Megan.

While I was in juvie.

And I dreamt of it.

 Can't help but wonder if the dream slipped into my mind
  the same night he slipped into her.

And I promised I wouldn't be mad.

But I never specified for how long.

My phone rings, and I see it's one of my guy friends. I pick it up. "What up, dude."

"Dude, you're alive."

"I'm alive."

"When did you get out?"

"Just yesterday."

"Oh man, ha, crazy Jojo over there. Well, glad to hear you're—"

Sitting beside me on the bed, Kolton snaps my phone closed, hanging up the call. I look at him confused. "Seriously?"

"Get off the phone." He looks me in the eye.

"What exactly is your problem?" I jerk back, glaring at him.

He doesn't bother with an answer.

From the second I walked through his bedroom door fifteen minutes ago, he's been withdrawn. I'm sure he can't believe I didn't flip out after he confessed to sleeping with Megan. He probably can't believe the calm I'm maintaining will last much longer.

One, he's right.

Two, he's beating me to the punch.

Tick-tock, Jojo, he prods.

Let's get this over with.

"Did you hear me? What is your problem? Why did you do that?" I shove him, jump off the bed, storming out of the room.

He doesn't like that.

He follows me out.

"Where do you think you're going?" he demands.

"Where do you think?" I spit back.

"Where are you fucking going?" his voice raises higher.

The increased volume of his voice throws me over the edge, and I spin around rapidly to face him. He wasn't expecting it, and practically bumps into me. I shove him backwards, like the slap of a ricocheted bullet.

"How *dare* you talk to me like that. Don't yell *at me*. You want to yell *at me?* I'm fucking going home," I spit through gritted teeth. He doesn't like to be challenged, but I'm fuming with adrenaline. I'm bigger than my body. No fear here. Only hate. Dark, dark hate.

"This how you gonna play it, Jordan? You gonna start shovin' me, huh? You want to play like that? Bite me, bitch. Do it again. See what happens."

There's no pause.

I hear the things he doesn't say.

The threat practically palpable.

"You fucking touch me again, and I'll make sure you wish you didn't, you piece of shit."

I shove him back again, wondering if he'll actually punch me. The one time he slapped me, it had been quick and out of peak annoyance, not thick with this kind of rage.

He catches backwards, steadying his feet once more, shaking his head back and forth, and looking to the heavens, as if asking for restraint.

His grasping for control, fighting himself not to put hands on me, doesn't stir anything in me besides more hate.

I'm ready to combust.

I'm ready to burn.

I just need him to light the match, throw it my way, give me a reason to burn him down.

I can't catch fire without him.

I shove him again, my hands exploding with the force of fire withheld. He stumbles back again, circling himself 180-degrees away from me so his back is facing me. I can still see him shaking his head back and forth, and he yells like thunder, "*Fuck!* Jordan..." He's pacing back and forth on an imaginary line, the width of five feet, back and forth, back and forth. "You don't want to fuck with me, Jordan," he says through gritted teeth.

Oh, but I do.

"Don't fucking turn away from me. I'm talking to you!"

"Fine. You want me to face you? You want me to face you? This what you want?"

He's turned around to face me, punctuating his questions by inching closer and closer to my face, until we're forehead to forehead, and I'm walking backwards, trying to break our contact, separate our foreheads, avoid the heavy hit of transferred energy from his thunderous questions. After six steps backwards, I hold my ground, and he stops stalking.

"You're fucking insane. Get the fuck away from my face," I slither in a tone dripping with poison, quieter than my previous screams.

"Don't turn away from you, but get the fuck out of your face? Which is it, Jordan? What do you want? Callin' me insane. Look in the fucking mirror, bitch."

He's backed away from me again, still pacing back and forth on his imaginary line, the width of five feet, back and forth, quick, pivot, pace, pivot, pace.

"I want you to leave me the fuck alone. Don't call me. Don't text me. Don't fucking talk—"

"Oh, here we go again. Is that what you want? Then do it. Do it already."

"Go to hell, Kolton. You're such a piece of shit. Cheating on me every time we get in a fight. Fucking Megan while I was in *jail*!"

"Calm down, bitch. You were in juvie," he dismisses with disgust.

"What the fuck ever. Same fucking thing. I'm done! I'm fucking done with you. You are *such* an asshole. I don't know how the fuck I ever dated you. I fucking hate you. *Hate you!*"

"Okay, Jordan. Okay, Jordan. So what does that say about you, huh? If I'm just so bad, so horrible, what about you? What's that say about you? Why are you with me? Why do you want to be with me, then? I'm just *so* terrible. So, what's that fucking say about you?" He practically rolls the questions into one another, not waiting to pause between each one, like the rapid rhythm of a rap song.

He looks at me expectantly.

Rant complete.

"Fuck you, Kolton," I scream through darkened eyes.

I open his driveway gate and let myself out, walking the entire way home, back to an empty house.

After an episode like that, I suppose there's nothing left to do but break up, right?

So, I did. I broke up with him again.

But this time, it feels different. More final.

Ha.

Haha.

Right.

I decide to pick out my first-day-of-school outfit, as if a planned outfit and a first day of school could help me now. Perhaps they could, though? Senior year. Last year. Familiar territory. Queens of campus.

I think of the tables in the quad, where all my friends will inevitably swarm before class, during Nutrition and lunch. The Senior Tables. No one needs to talk about meeting there. We all know these tables are a senior-year right. Our junior-year meeting spot in the hallways will inevitably be taken over by the new class of juniors. Just the way it works.

I anticipate the Senior Tables will feel slightly off at first, like they're not ours yet.

This is where Kolton used to hang, by the Senior Tables.

And a series of memories flood.

The days when he'd stand tall and looming on the bench of those red, crisscross lunch
tables, staring over at me shamelessly, me returning his stare.
    Did we smile at each other?
    Probably not.
He would call to me with the challenge of that relentless stare.
And I'd decline his invitation with my own blank stare.
I'd break our locked eyes, pretending to laugh at something Didi and Alsyn were talking about, look back at him once more, and decline all over again.
The whole thing was dumb.
He always knew I wanted to come over.
I can't recall how many lunches we'd stare at each other like this.
If he was feeling particularly persistent, he'd walk over to the short iron fence separating the senior tables from an area of grass that hugged the junior-year hallway spot, sometimes with Tobi, Georgie, and Nick in tow, sometimes by himself.
    When he made the effort that way, I always conceded.
    Met him halfway.
    We'd shoot the shit and giggle across the fence.
    Sometimes, Didi and Alsyn would join too.
    My favorite part?
        I'd always check down right, to the tables neighboring the Senior Tables.
        Jackie sat over there.
        I'd make sure she saw.
        On the brief occasion she'd actually make eye contact with me, she'd just squint her eyes in what I'm assuming was a dirty look.
        When we locked eyes like that,
            Kolton talking to me,
            me talking to Kolton,
            strong in numbers,
            Didi, Aslyn, Tobi, Georgie, Nick,
            all shits and giggles,
        I never looked away.
These memories fade, and I'm brought back to here-and-now, in my room, picking an outfit.
    I try on a strapless, off-white dress, covered with a top layer of tiny flower cut-outs, almost like lace but not quite. I pair the dress with strappy, second-

hand Steve Madden sandals, the black straps wrapped in flat, gold, chain-link metal, with a loop of strap around my heels. I slip that loop behind my heel and stand up to look in the mirror, take myself in. The sandals are a little small, my heel almost creeping out the back, but they work.

I'm still looking at myself in the mirror, cock my head to the right, and the only word that comes to mind is—*empty*.

Can't tell if it's me or the outfit.

Can't tell if it's the Senior Tables with me and no Kolton.

I try on a bracelet in hopes to bring the outfit to life, and as I go to close the clasp, I turn my wrist and run into the scars lining the underbelly of my arm, seven vertical pink puffs.

Newly healed, they're smooth, plump, and shiny like dolphin skin; and a shade of soft pink, almost like pink pearls. But against the contrast of my tanned skin, even on the underbelly, the soft pink squeaks brightly. It's alarming. I make a mental note to keep the inside of my arm turned toward my body at all times.

Will I ever be able to have a normal job? What kind of job can you have with scarred arms like that? I can't hide these scars in California, where the sun shines persistently. Maybe I'll have to move somewhere cold and dark, somewhere demanding long-sleeves and long faces. I'll fit right in. Won't even have to explain my sadness in a place like that. People will just assume it's the weather, and I'll nod and agree:

"Yep, just missing that Vitamin D."

BLUE WATER, *a year in the ocean.*

PART II: FLOATING,

& other things to do in limbo.

BLUE WATER, *a year in the ocean.*

OCTOBER 2009,
a punch of finality.

I figured they might show up. This is the Mexican-Nas party in Santa Ana. We've all been to this party before, with the same groups of people, so when I see Jackie and Kolton walk in, I can't say I'm surprised.

After Kolton and I broke up a month ago, he crawled right back to Jackie.

Jackie's in the same grade as me, so although Kolton's not at school with us anymore, I still have to see her during the week. My friends know better than to speak such nonsense, but random people say we look alike. Just because we both have brown hair and brown eyes. I don't think we look anything alike.

She's quiet at school. From time to time, we'll catch eyes and she'll do her whole squinty-dirty-look thing, and I'll just stare back at her until she looks away, similar to junior year. She doesn't make eye contact too often, though.

Kolton's wearing a black and blue, plaid, long-sleeved flannel with his solid black jeans, bottomed off with his black PF Fliers. He looks good.

I'm drunk and surrounded by Aslyn, Didi, and Amy. Amy's an acquaintance of sorts. Aslyn brought her into the group recently. She doesn't go to school with us, but she's been hanging with us on weekends. Aslyn's always inviting strays to the group, her temporary little minions, until she gets bored with them. I never get too close to her strays. They usually don't stick around long.

I don't mind Amy in small doses. We call her Crazy Amy.

If we decide to roll one night, each taking a hit of ecstasy, Crazy Amy takes four.

If we're hanging at Aslyn's for a low-key night of drinking, Crazy Amy spikes her mixed drink with cough syrup, sippin' on that purple drank, getting all dopey, slow, and sloppy.

If we're shop-lifting snacks and fruity chasers from CVS, Crazy Amy snatches *two* handles of alcohol.

She just goes that extra mile, so she's earned the nickname.

Plus, there's something about her eyes. They're a shocking shade of green, and she appears to be in a continual state of wide-eyed elation, almost a little *Here's-Johnny!*-esque.

"Eeeckh, fuck Jackie," I seethe.

"That bitch is so gross," Crazy Amy validates me. "Let's go."

She pulls Didi, Aslyn, and me along until we're standing directly opposite of Kolton and Jackie. Jackie crosses her arms, slanting her right hip upward as she leans back into her left hip, scowling at the four of us so hard her eyes are almost shut as she all but cowers behind Kolton.

"Kolton. Long time no see," I gush with a smirk. "Jackie," I clip, beating into her with my eyes for the briefest second before turning back to Kolton. "So, are you guys hanging for a while?" I ask while looking Kolton in the eye directly and playfully tapping his arm.

Kolton looks slightly amused and uncomfortable.

Jackie is fuming.

"Um, bitch, can you *not* touch him?"

Before I can even respond, Crazy Amy inserts herself, "Listen, you nasty little troll. Don't ever fucking talk to my friend like that again."

Jackie spits back, "Well, *maybe* your friend shouldn't be such a slut!"

But surely, Jackie should have known better.

You just don't mess with Crazy Amy.

She's crazy.

Crazy Amy drops her red cup to the grass and lands a quick punch straight to Jackie's mouth, right where her lips just tisked the *tttt* sound of her last word: *slut*.

If we're getting into a verbal catfight, Crazy Amy turns it into a brawl.

I don't even think it's because Crazy Amy feels that our friendship is held together with some iron string of loyalty. I think it's because she likes me *enough,* and she can turn any situation into a full-fledged scene when given the opportunity.

Kolton jumps in to break them up. I can hear Jackie yelling at us as he pulls her away.

I'm still a bit in shock as they disappear from the party.

Didi and Aslyn are laughing hysterically. Crazy Amy is riled up, likely swimming in adrenaline.

"Fuck that little troll. Thinks she can call you a slut? Uh-uh. Fucking bitch."

"Dude, you're nuts," I yell over the noise of the party.

"Nah, fuck that chick. Stupid fucking bitch."

"You just nailed her." I'm still in disbelief.

"She's lucky your man pulled us apart."

"Right in the mouth…"

"I'd do it again, she ain't careful. Uh-uh."

"Damn…you good?" I ask her, offering up my drink.

"Yeah, fuck her," and she takes a gulp of my drink. After a few breaths, she calms, and we begin to laugh alongside Aslyn and Didi.

I laugh because I'm drunk.

I laugh because I don't know how else to respond.

I laugh because I realize Kolton and I are undeniably done.

I laugh so I don't cry.

MARCH 2010,
carefully choosing college.

College commitments are due soon.

I had my heart set on University of California, Santa Barbara, for a while now, but as it gets closer, reality sinks in.

If I went to UCSB, I'd ruin my life beyond repair.

With last summer's track record, I'm quite confident of it, actually.

The party scene there is another world entirely. Step foot in Isla Vista and the buzz is palpable. I knew the only thing I'd walk away with after four years would be another arrest, a rape story, an STD, and a pickled liver. I'm raw and emotionally volatile. I don't have the self-discipline for any alternative outcomes at a school like that.

I still want to go.

But the ruin-my-life-beyond-repair fear is stronger.

This leaves me two options: San Diego or Long Beach State.

I didn't apply to many schools because, well, I don't care much at this point. And I don't have any pressure from my parents one way or another. I'm pretty sure my dad hasn't seen a single report card in the last two years. Since I'm the one who gets the mail, I always intercept them first, and my dad hasn't thought or known to ask. I don't think he's aware that I'm about to graduate with a 4.1 GPA. Or that I got into UCSB.

I asked him to visit the San Diego State campus with me last weekend, and this weekend we're visiting Long Beach State.

We park in the lot by the Student Health Center and get out of the car to meander through the campus, take it all in. Can I picture myself walking these sidewalks, lugging my books and bag from class to class? Can I see myself passing by this circular, spitting fountain?

We tour the on-campus dorms, and I hate them. Lack of light, brick walls. Then there's the worn, wooden closets. They feel suffocating and old. And not a charming, whisper-of-vintage kind of old, but like a house from the '60s without the pops of color. Stale.

Freshman are required to live in the dorms their first year. These dorms have me leaning toward San Diego.

"We also have our off-campus dorms, located a mile and a half from here. Those dorms were just renovated this past year, and there's a free shuttle bus that runs all day, transporting the students to and from campus," our guide gushes cheerfully. Perhaps she read the *no* on my face as we maneuvered around the tight quarters of this dorm.

"I'd like to see those ones," I say.

"Alright, let me give you the address, and there'll be more student guides to show you around when you get there," she explains.

"Thanks." I'm already turning to leave, and my dad shuffles behind me.

Hi

A text pings through my Blackberry. I don't have Kolton's number saved in my phone anymore, but no matter. I recognize his number and besides, I've been thinking of him. I believe in that sort of energy hoopla. I believe if I think of him enough, that energy can float right on out of my body, crossing freeways and cities, tap on his forehead, and proceed to seep right into his mind.

I miss him. Hearing from him feeds that need of mine to be on his mind. Satisfies that clicking need, if only for a minute. Doesn't mean I'm happy to hear from him. He's distracting, confusing, and no matter how we start, no matter what we do in between, the ending is a crushing constant. I'm always left wanting, itching, hungry, lacking. After a round-about of Kolton and me, I'll find myself unable to physically be anywhere for too long, because everywhere will feel stifling. Existing already feels like an effort. I don't need him yanking me around on top of it.

It takes everything in me, but I decide not to respond.

As advertised, the off-campus dorms are just over a mile away.

"I like how much light these ones get. The light-wood floors are kind of cool. And I like the mirrored closet doors," I offer out loud.

Just like that, it's decided.

I settle on Long Beach State—for the sake of natural lighting and mirrored closet doors, but mostly because I still don't have my driver's license. Long Beach is closer to home than San Diego, which, although streaked with horrible memories, is all I have.

This is how I make my decision.

A whole lotta fat, blubbery apathy with speckles of insight. Insight that isn't effectively insight at all. Lazy reasons I choose not to challenge inside my own mind.

Pick a school, any school.
Whoop, not that one.
Pick another one.
Just keep moving.
Ride the momentum.
Let the years of grinding through classes and extracurricular activities carry you through.
Ride the momentum.

I don't have a better plan than college.

Even if I don't care about it anymore.

As I conclude the decision aloud to my dad on our drive back home, I have a fleeting vision of a fresh start:

    College.

    No more DUIs, no more violence, no more stints in juvie.

    Back to the golden child I was before all the trouble.

    Back to happy.

    No more Kolton, either.

    Fresh start.

    College could be different.

    Life could be different.

    I could be different.

As quickly as the fleeting vision comes to mind,
    it dissolves,
        and I mock it on its way out.

Finishing senior year takes every ounce of strength I have left.

Every. Single. Thing. Hurts.

I've changed my definition of happiness. Because when you're down, down, down, happiness isn't what it used to be. When you're down, down, down, happiness lowers its standards, becomes simpler, only begs for the absence of despair, which isn't genuinely happiness to begin with. So, when you're down, down, down, happiness is just being able to float, hoping if you accidentally bump into a wall, it's made of matte indifference and not sticky guilt, hate, shame, or more misery.

Probation visits.

Hard knocks on bedroom doors.

Knocks on the door will never again make my heart beat in joyful anticipation, but rather with an adrenalized rush of panic.

Parties with friends that I know I'm not supposed to be drinking at, but do anyway.

If I get caught doing anything where the police are involved, I'm screwed. I'll get sent back, not to juvie, but jail now, since I'm eighteen.

But if I'm not at school or parties, I'm home.

Home.

Empty, empty home.

I never know where my dad is.

There's never much food in the house, usually only some frozen floutas from Costco.

It's a mess in every corner, in the sink, in the bathtub.

I get a boyfriend.

Doesn't last more than four months, and I don't care at all.

We go to prom together. Prom. Which makes me miss Kolton all over again.

When I break up with the new boyfriend, he cries. I feel nothing.

And high school graduation.

There's that.

And now summer.

Just one more stretch of days to kill until I can escape and begin my new college life.

AUGUST 2010,
what do you mean, she's mean?

I have two days left until I move into the Long Beach dorms, where I'll be semi-trapped because I'm still not driving.

Summer is wrapping up, and what better way to send it on its way than with a party?

At least with those of us left in Orange.

Aslyn and Didi are both gone.

As planned, Didi earned her full-ride to Oklahoma on a soccer scholarship. Training started earlier this summer, so she's been gone for two months. Aslyn was scheduled to move up to San Francisco a month after that.

After Didi left, Aslyn softened toward me immediately. Though our friendship had a delightful beginning, it grew complicated as the years passed. Aslyn hated me for reasons beyond my control, and I hated that she hated me, but I loved her still. She played hot and cold with me, and became subtly cruel, operating at a level of discreetness that typically only females can read– –psychological warfare.

When I started getting cold sores this past year, she pounced. "Maybe if you weren't always biting your lips, you wouldn't get those things."

Even worse than the cold sores, my deepest source of shame was this hidden habit I had since I was young—pulling my hair. I have no idea why I do it. My best guess is it serves as some sort of self-soothing technique, and it's incredibly difficult to stop once it starts. The urge to pull would disappear for years without me thinking twice about it, and then reemerge during periods of distress. My mom was the only one who knew. When I was little, we came up with a code word she would say gently to bring my awareness to what I was doing, and help me stop. The code word prevented deeper embarrassment in front of my brothers and dad. I have no clue when or how Aslyn noticed the habit, but once it was on her radar, she wasn't as generous as my mom. "Stop plucking your hair. You're gonna go bald."

She was also eager to share news of my reputation growing shifty when I started making out with random guys at parties once the drinking kicked off our sophomore year. "Nate told me the Villa Park guys were talking about you being kinda slutty. You should probably cool it with the make out seshes."

It's a complex dynamic to be picked apart by someone you love, someone who is supposed to be on your side.

I imagine this is why most of her stray, minion friends never stuck around long. Once the honeymoon phase was over, she dropped into the darkness that still had a hold on her heart. I knew her secrets. The ones she shared when we first became close. I knew why she was mean. I excused most of her behavior because of her secrets. I thought she deserved someone to truly love her. She did. We all do. But she acted in ways that made it difficult to do so.

My tactics switched between ignoring her and clawing back.

One particular claw-back of mine rivaled hers in cruelty. I had been passed out after drinking at her house with a small group of our friends. After being woken up with a pillow to the face from one of our dumb guy friends, I went on a rampage. She was my first target. Any day-to-day restraint I maintained in ignoring her accumulative digs at me, was long gone.

I called her fat.

I never actually thought she was fat, but I knew it was the kill shot. Her deepest insecurity. She didn't talk to me for a week after that one.

There was also the unspoken competition for Didi's affection—one I never opted into to begin with. Didi sensed it too. We were both intuitive enough to shrink the way we adored each other to keep Aslyn's wrath at bay. I allowed myself to be the third wheel in an attempt to keep the peace.

But the month before Aslyn left for San Francisco was different; she clung to me. Hate or not, she needed someone, and Didi was gone. We spent every day together until it was time for her to leave. I hadn't spent that much one-one-one time with her since freshman year.

I think back on those early memories.

The beginning of our friendship felt enchanting, like entering a made-up world we created ourselves. She knew how to dress up ordinary activities into worthwhile adventures—like the time she had Didi and I join her in making tie-dye shirts and wrapping our foreheads in paisley red, rolled-up bandanas before biking across town to watch one of our guy friend's baseball games. What could have been a simple bike ride turned into a uniformed girl gang, battling the heat of summer, on a mission to rally our friend's spirits against the opposing team.

Or, the times we had to get creative between our two-a-day cheer practices. We would prank call my dad's cell phone from an unknown number, and leave him voicemails of us singing along to *NSYNC's "I Want You Back".

You're all I ever wanted
You're all I ever needed
Yeaaaaayuhh.

We'd start busting up before getting too far into the song, and have to hang up before blowing our cover. As though he had multiple suspects in his life that would leave him voicemails like that…

Fast-forward to the last sweltering day before Aslyn left for San Francisco. After laying out at her mom's pool, she drove me back to my house. I got out of her car, said goodbye as normally as any other day, and she drove away. No hug. And the next day she was gone.

My heart ached when she left; perhaps even more than when Didi left. I still had Britney and Emily, but it wasn't the same. My two best friends were gone.

As I sit here on this couch at this pointless party, I miss them.

I don't want to miss them anymore so I drink myself into a stupor instead.

When I wake up, I manage to find a ride back to my house, back to my bed. My bed just isn't going to do it, though. A year out, and I still want Kolton's bed. With one eye squinted closed, I text him through drunken determination.

Kolton
jojo
I'm leaving
where?
School
cum over
Come get me
where?
My house
k

It's after midnight. I have no idea if anyone else is even home, so I walk straight out the front door. I trek down our long driveway to meet Kolton out on the street. I'm waiting at the end of our driveway, where a short, red-brick wall separates it from another long driveway. This paralleled driveway branches off into a spackle of four additional homes, each one on at least an acre of land, like ours. Another four homes. Another four worlds. All tucked away, branching off from this one paralleled driveway.

To pass the time, I hoist myself atop the red-brick wall, only a few feet high. I'm not thinking of this wall for what it is: a road to four other homes, four other worlds. I'm thinking of this wall as a place to perch my butt while I wait for Kolton. I'm thinking of this wall as a place to steady my angst, ground my ass, because even through my drunkenness, the height of the situation is not lost on me.

Kolton. Kolton. Kolton.

I get to see him.

I get to lie with him.

I get to be held.

Can we claim each other once more?

Can we dissolve past pains, lick each other's wounds?

Can we get back together?

I lose myself in the tunneled proximity of possibility. The possibility of us is so close. He has to be but minutes away. A car turns down the driveway, flooding my eyes with its headlights. I plop off the red-brick wall, in plain sight, ready to be reunited. Ready to begin again. The car slows down a few feet beyond where I'm standing. From this side angle, in absence of blinding headlights, it becomes recognizable.

It's Jason. My brother.

"Dude, what are you doing?" he asks as he rolls down his window.

"Nothing. I was walking home," I say nonchalantly.

My entire family hates Kolton. If he pulls up while Jason's lingering here in the driveway…well. No good can come of that scenario.

"You going home?" I ask Jason dumbly.

"Yeah, get in the car," he concludes the rendezvous.

I maintain my composure, acting like it's totally normal that I'd be *walking home* after midnight, especially when *walking home* looks like me perched expectantly on the red-brick wall, and not actually *walking* anywhere.

As we pull up to our house, I'm still acting nonchalant, and I head to my room, close the door.

I text Kolton.

Wait for me at the end of the driveway.

He quickly responds.

here

Be out soon

Great. It's going to take me a few more minutes to get all the way back down the driveway, and now I have to sneak past Jason. I take off my sandals, holding them in my hands, and turn my door handle as quietly as possible. Standing in the hallway, still holding my sandals, I slowly close my bedroom door, releasing the door handle so slowly that I succeed in not making a sound.

Our house is one big rectangle, my bedroom at the far right of the house, Jason's room in the middle, and the front door at the far left of the house. It's riskier to try and sneak all the way through the kitchen, past the hallway leading to Jason's room, past the living room, past the dining room, all the way to the front door. I figure the back door, spilling off from the laundry room into the backyard, is my safest bet.

Our backyard is a whole hill of dirt. There's not much light from the night sky, and I can't see a thing. I tip-toe as quietly and quickly as I can through the backyard, trying not to crack any twigs beneath my bare feet. I make it all the way around to the front of the house.

Uh oh.

Problem.

Kolton's car is *in* my immediate driveway, not over 250 yards away at the very end of the driveway that meets Orange Park Boulevard, not safely away from my house, not far away enough from Jason's close gaze. Jason could walk outside and—

Shit.

There he is.

Jason opens the front door, yelling at me, "Damn it, Jordan!"

I'm closer to the car than Jason is, so I make a run for it.

I open the backseat car-door closest to me, and realize Kolton's brother, Cyler, is driving.

"Go!" I yell.

"Are you sure?" Cyler asks apprehensively, looking to Kolton for confirmation.

"Go, Bro," Kolton urges.

Jason yanks open the car door I just closed and grabs for me. I scoot to the other end of the backseat, but he juts his head inside, taking hold of my arm, and rips me out of the car. I'm absolutely heated and still drunk enough to do something about it.

Plus, the tunnel vision.

I'm still intent on the possibility of Kolton and me. Seeing him. Lying with him. Being held by him. Nothing's getting in my way. Nothing. No one.

I shove my brother away from me with a force beyond myself. I whip around, clambering back into the car, screaming at Cyler once more to *just go*.

Jason yanks the door open again, grabbing me with more force than the first time. But I yank away from him with more force than the first time.

Suddenly, he drops my arm without warning, shuddering backwards with a yelp of agony that he tries to contain. I pulled his shoulder out of its socket. This has happened before. Well, I haven't pulled it out. But it's been pulled out before. When shoulders get yanked out of their sockets even once, it's a lot easier for it to happen again. So, yeah, here we are.

He retreats to the house with his limp shoulder, spitting and muttering the whole way in, shaking his head back and forth, matching the cadence of his angered, frenzied thoughts as they spill aloud: "Fucking piece of shit. Ends tonight. This shit's over. That fucker. Swear to God."

With Jason out of the way, I scream at Cyler once more, "Let's fucking go!"

Cyler doesn't say anything. He puts the Benz in reverse and drives the three of us back to their house. I'm still drunk, emotion oozing frantically, still alive and raw from the chaos of the whole ordeal, heightened further by the fact that I'm with Kolton. I'm here. At his house. I'm with him. We retreat to his room. I keep wiping angry tears away from my face, muffled chokes of air escaping every few seconds, as I try to catch my breath and calm down.

I don't know how many minutes pass before Kolton's parents burst through his bedroom door. Nancy's voice crackles with haste. "Jordan, you need to get out here. Now."

"Great," I mutter in anticipation of what's to come, wipe away more angry tears, and put on my game face.

I walk out of Kolton's room, past the kitchen, towards the wide-open front door. Outside the front door, Jason's standing with Justin, both their arms crossed against their chests, like body guards, waiting to escort me home.

"Let's go," Jason says through a clenched jaw.

"My sandals." I go to turn around.

"Nope." Jason reaches his arm inside the house, wrapping an excruciating, pinched grasp around my arm. In the instant I turn my head, trying to retreat back in the house, I am momentarily released from my tunnel-vision, seeing for the first time the extent of the situation as it's unfolded.

I see Kolton, Cyler, Nancy, James. I see their expressions—ready to throw down, fear, anger, concern, respectively.

Of course, Kolton's ready to throw down. I'm nowhere near his thoughts. His face looks like a growl, like he's begging my brothers to step foot inside his house, to give him somewhere to dump his anger.

Cycler looks out of his mind. Like his dad, eccentric is his thing. Not anger and aggression. Between a forced hand at driving the getaway car, to my brothers hopping their ten-foot iron fence, breaking their safety barrier, to show up at their front door, I'm sure he's traumatized.

Nancy's fight-or-flight kicks in, and Mama Bear's gone into fight mode. The safety of her house and family threatened, she looks absolutely pissed. And I'm the one who brought it in. Kind of. Me *and* Kolton, but Kolton's protected by her loyalty, so I'm guessing all her anger is directed at me.

James. Sweet, sweet James. The calmer, kinder of the two parents, James' face drips with concern as he makes eye contact with me. I think he feels bad. Kolton and I caused a scene, but he knows me. Knows this isn't how I want to be. If it were up to him, I bet he'd love nothing more than to keep the peace and resolve the situation right here and now.

Jason's pinched grip pulls me back to reality.

Through this last sliver of a wider lens beyond the tunnel-vision, I decide to surrender, and I follow my brothers out of the house.

On the street, I see my Jetta parked idly. With all four doors wide open, I can see my dad in the driver's seat and Jackson in the back seat. When's the last time the five of us were all in the same place at the same time? My own family reunion. How sweet.

I willingly get in the backseat, squeezing between Jackson and Justin. Jason gets in the front seat. Each of them shut the four car-doors separately, the timing so close together, it sounds like a round of shots.

Slam, whack, bam, clap.

Slam, whack, bam, clap, and I feel entirely trapped.

My dad peels away from Kolton's house, screeching tires and all. He doesn't say a word to me. And it's too much to sit with, sit between, sit in.

I can feel their collective rage towards me.

But what about *me*?

Huh, what about me?

What about *my* rage?

What about *me*?

No one cares when I'm behaving. No one cares when I'm sad. But, oh, I make a scene, and now it's all my fault? I'm trouble? I'm the creator of all chaos? All on me, huh? All my fault, yeah?

Fuuuuuuuuuck all of you.

Fuck you all.

Fuck you guys!

I think it.

And then I say it.

I claw at the back of my dad's neck from the backseat. Keep screaming. Keep flailing around, even though there wasn't much room to flail, the small Jetta containing all of five of us. Too much. Too much anger. Too much to sit with, sit between, sit in.

My dad stomps on the breaks, making all of our heads whip forward, throws the car in park, busts out, yanks the back-door open—Justin's already stumbling out of the way—and grabs me by the hair, throwing me out of the car.

I lose my fucking mind.

I lose my fucking mind.

I lose my fucking *mind*.

He's got me flat on my back, flat on the gravel.

I scrape, scratch, claw, and flail upwards.

I make for his junk, kicking straight where it hurts.

> Black, black, black.
>> The night sky so black, so dark, I can't see.
>> My anger so black, so thick, I can't think.
>> His grip so black, so tight, I can't breathe.
>>> Black, black, black.
>>>> He chokes me out, my body finally going limp, my mind fading.
>>>> Choked out to blacked out.
>>>>> Black, black, black.
>>>>> *Black out.*

I come to as we're pulling into our driveway. I'm still seething but weakened. Back inside the house, I beeline for my room, slamming my bedroom door with rage, locking it behind me. Before I know it, I hear the high-pitched hum of power tools, and once boosted a half-inch from the floor, my bedroom door suddenly falls with a thud, punching the wood. A second later, it's gone. They took off my *door*.

I chase them into the kitchen, screaming and yelling.

They ruined my chance of possibility with Kolton.

> Destroyed everything.
>> Stripped me of love.
>>> Ripped apart my chance of being held.
>>>> Somewhere in between hating them and—
>>>>> *Whoosh—shatter—*

There goes one of the bowls.
Misses Justin's head.
Shatters on the ground.
Slam, whack, bam, clap.
I copy the cacophony of the car-doors from ten minutes prior.
Duplicate the noise, release the force against anyone getting within arm's reach.
Slam, whack, bam, clap.
But it's me this time.
I'm slamming, whacking the floor beneath me.
They have me.
My right arm pinned under Jason's force.
My left arm pinned under Jackson's force.
My legs pinned beneath Justin's force.
It takes all three of them to hold me down.
But, power in numbers, they have me.
All three of them, sweating and grunting.
Restraining me, as my screams curdle the sticky summer air.

    & I rip back and forth,
    back & forth.
    Screaming like this is rape.
    Screaming all the screams
    I'd been holding in.
    I'm screaming at Kolton.
    I'm screaming at my parents.
    I'm screaming at my life.
    Why am I *still* here?
    I scream for questions
    unanswered.
    I scream for anger.
    I scream for sadness.
    I scream for injustice.
    I scream for hate.
    I scream for death.
    I scream for me.
    I scream because I tried to
    give up & the world kept

> bringing me back.
> I scream & I scream
> & I yell obscenities.
> *Fuck* streaks every sentence.

What is it about summer? What is it about August? What is it about Kolton? What is it about me? Last year, it was the police pinning me down. This year, it's my own family. How am I still here, even one year later? I'm still so sad. I'm still so angry. Why didn't anyone help me? Why didn't anyone see me? Why didn't anyone hold me?

I run out of fuel, so the screams subside for a bit.

My dad called the cops when my brothers first pinned me down, and shortly after, I hear pounding on the front door. Two cops pour into the kitchen, trailed by a woman with a metallic, silver clipboard. In a matter of seconds, I'm flipped onto my stomach, my hands brought together and handcuffed behind my back, the boys released from restraint-duty.

"You gonna cooperate?" one of the cops asks.

A memory of the cold, lonely, yellow-white walls of my cell from last summer stabs my mind, reminding me of the isolation I know I'd never be able to handle again. I respond through gritted teeth, "Yes."

"'Kay. Get up on your knees. I'm gonna stand you up," the cop instructs.

Once I've risen to my knees, he props me up the rest of the way to a standing position,

maneuvering me to sit down at the kitchen bench behind us. It's the woman's turn now, the one with the cold, silver clipboard. She takes great pause before she begins her series of questions. I don't say a word in response.

Instead, I glare up at her through dead eyes.

She looks altogether confused and scared, but continues moving through the questions, concern carving a deeper and deeper furrow between her eyebrows.

"Oh, *sta-foo!*" I suddenly scream at the woman with her silver, clicking clipboard.

My dad looks at my brothers in question, wondering what that means, while voicing the question aloud: "Stafoo…? What does— "

"It means *shut. The fuck. Up,*" I educate them on the acronym—S.T.F.U.

The woman looks down at her clipboard and back up at me, as if somewhere in between lies an answer for what I am. What am I?

Why am I so hateful?

Why am I so aggressive?

Why am I so angry?

Why am I so mean?

5150—involuntary confinement of an individual suspected to be a harm to themselves or others.

Deciding I'm certainly a harm to others, she gives up on the questioning and says it's time to take me in.

I'm sure she's eager to do so.

Take me away.

Analyze some more.

And send me back after a seventy-two-hour hold, cleaned up and contained in a category.

Diagnosed with a name.

    Something to be contained by that name,
    fixed with medication,
    doped up into shaping up.
        Contained by that name, huh, lady?
        Fix me, fix me,
        Med-i-cate me.
        Dope me up.
        So we can shape me up.

I'm released from my seventy-two-hour hold.

Diagnosed with nothing.

They said the behavior was alcohol-induced, not psychological.

They told my dad I should look into AA, rehab, things like that.

In the car on the way home, I say I'm sorry.

And I am.

I feel horrible.

I see burgundy scabs across his face from where my nails ate the skin nights before, think of him going into the office like that, and I can barely hold myself together.

I am so, so sorry.

I am a monster.

I am so, so sorry.

He knows.

But he doesn't know what to do with me.

"What are we gonna do?" he asks me.

"What do you mean? I have to go to school," I answer desperately.

"The boys think you shouldn't go. They said to send you to rehab," he tells me.

"I can't go to rehab. I can't do that. I have to go to school. I have to keep my momentum. It'll screw up everything if I go to rehab. I'll have to drop from all my classes. I'm supposed to move into my dorm *today*."

I'm in frantic tears, fear welling up in my chest. It's the same fear that washes over me when I think of the yellow-white walls of my cell from last summer.

Rehab sounds like isolation.

No control.

Trapped.

Cut-off.

Cold.

Lonely.

"So what do we do?" he asks again, weighing the options.

"School. Dad. School! I have to go. We'll go home, I'll pack my stuff, and you can drop me off in Long Beach," I say urgently.

"Okay," he says, his voice heavy, uncertain, and I think a little sad.

"I'm sorry," I say again as I look at the scratches on his face once more, the apology on repeat in my mind.

"I know," he says, still sounding heavy, and there's sadness there. There's definitely sadness. It scares me. He can't be sad. He can't be uncertain, dropping me off at school, like he doesn't know exactly the right thing to do. He can't be the one not knowing. That's his job. He has to know. It's *my* job not to know, to be the one running out of solutions. He has to have solutions. Boundaries, rules, punishments, solutions, course-corrections. That's his job! He's supposed to know what to do.

But I can hear it in his voice.

He doesn't know.

He doesn't know what to do.

He doesn't know what to do with me.

Uncertainty.

And sadness.

The uncertainty is scary.

The sadness is unbearable.

    The sadness feels like he's giving up.

    It sounds like he believes I'm undoubtedly going to fail.

    To continue wrecking my life.

We remain silent the rest of the drive home.

"Just give me thirty minutes. And then we can go. I'm mostly packed up," I urge as we pull in our driveway.

"Okay," he says.

We walk into the house together, and the boys are all laughing in the kitchen. They look up at us and quiet down a bit. Jason and Justin disperse to their rooms, not saying a word. Jackson lingers, still picking at a plate with a chicken flouta on it.

He looks up at me as I approach the kitchen.

During my rampage a few nights prior, I had screamed and spilled some of Jason and Justin's secrets that my dad didn't know about. I hadn't made any digs at Jackson. Everyone knows he's the favorite. You're not supposed to do things like that—have a favorite—but whatever. Somewhere in my drunken rage, the favoritism apparently shielded him from the onslaught of incriminating disclosures.

He's standing on one side of the island, in the middle of the kitchen, following me with his eyes until I'm standing on the opposite side of the island, directly in front of him.

My dad walks past us, headed for his room.

Jackson's elbows are both propped on the island, one arm lying flat and parallel to the counter, the other arm at a forty-five-degree angle, holding the chicken flouta he's taking bites from.

"I'm really sorry," I say, bursting into tears.

"Come here," he concedes.

He embraces me in a full hug while I cry.

"I have to pack," I say with a wet face and a snotty nose.

"'Kay, come on," he says, and walks with me to my room.

I tell him stories from the looney bin, explaining how when I was sleeping one of the nights, I woke up in the middle of the night to hissing, satanic-like mutterings. I thought to myself that I literally might be down-right crazy, or this is a nightmare. But then I got up and went to the bathroom, and it still didn't stop. I realized it was one of the *actual* crazy girls across the hall from my room. Terrifying nonetheless. I explained how even if you weren't actually crazy going into a place like that, how easy it'd be to get confused by the time you left.

"Do you think I'm crazy?" I ask Jackson, after finishing my story.

"Nah, you're wild. And you *act* crazy sometimes. But you're not for-real crazy," he dismisses the idea.

"I feel crazy sometimes," I admit.

"I know, fool. We all do," he answers with a shrug of his shoulders.

With limited time, I shove what wasn't already packed into black trash bags, and Jackson helps me pack me up the car. When we're finished, I grab my dad, and it's time to go. Jason and Justin are still avoiding me in their rooms, and I make a mental note to write them both apology letters. Jackson gives me a final hug.

"You'll be fine. You can come home on the weekends. You're not far. Chin up." He releases me.

"Thanks," I say with a wimpy face. He kisses my hair where it meets my forehead, and I leave.

On the drive to Long Beach, a subtle numbness settles over me.

A wall.

A shield.

A barrier.

If I'm going to survive this, I've got to separate myself. Separate myself from myself, from the world, from others, from my feelings.

Chin up, I put myself away.

OCTOBER 2010,
what do you do in a dead sea?
Float.

School is easy.
Getting up is hard.
I hate Long Beach.
But I don't want to be home, either.
I'm scared to drink.
Being sober means I don't know how to make friends, though.
I don't know if I actually want friends.
But isolation sounds like a death-sentence.
I block Kolton on my phone.
Wishing, every minute, he'd somehow show up at my dorm room.
I want to be saved.
But I repel even the slightest of niceties.
I move.
    From my bed to class, to eat, back to my bed, back to class again.
Yet I'm stuck.
    In my head, on Kolton, in my sadness, back in my head.
This is limbo.
    It's not much.
    Only a few things to do here,
    Like:
        Cry.
        Be afraid.

Do the bare minimum to keep life afloat.
Hug myself in the misery.
Fake a smile.
Be quiet.
Let my heart catch on glimpses of hope.
Mock myself when the glimpses fade back to black.
Float.
Repeat.
And so it goes.

APRIL 2011,
pick your poison.

I block Kolton.
I unblock Kolton.
I block Kolton.
Then I unblock Kolton.
But now, I'm about to see him.
It'll be the first time in months.
He's been texting me for a few weeks, and I'm home for the weekend, partying in Orange.
He tells me to come over.
So, I do.
I patter into his house, trying not to be heard.
When I find him in his room, he's romancing with his new poison. Apparently, he's graduated from daily weed to oxy since I last saw him.
I begin to protest, but his eyes simply reflect back an image of myself, and I rescind to silence.
Hypocrisy withholds my whiny words.
For I, too, have toyed with my poison tonight.
He's high on oxy.
I'm drunk.
Leave it to our poisons to envelop us in a blissful state of carefree play and banter.
A state in which I love him, and he loves me.
We're lying down together, face to face.

"I missed you," he gushes at me.

I can't believe he just offered that up for free.

"You always miss me," I respond.

"Don't tell anyone."

"No one would believe me."

And he breaks into a slow giggle.

He stares at me openly, and I wish, not for the first time, I could show him this version of himself—the good version—when he turns into the monster version of himself. Say, *Kolton, look, this is the real you. You don't have to be mean. This is who you are. You're good, I promise.*

"How's school?" he asks.

"I hate it."

"You should quit."

"And do what?"

"Come live here. With me."

"What will Jackie think of that?"

"I already told you we're done."

"Well. We both know I can't live here."

"You're right. We never get along for long."

"Never." I burst into an unexpected laughter, which then triggers a few tears, which I wipe away quickly.

"Don't cry."

"Why?"

"'Cause I don't know what to do when you cry." He laughs again. Gently.

"No. I mean, why don't we ever get along for long?"

"I don't know. We're too crazy."

"You're too crazy." I lightly tap his chest.

"I know. You are, too."

"I know."

Tonight is one of those rare occasions when we just work.

We're not even touching the ground.

We're floating, but it's the good kind: elevation, not oblivion.

The next morning, I leave Kolton's because I need to get a ride back to Long Beach. I have to study for a test. Later in the afternoon, I figured he would have at least texted me by now.

Nothing.

Before going to bed, I call him.

Nothing.

I should have known. We said it ourselves just last night. We never last long.

Growing more and more infuriated by his lack of response, I call her. Jackie. Tell her everything. Tell her how he's been texting me, how he told me they were broken up for good, how he keeps inviting me over.

"So I hung out with him last night. But you know how he is. When I was with him, we'd have a fight, wouldn't even be broken up, and then I'd hear he'd run off to *you*, claiming we were done. When, of course, that wasn't the case. He's a liar, which is why I called."

I take a slow, shaky breath.

"You guys are still together, aren't you?" I finally press.

The pause in her response tells me everything I need to know, but instead of answering, she asks a question to my question. "Did you guys sleep together?"

"We did." I say it like a smack.

"Okay," she responds flatly.

"Well. Now you know. Good luck, Jackie," I hang up.

Predictably, my phone rings only minutes later. Here we go again. Here it comes.

> *Ring around the rosie,*
> *A pocket full of posies,*
> *Ashes! Ashes!*
> *We all fall down*
> ♪

I don't answer the first three times Kolton calls, so he resorts to firing off some fun texts:

Why the fuk would u tell Jackie?
Ur a dum cunt. I got what I wanted from u. thx.

And, of course, he calls once more, and I pick up. "Oh. Look who wants to talk now."

"Fuck you, Jordan. You think telling Jackie does anything? She'll come running back to me just like you did. Fucking dumb cunts."

"*Fuck you, Kolton!* Go fuck yourself!"

"You already did, bitch."

"You're a piece of shit. Fuck the fuck off and don't ever call me again."

I hang up and hate him.

We should have never succumbed to sleep last night.

We should have fought it.

We should have stayed awake forever. Stayed in our own little love affair—him, me, and our poisons.

Because it should come as no surprise that as today came and daylight broke, so did we.

Ring-a-round the rosie,
A pocket full of posies,
Ashes! Ashes!
We all fall down
♪

Together. Not together. Make up. Fight. Jackie. Back to me. Back to her. Ignore me. Ignore her. She's mad. I'm mad. He's mad. Make up. Fight. Together. Not together.

We all fall down.

Jackie breaks up with Kolton for that one. And it doesn't take long for him to come crawling back to me in her absence.

I fall asleep on his bed while we're watching *Bad Boys II*. When I wake up, he's gone. I wander groggily into the kitchen, then the living room, then out onto the porch. He's nowhere to be found. I go back in his room and call his phone.

"Where are you?" I ask, a little annoyed.

"My parents' room," he answers.

I hang up and head into his parents' room.

"You are grotesquely predictable," I mutter in disgust upon realizing what he's doing.

"Stop trying to sound smart. It's annoying," he delivers back, as evenly and nonchalantly as delivering the weather, not breaking focus from the jewelry he's turning over in his hands.

"Kolton," I bark, trying to get him to look up at me.

Exhaustingly, he glares up at me from under his dad's wire-frame glasses, saying nothing at all. He looks old in those glasses; old and stupid. God, he looks so stupid. Neither of us blink, and he turns his attention back to the jewelry, putting down one ring and picking up another, slowly turning it round and round, a circular hunt for value.

He could do worse than pawning off his mom's jewelry. In fact, he has. Past incidents jump to mind.

A few years back, Kolton and his friend Patrick needed cash. Not like they didn't both come from families where cash was plentiful; they just needed *more*. Enough to suit their pharmaceutical extracurriculars.

They had an acquaintance who'd recently sold a significant amount of coke and came upon a fresh sum of cash, just over $800. Logical next steps ensued.

Kolton and Patrick drove over to the kid's house, rang the doorbell, and, upon the kid opening the door, Patrick punched the unsuspecting kid in the jaw, knocking him on the floor. Kolton raced into the kid's bedroom, somehow found the cash, and they left.

For that little stunt, Kolton was thrown in juvenile hall for two months, locked up in isolation, and Patrick was sent to an all-boys boot camp in Ohio for nine months.

There are moments like these when I recall details of Kolton's past, and sometimes they're so inexplicable, I don't know what to do with them, because my need to be with him is equally puzzling, most likely larger, and downright blinding. I push the horrific details out of mind, not without consequence, of course.

The consequences are always the same:
    a little more venom to entangle and darken my spitting words,
    a little more fire to flare my too-quick temper,
    a little more rage to heighten my outrageousness,
        all subdued until the next time I get drunk and spill it on everyone.

I consider berating his behavior but stop.

For, truly, what am *I* to say to *him*?

After all, I'm with him in this moment.

I walk out of his parents' room, a little meaner, a little colder than before.

The nights begin to blend together.

When's the last time I talked to Kolton?

Haven't heard from him in weeks.

It's another aimless weekend, another aimless party back home in Orange.

What can I tell you about this party that you don't already know?

All these interactions, these nonsense conversations. They seem important in the moment, bloated with warm alcohol rushing through our bloodstreams.

We think we're getting somewhere in the bare-naked truths we spill, but we spill aimlessly, with no regard for who we're even talking to.

It could be a wall.

It wouldn't matter.

But none of it's important.

Yet, it's all we have.

So, I'm spilling some story to Klarissa, who happens to be a person but could be a wall.

Where are my friends, anyway? I wonder as I tell Klarissa I'll be right back and go looking for Emily and Britney. I find them in the living room, interrupt their own meandering conversations, and tell them it's time to take more shots.

In the kitchen, we each take two more shots of vodka, chase with Red Bulls, and we're laughing and talking nonsense.

We move back to the living room, and sink into the couch.

Britney spits out details about some fling that isn't unfolding as hoped.

Emily echoes Britney's woes. "I thought Jackson was coming tonight. He told me he was going to come." And she begins to cry. When did she get so drunk? I start to cry myself. When did *I* get so drunk?

"Kolton won't even talk to me. It's been three weeks. I'll get a call from him at 4 a.m. and try to call him first thing in the morning"—I choke up and breath a ragged, moist inhale of breath—"but he never answers. He just…disappeared. Again."

Besides us girls, there are two guys in the living room, wrapped up in their own drunken nonsense. Emily won't let up, though. Either she's the drunkest of the three of us or she's just the saddest. Her cries deepen, she buries her face in her hands, and in the wake of her need, Britney and I compose our blurry, drunken selves as best we can to console Emily. Her cries grab the attention of one of the guys, and he tries to help.

"Hey, don't be upset. It'll be okay."

Emily pauses, looks up to find the voice throwing sweet attempts of comfort at her, squints her wet eyes into a scowl, and spits, "Fuck you man. I don't even *know* you."

Well, shit! Emily's typically sweeter than all of us. Britney and I exchange sloppy smirks through glossy eyes, and start laughing.

We need to get out of here.

I find us a ride home and offer some condolences to the guy who tried to offer Emily some. "Don't take it personally. She's actually really nice. She's just super drunk."

Back at my house, we find Jackson. He's with another girl—probably why he didn't end up coming to the party—and Emily is devastated all over again. Emily and Jackson started hooking up about a month ago, but it doesn't seem to be going anywhere serious. She isn't the first one of my girlfriends to fall for one of my brothers. I don't mind, but I also don't get involved. She goes to my room to curl up in my bed and pass out.

Britney and I drink a little more in my kitchen. Fifteen minutes pass, and Jackson eventually walks the girl out to her car. As he walks back through the kitchen, I've begun crying again, and Jackson's concerned.

"Dude—what happened?" Everything is already a spinning blur and I have to shut one eye just to see Jackson clearly. I start to blab on about Kolton, and that's the last thing I remember.

The next thing I know, I'm waking up with my least favorite, most familiar headache.

It has to be 6:30 in the morning, and Emily is wide awake, sitting erect on the edge of my bed, wrapped in my white, fuzzy robe.

"I couldn't sleep," she offers through puffy, red eyes.

I sit up in response.

"I went and walked down the driveway, just to move," she continues.

"We're gonna be fine," I say unconvincingly as I put my hair up in a bun and rub my face, still waking up.

Emily doesn't need to explain. I know what she means. I'm in my own restless pain. The type of pain that keeps you moving from place to place, nowhere quite satisfying. The type where a whole day is spent moving from home to the store, from the store to the gas station, from the gas station to a friend's house, from a friend's house to another friend's house, until you're finally back home, falling into bed, exhausted from all the moving. No matter how much moving is accomplished, the pain is still there, close behind, like a shadow.

I'm thinking about Emily moving, her stroll down my long driveway, finding nothing, turning around, and coming back to my bed. I'm thinking of this and grab for my phone.

Kolton called again.

But this time, he left a voicemail.

He never leaves voicemails.

Britney and Emily begin to talk, so I walk outside. The concrete walkway stretches past my front door, leading to our front steps made of bricks—some intact, some crumbling, some missing altogether. There's a chill to the spring air, and it's bright outside, hurting my eyes and amplifying my splitting headache. I feel depleted and sad, and the morning sun feels wrong. I plop down on the first step and listen to the voicemail.

"So…I got a call from your brother last night. I don't know which one because he wouldn't say. Told me I needed to leave you alone, he doesn't want to see his sister cry anymore. Said you were crying a lot last night and pretty upset. He also said that if I ever talked to you again, that me and lil' homeboy would have trouble."

He pauses, exhales a dramatic breath out, and continues, "I don't know about all *that*."

"But whatever. Look, just call me back. We can talk, and I'll explain everything. No one needs to be confused. No one needs to be upset."

My heart jumps a little at the satiating thought of an explanation, some validation to sink my teeth into, some reason for his disappearance, the hope that he did, indeed, love me after all.

I call Kolton back, and he answers. It's the first time I've heard his voice in weeks. The questions practically pour out of me:

"Where have you been?"

"Why haven't you been answering my calls?"

"Why do you keep calling me at four in the morning and then disappearing again?"

"Where have you been?"

I end the interrogation the same way I opened it up.

But, of course, it's precisely the questions I'm not asking:

Why did you leave me? (Again.)
Do you still love me?
What did I do?
What didn't I do?
Am I losing you? (Again.)

He doesn't give much in the way of answers. "Which brother was that? Whoever it was, he's a fucking douche bag."

"Kolton…" I try to refocus him.

"Look, I haven't been ignoring you. I've just been busy. And I've been with my family. I just need to spend time with them right now, okay? Not everything's about you, Jojo."

"*Nothing*'s about me," I say under my breath as I glare back at the bright sun, wishing it would stop shining brighter and bigger while I dimmed darker and smaller by the second.

"What?" he asks.

"Nothing. I just don't get it. Even if you're with your family, you can still text me back and tell me that. And the calls at four in the morning? Like, what in the world. That doesn't make any sense," I push back.

"Look Jojo, I got to go. I'm going to a baseball game. We can talk more after the game."

"Promise me you'll call back," I say firmly.

"I promise."

Minute by minute and hour by hour, the day goes on, as days tend to do.

Evening arrives, and it's Sunday, so I have to get a ride back to Long Beach, back to the dorms. Back to my room, all saturated in pink décor.

As if all that pink could somehow save me.

A few days pass, and Nancy calls me.

"Hi, honey. Just wanted to see when Kolton and you were getting back from Long Beach, so I know when to make our dinner reservation."

"Hey, Nancy. You know, that's funny. I'm actually not with Kolton right now. In fact, I haven't heard from him in days," I gladly report.

"Okay, honey, I figured. He told us he was with you today but we suspected otherwise." Then she switches to a more authoritative tone. "Honey, if I were you, I'd stay away from Kolton right now. He's not in a good place and just about the worst thing for you," she finishes hoarsely.

I already know that.

She's referring to him being on drugs.

Which I already know.

But it's obviously getting worse because he keeps disappearing for longer and longer periods of time. I suspected this may have contributed to why he's been ignoring me on and off the last few weeks. But then again, he does that all the time. What tipped me off that things were *actually* getting bad was the 4 a.m. calls.

Drugs or not, I hang up with a smug look on my face, hoping Kolton will get in trouble.

Later that evening, I'm lying in my dorm room bed, my roommate gone, and whatever satisfying sentiment emerged from the thought of Kolton getting in trouble is now overshadowed by the reappearance of that restless pain, resilient through and through.

"Can you fucking *stop*?" I scold myself aloud.

Stop what exactly, I'm not even sure.

All of it.

Stop caring.
Stop being sad.
Stop going back.
Stop being involved.
Stop thinking.
Stop the mental anguish.
    Just. *Stoooooooooooop.*

JULY 2011,
a penny for your thoughts.

"Jordan's a good kid. She's gotten into a bit of trouble these past few years, so I just want to tell you some background on what happened and preface with the impact this may have had on her. Jordan has three brothers from me and my ex-wife, April."

Therapy was my dad's idea.

I'm home for the summer, having finished my first entire year of college. August is nearing, marking the anniversary of not only my DUI but now my 5150 as well. No matter what I did (school) or didn't do (drink excessively, talk to Kolton), I still felt a black cloud following me around, still fighting the depression and anxiety. I was terrified and desperate to avoid whatever catastrophic episode August had in store for me this summer, and I shared as much with my dad.

He suggested therapy. I said okay.

He told me to find a therapist and he'd pay for it.

I kept it on my to-do list but felt entirely daunted by the task.

I kept extremely busy, picking up old babysitting jobs I'd had in high school.

My dad picked out three therapists, gave me their numbers.

Penny's was the only voice that sounded warm enough over the phone.

So, here we are.

"The kids had a very solid foundation growing up. In about 2005, though, things really started to shift. April and I split up, and she moved out of the house. We were also both using drugs for about two years during that time.

I've been clean since 2007, but April's use has been up and down, kinda spotty. This has created a strained relationship between Jordan and her mother, which she's expressed has been hard on her.

"And the last few years, Jordan's been running into some trouble with drinking. It's not that I think she has a drinking problem, but rather a problem *when* she drinks. Straight-A student, super bright."

Guess he was paying attention to my grades after all, I think to myself.

And then he gets to the punch line. "With everything that's happened, though, she struggles with depression and anxiety and had a suicide attempt a few years ago."

alkdjflke.

There it is.

It sounds so insane, out loud like that.

With it spoken aloud, I can't help but wince and scoff at it.

I judge my actions well before anyone else can.

I'm saying sorry before I even know what I'm sorry for.

I don't like it being said out loud.

I know I did it, attempted suicide, but it still feels out of place to me.

Some years later and I still don't fully understand those actions, those dark parts of me.

Those parts feel like they belong to someone else entirely, so much so that after my dad discloses this piece of information about my suicide attempt, I feel myself separate into two people.

Crazy Jordan and Perfect Jordan.

Crazy Jordan's, well, crazy. She hates, drinks, bites, shrieks, and apparently tries to kill us.

Perfect Jordan's, well, perfect. She's kind, disciplined, smart, well-behaved, funny, and playful.

I can feel Perfect Jordan inching closer to my dad and Penny, sitting beside them, all three looking on at Crazy Jordan, bewildered, curious, concerned, but lost in understanding why. Why would someone do that?

With an audience, albeit just my dad, Penny, and Perfect Jordan, the suicide attempt feels juvenile. Stupid. Embarrassing. A child's post-tantrum hate letter scrawled in blue and red crayons, on the living room wall no less, because, you know, defiance. A scribble-scrabble reading, "I hat you all," missing the "e" on *hate* because it's a child, and while the passion's there, kids don't have it all quite down yet.

The whole time my dad was bringing Penny up to speed, I was sizing her up from where I sat on the couch, deciding on her. She had short hair, kind of like Jamie Lee Curtis. A gentle voice. Eyes that pinched shut when she smiled. And a soft, full roundness to her frame that made her feel nurturing and motherly in nature. But when my dad delivered his final kicker about my suicide attempt, I broke away from Penny, rolling my eyes, and staring out the window.

"Sounds like you've had a bit of a tough go, here, huh?" her voice directed at me, pouring like nectar.

My arms are still crossed tightly against my chest, my left hand popping out of the nook of my right elbow. I slide the pad of my thumb over the top of my middle-finger nailbed, back and forth, up and down. I don't know what to say, so I don't say anything. I just keep rubbing the top of my nailbeds with the pad of my thumb, hopping from nailbed to nailbed, mostly between the ring-finger and middle-finger nailbeds, but sometimes my index-finger nailbed, too.

Back and forth, back and forth, back and forth.

Up and down, up and down, up and down.

I still haven't come up with anything to say, but I find myself calm slightly with the repetition of my thumb against the smooth top of my nailbeds. Slowly but surely, slide by slide, I'm releasing something, even if it's the tiniest something.

I'm releasing something tightly wound, something pent up.

In miniscule quantities, but releasing nonetheless.

Back and forth.

Up and down.

Release, release, release.

The release doesn't have any words. That's okay. It's still something. Something small but mighty, and in a way, that works for me—pinpoints of relief.

Not all encompassing.

Not a landslide.

Not drowning.

Not too much.

Not so much that I can't handle it.

The remaining ten minutes go on like this, Penny asking questions, me sliding my thumb across the top of my nailbeds, looking out the window, my dad answering for me.

It's not much.

But it *is* something.

At the very least, it's one additional thing to do in limbo.

This is limbo.

Only a few things to do here,

Like:
> Cry.
> Be afraid.
> Do the bare minimum to keep life afloat.
> Hug myself in the misery.
> Fake a smile.
> Be quiet.
> Let my heart catch on glimpses of hope.
> Mock myself when the glimpses fade back to black.
> Float.
> Slide my thumb across my nailbeds.
> Repeat.
> And so it goes.

It's been three months, once a week.

I see Penny once a week, and some sessions I leave with more pinholes of teensy-weensy relief. Hope that I might actually crawl out of this darkness. Other sessions, not so much.

Our sessions always begin with her twinkly smile and a report of my past week's events, which always picks and plucks at the different layers of myself, my emotions, always trying to unearth answers that will make sense of all this—who am I? How do I feel? Why do I feel this way? Why am I here?

"My mom called me this week because Jason's birthday is this month and she wanted to plan a dinner thing for him. But I was babysitting, so I was taking forever to respond, and she sent like fifty texts with a million questions, and it was so annoying. It made me completely shut down. Like, leave me alone. I'm actually working. You should try it sometime, you know? It's just frustrating. She doesn't understand how stressful it is to always be in school or working. She doesn't get any of that because she doesn't have to do anything. Except be a screw-off and do drugs." I pause from my rant before adding, "Look, I know that sounds dramatic. But there's just stuff about her that really bugs me. And makes me feel like I just want to shove her or scream at her," I explain.

"You're mad at her," Penny offers.

"Yeah, probably," I agree.

"You're mad at her for leaving all those years ago," Penny continues.

"Yeah, I am. Like she got to do whatever it is that she wanted to do and left me with the boys. Who smell. And are dirty." I snarl my nose, indicating just how gross the boys can be.

"Do you love your mom?" Penny asks.

"Of course I love her. I mean, she drives me nuts, but I love her. I miss her. Or the way she used to be. I miss the way she used to be. Before all the drugs."

"Tell me about that," Penny directs.

"Well, it's kinda all over the place. The memories that come to mind don't even make sense. Like, I'll miss things that just remind me of our family as a whole.

"There's this one memory of the Orange house that I just can't get out of my head. It had to have been summer or spring. It was warm. And I guess it's not really the Orange house itself, but it's a memory of the creek down the street from our house.

"Jackson and I used to ride our bikes down there, meet a few friends, build rope swings, try not to fall in the creek, fall in the creek anyway. That kinda thing.

"But the memory isn't of the creek itself, either, I guess, but the scenery, like the setting, the background kinda? I don't know. It's weird. It's like the trees and trail leading down to the creek, and a soft, quiet breeze.

"But it's super calm and peaceful. And the memory feels kinda…almost blank…like nothing actually happened there, just a blank feeling of calm attached to the horse trails and the trees near the creek. That's it. But that's something that will make me miss her. What does that mean?"

"Well, it makes sense. There was a time, although short, when the Orange house was calm and peaceful for you guys, where things were safe, before your mom moved out."

"I can't remember the day she moved out. It all feels fuzzy. It almost makes me feel crazy, because I'll feel so angry or sad about random things, and usually I know the emotion stems from being angry at my mom or my dad, or whoever, but I can't always remember the particular moments. Like her moving out. I can't remember that. It's just mushy. She was there, and then she wasn't. And when she wasn't, she never was again. You know what I mean? Like, once she moved out, which I can't even remember, she was just gone."

I pause for a moment, but Penny doesn't respond yet. She holds my eyes and waits.

"She was supposed to take us. Jackson and me. We still wanted to be with her. But it never happened. I don't really know why. But when she moved into her new apartment in Newport Beach, she was supposed to take us. She told us she would."

"What happened?" Penny asks.

"Nothing. That's the thing. There was just a whole lotta nothing. That's why it feels stupid to be as angry or as sad as I am, sometimes. I'm mad. I'm sad. About nothing. Nothing *even* happened. Well, I mean, things happened. My parents got nasty a few times. And there was that one fight—to this day, I don't know the truth of what actually happened."

"And what fight was that?"

"It was Valentine's Day. I remember because I'd been wearing a pink shirt and white shorts with my hair all curled. I was a freshman in high school, and was hanging with a group of friends after school. I had this huge crush on one of the guys in the group, Kenny. I was sitting on his lap, and we were all off at some abandoned field, under a tree-fort. The guys were all drinking beer. I didn't drink until my sophomore year, so I wasn't drinking yet. I just remember being so excited about sitting on Kenny's lap.

"And then I got a call from my mom. She sounded frantic, telling me my dad hit her. I asked her where she was, and she said she was at the hospital. I think it was Kenny who gave me a ride back to the house. Jason was there and had heard what happened, so we drove to the hospital to go see my mom.

"My dad was nowhere to be found. I called him to tell him that I hated him, that I was moving out and never speaking to him again. I was so mad.

"When Jason and I saw her at the hospital, she was super out of it. Granted, she *was* bleeding a little, but she didn't look swollen or puffy, like someone had beaten her up.

"To this day, my dad denies ever hitting her. He even says he believes her—that she really *thinks* he hit her—but the way he explains it, they were having a pretty heated fight, and she was coming after him. He blocked her from swinging at him, but when she kept trying to claw at him, he had to shove her back, and when he did that, she fell and hit her head on the bed frame going down.

"So, sure, there were things like that, but most of the time, it was just a whole lotta nothing. No one home. Or, if they were home, they'd be holed up in their room with the door locked. Their door was always locked. And if we ever did get a chance to peek in their room, it was always dark and stuffy. It was just weird. They were so weird."

I finish my thoughts and take a deep breath, feeling kind of weird, myself. Exposed.

Penny nods a heavy nod and takes in a deep breath. It's as though saying all these words out loud—putting sound to quiet, mute memories—gives them life, grants them physicality. It feels like I'm removing the memories from my body and placing them to hover in the middle of the room, vulnerable to whatever Penny decides to do with them. There they are, just hanging out. And when Penny nods her heavy nods and breathes her deep breaths, I can tell she's holding them—my words, my memories, my feelings. She's holding all of it, creating space for it.

She isn't touching me, yet I feel held.

"Jordan, that's not nothing," she finally says, gently. "What you went through is *not* nothing. When parents are using drugs or alcohol, a lot of things can happen. But it's never just nothing."

"Well, fine, whatever. It was something. But it was something that happened a while ago, so I don't see how any of that should be bugging me now. I honestly don't care what happened with my family. When I get upset nowadays, it's all related to Kolton. That's why I'm here. To figure out what's wrong with me, why I can't get over him. He's terrible, but he's all I want."

"Okay. We can talk about Kolton. That's okay. And it's okay that he's the person you want to be with right now. That's all okay. I do believe, however, someday he'll no longer be that person for you. Someday, I believe you won't want him anymore."

"Right," I dismiss her, crawling back into my head, beginning to shut down.

"You don't think so?"

"Don't think what?" I stare back at her.

"You don't think you'll ever want someone besides Kolton? Someone who treats you with the love and respect you deserve?"

"I don't know?"

"You don't know what?"

"I don't know. Sure. Yeah, someday I'll get over it," I deliver, clipped and sharp.

She keeps poking. "Don't you want that? Don't you want to be with someone who treats you with the love and respect you deserve?"

I don't answer her.

My eyes brim full as I try to hold back my tears indefinitely and refocus my gaze downward at the carpet. It's brown—a natural, non-threatening brown—inter-looped with a lighter shade of brownish-beige. With the sun seeping through the blinds, I can see the lint fuzzies in the air, circling downward in lazy spirals like fall leaves to rest on the rounded tops of the carpeted loops.

I uncross my right leg from over my left leg, switching their positions. The motion stirs the lint, disrupting their lazy spirals, dispelling them in chaotic directions. After some time, I watch as they slowly fall back to their original rhythm, spiraling down.

Their path of motion is Sisyphean—fated to repeat itself on a loop, forever.

When Penny and I are still, the lint falls slowly, but add some commotion to the mix and they inevitably rise to the occasion, shooting upwards into the limitless atmosphere, interacting with the commotion, becoming part of it. When the commotion ceases, the lint returns to its slow descent down to the carpet once more, just waiting for the next time someone stirs it up, brings it to life. Only to ultimately fall to the carpet again.

Forever up and forever down.

"I don't know what I want. I think I want a healthy relationship. But, then again, I still want Kolton. So, what's that say about me? That I'm a dirty, dramatic sadist who likes chaos?"

"No. That's not what that says at all—" she begins to answer.

"I keep thinking about him," I interrupt.

She nods, leaving space in the silence for me to continue.

"I just miss him. I miss him so much. It feels like I'm hitting a wall. Like, I miss him. I can't be with him. He's not good for me. But *bam*, that's the wall. Because there's nothing to do with that information. So, what do you do with that? What do you do then?"

"You let yourself miss him. Invite the feeling over for tea. You let yourself be sad," she responds gently. She links the feelings-and-tea concept back to *Tuesdays With Morrie*, a book she also recommends I read if I have time.

"Everything makes me think of him. That show everyone loves, *Breaking Bad*? It has a lot to do with drugs, and the main character reminds me of Kolton's friend, Patrick. I don't miss Patrick by any means. But it makes me think of Kolton. So then I'll miss Kolton all over again. How do you make that stop? How do you stop the thoughts?"

Penny pauses, taking my question in, thinking it over before answering. "I'm not sure it's so much *stopping* the thoughts as much as it's creating new thoughts. And allowing space for those thoughts when they *do* come, instead of trying to push them down."

"Maybe…" I nod my head up and down, slowly, contemplating what kind of new thoughts I should create.

"When you miss him, what do you miss?"

"I don't know. Hugging him. Being held. His laugh. His voice. He has this weird, slow tone of voice. Low. Distinct. I thought he was kinda dumb when I first met him. I mean, his voice was so slow, so different. I thought he was stupid. He's not. Don't get me wrong, he's definitely quiet. But not dumb. He just observes people, like, all the time. Observes everything they do and say."

"And he observed you?"

"What do you mean?" I shoot back defensively.

"I just mean, did he pay attention to you, too?" she asks.

"Well yeah, obviously." I cross my arms, sitting back into the couch a bit.

"Okay, good. That's all I was asking." She smiles back.

I don't believe her, though. I feel like she's getting at something, something she wants me to disclose or discover, but I immediately feel stupid, and I'm not entirely sure why. I shut down completely now, not wanting to expose even another inch of myself.

"When he paid attention to you, what did that feel like?" she presses after about thirty seconds of silence from me.

I stare out the window and don't answer. I'm mad at myself for still feeling this intensely after all this time. I'm disappointed that I've become *that girl,* stuck in *one of those* relationships. I still don't understand it, and I just want to be done with it already.

"Jordan?" Penny tries to gather my attention once again.

"Hmm?" I ask, giving Penny my most expressionless deadpan look, holding her eyes, and providing nothing else.

She moves on to the next question. "What about you? Would you like to talk about you?"

"No. Like what?" I contradict.

"Well, in your first session, your father shared about your suicide attempt. We haven't talked about that. Would you like to talk about it?"

First, I smirk at her. I don't say anything. When she doesn't continue, I pull my eyebrows in a scowl and look back at her as if to say *seriously…?* She never throws me a bone, though. She stays silent and waits for me.

In response, I only furrow my eyebrows more and whine at her pleadingly with my eyes, begging her with my thoughts: *Don't make me think about this. Don't make me talk about this.*

She doesn't concede. She continues to wait patiently.

"I don't see why I need to talk about that. You already know about it. Isn't that enough for you?" I spit.

"Is it enough for you?" Penny flips it back.

The tears start seeping out of the corner of my eyes. I try to withhold them as I tighten everything in my body. I hunch my back down, tighten my left thigh over my right leg, cross my arms, pulling them closer against my chest, dig my nails into my arm, and turn my face towards the window.

Five minutes go by. Five whole, silent minutes.

"People live for people," I whisper through the saliva gathering at my lips. I continue to stare out the window. It's easier than looking at Penny directly.

"Can you explain that a little more?" Penny prompts in a quiet, lulling voice.

"I mean, people live for people. They live for each other. People don't live to go to school or work. Those are just things *to do*. We *live* for each other. The point is each other. So, when everyone's gone, there's no point," I explain in a whimper.

I'm crying now. Sometimes I can control the tears. Today, I can't. I surrender my head to my hands as I smear them with my tears.

"Who's gone? Who is everyone, Jordan?" Penny tries, ever so gently.

"Everyone is everyone. Everyone's gone," I answer slowly. I grow quieter, entering a trance-like state, avoiding Penny's eyes. "So, there's no point."

"And who are those people? Who is everyone?"

"Everyone," I say expansively, dramatically, still crying.

"Okay. So, if everyone's gone, I'm guessing you don't think anyone loves you, then?"

"I *know* no one loves me."

"Do you really believe that?"

"Yes."

"I think you and I both know that isn't so, but let's just pretend for a moment that it's true. What about you? Do *you* love you?"

I keep my face still but flash my eyes upward at her, glaring. "That's a stupid question."

"Why is it a stupid question?"

"Because it is."

"What makes it a stupid question?"

I pause before I give her what she's looking for. "Fine. I get it. Yada yada yada. I'm supposed to love myself. I get it. And fine, I'll do it. I'll love myself, but you know what? Fuck everyone else, then. No one else gets any love. I'm not doing it again. Fuck Kolton. Fuck my mom. Fuck my dad. Fuck Aslyn. Fuck Didi. Fuck all of 'em. No matter how much I loved any of them, they never showed up for *me* in the ways I showed up for *them*. They didn't love me back. *Fuck. Everyone.*" I sink back into the couch aggressively, satisfied with myself.

Penny takes me by surprise and shakes her head in agreement. "Alright. Fuck 'em," she concludes. "But not you. Not fuck *you*. You need to love you. As for everyone else, that's fine. Fuck 'em."

I wait a few seconds, feeling her out before responding.
"Okay," I finally say through the smallest hint of a smile.
"Okay," she echoes.
"Okay," I say again.
That's all I got.
Okay. Okay. Okay.
Okay.
Fuck 'em.

2012,
ring around the rosie
♪

I get another boyfriend.
This time, perhaps, the most real it's ever been.
Nine months: the longest relationship I've had to date.
It's good.
The relationship is good. Healthy.
Which is, of course, the problem.
I'm not good yet.
I'm not healthy yet.
    He loves me purely and wholly, all the way past my glaring flaws. He loves me in that unconditional kind of way that I should be loving myself.
    So, maybe I'm not ready.
Or maybe he's just not the right one.
I know it's over when I no longer want him to touch me.
    This shift becomes so palpable that, no matter how good, how healthy, how unconditional his love is, I know without a doubt it's over for good.
    When I break up with him, he informs me, "No one is ever gonna love you as much as I do. Good luck out there." I hate him for saying this because I kinda believe him. But I hate myself even more for being the person he loves who can't love him back.
    I'm devastated.
        Not so much over losing *him*.
        But losing someone good.

Feeling like I'll never be able to be with *good*.

And, mostly, because I'm terrified of being alone.

The entire time we dated, I convinced him and myself that I was over Kolton.

It takes me to a while to realize I'd been lying to both of us.

I truly believed I was over it.

Spoiler alert:

I'm not.

I'm holding onto something.

I just have no idea what.

And I hate myself for it.

I hate myself for not being able to love the right person. The *good* person.

It makes no sense.

Why did I pass on a love that could weather the days, weeks, months, and years, holding out for one I can't count on to survive the hours?

I survive being alone. Go figure.

But it's hard.

The year is hard.

I fight myself to be normal, stay afloat, not be sad, be open in therapy, work on things.

Perfect Jordan wants us to make it.

Crazy Jordan wants to demolish everything.

They fight constantly.

About school:

    "Get up."

    "No."

    "Get up!"

    "*No!*"

    "Get up right now! You're going to class."

    "I'm not going to class. I don't give two shits about class."

    "Well, I do. I care about class, so get up!"

    "Fuck off."

    "Stop it. Get your butt out of bed and get to class."

    "Will you shut up if I go?"

    "Yes."

    "Fine."

About drinking:

"Don't take that shot. You don't need it."
"Blahhhhhhhh bllahhhh, wooooo! Bitch, be quiet!" (Takes shot.)
"We're going to regret that. Why do you always do this to us?"
"Why are you always bitching about everything? Why are you so boring?"
"I'm trying to take care of us!"
"Take care of us, huh? You sure you're not trying to just *appear* together so no one knows we're actually crazy?"
"We're not crazy."
"Yes, we are."
"No, we're not."
"I am. And I'm just as much of *us* as you are."
"Just drink a glass of water."
"Don't tell me what to do."

About Kolton:
"You know who we should call?"
"Don't even think about it."
"Too late. We're thinking about it. You're welcome."
"Why do you always do this? He screws us over every time. We're not calling him."
"But what about how good he smells…"
"Stop…"
"Or how amazing it is when he just cuddles us. Don't you want to be cuddled?"
"No. He's a jerk! Stop thinking about him. Let it go."
"You know you want to call him. Text him, at least."
"Drop it."
"Oh my god, I totally just texted him. Hehehehe."
"Great."

About surviving:
"Let's die."
"Let's not."
"Remember how sad we were yesterday, though? Ugh. Screw it, let's give up now."
"That was temporary. We laughed today, remember that?"
"Live fast, die young. We've had a good run. Let's just gooooooo."
"We're staying. Now shut up. I have to finish this paper because it's due tomorrow."
"Forget the paper."
"You'll thank me later."

Long distance is hard on friendships, but especially with friends like Aslyn and Didi. They're difficult to connect with even in close proximity, so throw some distance in there, remove the shared commonality of partying, and things just continue to fade. I make efforts to call them both. Sometimes they return my calls. Mostly they don't.

To my surprise, Emily and I grow closer, extending our conversations beyond the weekend parties in Orange. Texting and calling, swapping support.

When we discover Britney's secretly been hooking up with the same guy Emily's hooking up with, Emily and I grow even closer. Emily won't confront Britney about it, but I will.

Britney and I are talking on the phone one day, just the two of us, and before we hang up, I broach it. "Look. I know you've been hooking up with Emily's boy toy. You know she's into him. Why?"

"You know how Emily is. It's just…too easy."

Her answer stuns me.

"Dude."

"I know, I know. But you *know* what I mean. She just never stands up for herself."

"Britney. That doesn't mean you *screw* the guy she's into. And then make an effort to *hide* it and lie about it. I don't know, I just don't get how you can do that."

"Well. If it bothers her, she should say something."

I don't need to hear any more, so I end the conversation.

"'Kay, well, I'm gonna go. I'll talk to you later."

I *know* all of our friends are messed up. They're messed up. I'm messed up. I know that. We're all broken. But to not even *try* to be better? To turn that brokenness inward on the group? It's beyond what I can stomach.

Aslyn and Didi are back in town for the holidays, and I can't stop running Britney's words through my mind. *It's just…too easy.*

As everyone talks about meeting up at some party in Orange tonight, it's business as usual. Don't talk about anything real. Sweep it under the rug. Secretly hate and betray each other, but hey, cheers to that. Drink up.

It's not long before a bunch of our rowdy guy friends show up at this party. One of them pees on the front lawn and subsequently we all get kicked out.

The girls and I are walking in the middle of the street, trying to figure out where to go next, when I explode at Britney because I know she's the one who invited the guys. And because Emily won't.

"I told you we weren't allowed to invite any extras, Britney. They specifically said *no guys*. Now *we* can't even party there because you just *had* to invite the guys."

"Jordan, shut the fuck up. That party was lame anyway!" Britney yells back at me.

"Jordan, don't yell at Britney. It's not even—" Aslyn starts to interrupt.

"Aslyn. Shut. The *fuck* up, and stay out of this. This is between me and Britney. You haven't even *been* here, so you don't get to jump in. *Also.* Why are you standing up for Britney when you know she just fucked your ex while you've been up in San Francisco?" I turn to Britney. "Yeah, we know about that one, too, Britney. Aslyn's ex, Emily's dude. Who's next? Kolton? And then *you* come back down here," I say, turning back to Aslyn, "and fuck your ex, too, while your new boyfriend waits for you up north. Sloppy. You guys are fucking sloppy," I pour out.

"Fuck you, Jordan! You don't even know what you're talking about!" Aslyn screams back.

And the screams become louder, back and forth, until I finally just walk away.

Our group splits.

Britney stays with Aslyn, and so does Didi.

Emily comes with me.

And we go our separate ways.

I wake up today, recalling the details of last night's fight. Didi sent a text around 2:30 a.m. to make sure Emily and I got home okay. It didn't surprise me that Didi went with Aslyn and Britney. If she had left Aslyn's side, she would have never heard the end of it. Path of least resistance is and has always been the name of Didi's game, no matter the cost.

At this point, I finally understand *no matter the cost* includes losing me.

I call Britney, and in five minutes' time, the quarrel is behind us.

At this point, I don't care enough about our friendship to expect more from her.

Aslyn? I truly don't know what to say to her. Because I'm not sorry. So, I say nothing.

At this point, I'm surprised to find I feel relieved.

2013,
a pocket full of posies
♪

I wake up with another hangover and think about my life.
I think about drinking.
I think about why I drink.
I don't have any answers.

My dad and brothers moved out of the old Orange house to a new one in San Clemente. Fresh start. I finished my sophomore year at Long Beach living in an apartment off-campus with a few roommates. When my favorite roommate moved home unexpectedly, I decided I was over it and moved back in with my family for year three. The commute is long, but I jammed my classes into two days a week, so it's not so bad.

I change out of my pajamas and go downstairs to cut my dad's hair like I said I would. He already set out the buzzer kit on the kitchen table, and I find him sitting on the couch, watching a Green Bay Packers game.

"You ready?" I ask him.

"Yep." He gets up from the couch and sits himself in the kitchen chair with a straight view to the TV.

During a commercial break, he asks me, "What do you got going this week?"

"Just classes and work."

"How you been feeling?"

I decide to answer honestly, jumping straight to it. "I don't know. Okay, kinda, not really. I don't know. Every day feels like I'm stuck. Like I'm waiting to be okay, to feel okay, and I just keep waiting. Every day."

"Ahhh, Jordan. I'm sorry." He pauses for about ten seconds, like he's gathering his thoughts. "Eventually, you'll come to a place where those days will be farther and further between. Instead of seven of those days, there'll be five, and then four, and then three, and then maybe one," he explains.

"Hm." I consider the concept.

"You'll get there," he concludes.

After some pause, I change the subject. "Does Sonia mind the two-hour commute each weekend?"

He side-steps the question. "Well, we switch off every weekend. I drive up to Palm Springs, too, so she doesn't always have to make that drive."

"You didn't answer my question," I point out.

"I don't think she minds," he responds.

"I would mind," I rebut.

When he doesn't respond, I continue, "After a few years, there's no way I would put up with a two-hour commute every other weekend."

"Well, she doesn't seem to mind," my dad answers neutrally.

"So, how often do you guys talk when you're apart, then?"

"Oh, every day," he answers.

Every day?

Every fucking day?

A pang of jealousy stabs through me as I think of him talking to her every day. I *live* with him, and he doesn't even talk to *me* every day. She's been around for a few years. So what? How does a few years earn daily conversations? I'm his *daughter*. He doesn't talk to me or any of the boys much. He comes home from work, says hello, and goes up to his room.

The San Clemente house is big but empty. It's better than the Orange house. Clean, whereas the Orange house was a mess. But it lacks warmth. Living with my dad and brothers here feels like living with roommates.

It makes me miss my mom. She used to make anywhere and everywhere feel safe and alive.

"What do you think about seeing Penny less? It's costing me five-hundred bucks a month. I got this San Clemente house on a lease, with an option to purchase, and I'm thinking of buying, after all. Just trying to save expenses where I can," he interrupts my thoughts.

"I'll talk to Penny," I respond.

"Not to be derogatory, but does it really help?"

Without missing a beat, I continue cutting his hair. I'm not a hairdresser by any means, but it's rather straightforward. Clip to the desired length, put the plastic guide on the buzzer, trim everywhere, remove the plastic guide at the end, and use the sharper, intimate teeth of the bare buzzer to clean up sideburns, missed details, and the hairline at the back of the neck.

This is the part that requires some level of skill—the end—to avoid cutting the person on accident, the teeth of the razor much closer to the skin.

I continue to cut his hair, consider his question, and wonder how he could ask it when I'm trimming his hairline at the back of his neck, his skin only one level of pressure away from the bite of the bare buzzer.

I could so easily, so accidentally, so quickly, nick his neck.

But where there used to be my fight now sits my apathy.

"Jordan?" he asks in response to my lack of response.

"No. I guess it doesn't," I answer distantly.

I thought it did. Help.

I thought therapy helped.

But with the sting of confronting both the high costs—*$500 bucks a month*—and my dad's question—*Not to be derogatory, but does it really help?*—more than both those things, it's the questions he didn't ask.

Why aren't you getting better?

All this time, all this money…why aren't you happy yet?

Why are you still this upset? This emotional? Why are you so much?

I wanted to return his unasked questions with questions of my own.

Do you want me to be done so you can stop looking at the mess you started?

Do you want me to be better so you can believe your mistakes were minor, not colossal?

Do you want me to lie about my wellbeing for the sake of yours?

My anger settles as my apathy washes over me anew. Besides, I know it's not *all* my dad's fault. Nothing messy begins with that much precision. It's his fault. It's my mom's fault. It's Kolton's fault. And then it's my fault for making it worse. It's all of ours.

I still bet he'd like for me to be done with therapy: to be better, to be happy. To be done.

To relieve a layer of his guilt.

I should fight for it, fight to continue with therapy, explain how and why the weekly sessions not only help but are necessary. I should ask to reduce my weekly sessions to bi-monthly. I should do these things, but I don't. My apathy hangs heavier, so I opt out altogether.

And that's the end of therapy.

I carry my laptop downstairs to escape the distractions and sleepy aura my room is putting off. I need to knock out a homework assignment.

As I finally finish it, I decide to push myself to get ahead and complete the next few weeks' assignments. Despite my good intentions, Justin has other plans. He keeps walking around the dining-room table, cooing at his deaf American Bulldog, Belvedere, spurting out laughter and general teasing aimed at me. He just wants some attention.

"Belvedere! Over here! Right here, Buddy! Uh oh. Jordan, he's not looking! Get it, because he can't hear? Ahhhhhhh!" Justin squeals with pent-up energy.

"I'm trying to do homework," I deadpan.

"Okay, so what are we having for dinner?" he asks, determined.

"I don't care," I answer.

"Well, we've got frozen pizza, frozen pizza, orrrrrrr frozen pizza. Ahhhhhh! Do you want frozen pizza?"

I keep my eyes on my laptop, not answering him.

He comes over and bops me on the head playfully. "Head spank!" he yells as he runs away.

I don't get up to chase him, so he comes back. "So, you want a few slices?"

"Sure," I say so he'll leave me alone for a few minutes.

No such luck.

"Jordan, do I put the pizza in at 400 degrees or 425?"

"I don't know," I spit out, annoyed.

"I'm Googling it," he informs me.

I don't respond.

Thirty seconds pass and he squeals again, "*Ha!* It was 400 degrees! Belvedere, it was 400 degrees. I knew it! Jordan, you were wrong!"

"Mmmmh," I mutter.

Hunger brings my dad downstairs from his lair. He briefly engages with Justin and me, then walks outside. He's gone for some time until the door opens again, and to my surprise, Jackson walks through the door, my dad trailing behind him.

Jackson's in one of his witty, cocky moods. I can tell because he's walking with that brute swagger, smirk in full-form. Plus, it's Sunday night, meaning he's probably coming home from a weekend full of binge-drinking and partying, making him slightly hungover today, boosting him with an extra layer of disregard for giving a fuck about much. I like when he's like this. I think it's funny.

"Jackson, I need you to actually move your truck so I can take the trash out," my dad says.

"Jeff"—a dramatic, deliberate pause, and a wide smirk with cocked eyebrows—"why didn't you tell me this when we were outside?" He looks directly at me, rather than at my dad, sure that I'll give him the reaction he's looking for.

And I do. I giggle in response. My dad doesn't even protest the first-name calling—*Jeff*. They walk back outside to maneuver the cars around.

Once back inside, Justin's taking the pizza out of the oven, and Jackson starts talking about his weekend, telling us all about the Little Miss Red Riding Hood he met at some Halloween party. I'm following most of his commentary with laughter.

Justin gets up and closes the swinging kitchen door to the dining room, shutting me out of the conversation. Four seconds later, Jackson reopens the door and picks up where he left off in his story.

"Ignore him. He's just jealous because he's been bugging me for the past half-hour and I haven't paid him any attention," I explain to Jackson. We both laugh at that.

Jackson shuffles two slices of pizza onto his plate and comes to place the plate down on the dining room table directly across from me. He then makes his way back into the kitchen to retrieve the Parmesan cheese, ranch dressing, and Cholula sauce.

"Where are you going with all that?" Justin asks him.

"To distract Jordan," my dad answers for Jackson.

Justin follows suit, coming into the dining room to place his plate at the dining room table, as well. I ask Jackson to grab me some pizza. He answers with a playful, smart-ass comment, but I don't bother to tease him back or ask again. As predicted, he shovels two slices on a plate and brings it over to me.

It would have been awkward if my dad sat at the kitchen table by himself while the three of us sat together at the dining room table, so he brings his plate over to our table, as well.

I'm so caught off guard by this unplanned family dinner that I start to tear up a little. The tears are automatic, weird, and don't match the jibber-jabber mood the boys have created. I quickly pull the tears into check, playing them off as a side effect of my laughter.

My dad even asks me what I'm studying. This so closely resembles a normal family dinner, when a question such as his would be completely normal and flow naturally into the conversation, but since we don't *do* family dinners, it sounds stuffy, out of place.

The physical act of eating never takes long, though, and about seven minutes pass before my dad and most of us are through with our dinner.

Seven minutes.

My dad stands up and walks his plate over to the sink, then shuffles past the three of us still sitting at the dining table. "Gonna go watch my World Series".

Justin vocalizes it after my dad is up the stairs and out of earshot: "He can't stand family time."

Seven minutes together.

I can do a lot of things in seven minutes—wash a few dishes, pack a lunch, drive to the grocery store—those sorts of things. But I just can't figure out how I'm supposed to make a home feel like a home in seven minutes.

Kolton, I dreamt of you again last night.
It's been almost two years since we last saw each other.
Two years.
Does that mean anything?
Isn't that supposed to be a long time?
Shouldn't I have let this go by now?
Why are you still so alive in my mind?
Where did I put you in there?
Why can't I extract you?

I don't remember how the dream began. Suppose that's how most dreams go, anyhow.

We were together in your room, staying a safe distance apart from each other. It was calm. I tend to dream in colors. This one had a layer of hazy yellow-gray to it, like an old movie.

Instead of your bed positioned against the wall near the light switch, it stuck out in front of the mirrored closet doors. We were both lying on the bed, not touching, just talking and getting along peacefully.

I started to tell you about this song you'd never heard. I sang it for you, even though I'm not a good singer. You laughed warmly and said you loved that song.

You had this lined notepad where you were keeping a list of songs you wanted to buy on iTunes. You scribbled numbers on each line. Some numbers had a song written next to them, some were left blank. You told me to add the name of the song I sang for you on one of the blank lines. I wrote it down.

Then we were moving around on the bed, just kind of rolling into different positions. We stayed in one position, where you were lying all sprawled out, parallel with the bed, and I was lying with my head on your thigh, my body perpendicular to yours. Like we were best friends, just hanging out and talking together.

I heard your parents walk down the hall, and I haven't seen them in forever, so I decided I wanted to say hello. I walked into the kitchen, where they were chatting away happily. I said hello to both of them, embracing them one at a time.

Dreams are scattered fragments; some details carry through and others don't.

Some dreams are fast; some are slow.

The good ones seem to be the quickest.

This one is good.

By the time I wake up, I know I've lost most of the details.

The part I keep with me is simple: You, lying on the bed, my body perpendicular to yours, my head on your thigh, an aerial view of our bodies from overhead, like the image in my mind was captured by a spinning baby-mobile hanging from your ceiling, smiles beaming from both our faces, murmuring of songs and nonsense, feeling all sorts of nuzzled safety like we were babies in some cozy cocoon-nursery.

2014,
ashes! Ashes!
♪

"You're not even with me," he practically spits at me, still managing to keep his car on the road.

"Excuse me?" I ask bitingly. I'm not sure where he's going with this yet.

"You're not *with* me, Jordan. I mean, sure, we're together. But I'm in this, and you aren't. You say you are, but you make it pretty hard to tell sometimes. Makes me wonder what we're even doing here."

"What the fuck is that supposed to mean? Ben, obviously, I'm with you. What are you even talking about?" I'm in full fight mode now.

"You're unbelievable. I mean really, really unbelievable. You wanna say you don't love me? After a year? After everything I've done for you? Everything I've given you? Fine. You don't have to love me. I can't control that. But to say the only person you've ever loved…was him? Kolton?" Ben stutters out the last part, the bewilderment in his voice so pungent, I can practically taste it in the confined car.

"He treated you like crap. I don't understand what you don't understand about that. And to say he's the only person you've ever loved? Why are you even dating me? This is just effed up. And selfish."

Ben doesn't use curse words. I don't think I noticed until a few weeks into dating him, and when I asked him about it, he just explained simply, "I don't see the need for them. We're all perfectly capable of communicating without those types of words."

He wasn't saying this to add a cute quirk to his character. No, Ben actually meant what he said. He doesn't curse. The entire year that we've been together, I think I heard him say "fuck" once. And it's because I practically forced him.

"So, what, you just never use curse words? Like ever?" I'd asked.

"I wouldn't say never. But I try to keep them out of my vocab," he'd replied calmly.

"Fuck."

He stared at me blankly.

"Fuck, fuck, fuck. Does it bother you?" I pushed.

"No," he shrugged easily.

"But you won't say it."

"I don't need to say it," he explained.

"Now I really want you to say it. Just say fuck. Just once," I insisted.

"What? Why?" He was giggling under the pressure.

"*Fuck!*" I yelled.

He giggled again.

"*Fuck balls!*" I yelled again.

"*Fuckity fuck fuck ballsacks!*" I screamed.

"Dude, my brother's home!" Ben laughed again.

"I guess you better say it then."

"No…" he said, but I swear I saw his teeth pushed at his bottom lip in the shape of an "f" seconds before he said no, so I just waited. And stared at him expectantly.

"Fuck," he giggle-whispered.

That was in the beginning of our relationship, and to date, I've never heard him use a curse word again. I'm running through this memory so thoroughly that I only realize I haven't responded to Ben's monologue when he speaks again, the combativeness gone from his voice, the only tone lingering defeat. "I love you, Jordan."

The knot in my stomach flips, twists, and doubles in size, so I know I can't speak or I'll cry. It's all I can do to stare out my passenger-side window at the zooming cars on the freeway.

I don't need to say anything, though.

That's why he delivered it with defeat.

I don't love him back.

And we both know it.

Music picks up where words fall short:
["San Jose" by Joe Purdy]

♪

Ben gave it all he could.
    And it still wasn't enough.
    Not because of him.
    Because of me.
    Nothing is enough to save me from me but me.
    I'm still not quite sure how to do that yet.
    I do my best, though.
I'm busier than I've ever been.
Perfect Jordan is in full swing.
I'm in school full-time and working part-time.
But I still feel Crazy Jordan brewing below.

Bring up Ben's name in conversation and I'll be fine. I can discuss it all with ease. I'll smile, and the smile won't hurt because there was nothing bad there. It was all good, all the time.

And for the times it got to be unbearably good, I made sure to slip in an arbitrary complaint, pick a fight or two. Until even *that* wasn't enough. The fights, the self-made toxicity, the complaints weren't enough to make my relationship with Ben feel familiar. He remained good through it all.

So, yes, when Ben gets brought up, I smile, and it's a light smile.
    It's easy,
    it's painless,
    it's accompanied by memories that are warm and safe and slightly uncomfortable.

And when I grow bored or lonely enough, or if Ben pushes to make that *catching-up lunch* actually happen, reminding me of the good, easy, harmless memories we have together, then I'll admit I could probably be convinced to play again.

    Ben and me.
    Playing house and all that.
    I could probably be convinced.
    But Kolton?

If Kolton's brought up in conversation, nothing further needs to be said. Nothing needs to be discussed. I need no convincing. His name alone is startling. It's unnecessary for the memories to be extracted or unearthed, because they'll be waiting.

Kolton's name bears two possible reactions: hiccup or hyperventilate.

If I can help it, I'll hold my breath before the memories can be thought, before they seize the opportunity of thudding through consciousness. If I hold my breath quickly enough, before the memories materialize, he's just a hiccup. His name and our memories squeeze through me at the rapid pace of a breath but are forcefully expelled before they have the chance to settle on my awareness.

Kolton?
Shoot—hold your breath!
Hiccup.
Memories withheld.
Gone. Done. Not going there, not today.

Upon hearing his name, if I wait even a second too long to hold my breath, the ice-to-fire battle begins. My body feels airily cold and yet densely hot all at the same time. The tender insides of my hands come alive with tiny, intimate breezes of air-conditioned tingling, yet when I touch my fingertips to my face, I can feel heat emulating from my cheeks. The ice-to-fire battle rages beneath my skin. My thighs tighten. My shoulders tense. My eyes widen. My heartbeat quickens. All at the same time, the dam is withdrawn, spilling our memories everywhere, flooding my mind. Blinding flashes and blurred images pour into my awareness—a slow smile blooming from the right-side corner of a mouth, a leaf-green T-shirt, embers dropping from a defiant cigarette, an indulgent kiss from a soft bottom lip, a sour slap, buzzing wasps, Jackie's scowl, a bubbling jacuzzi, whispers of love, a hug that melted away wiggly restlessness, a pair of concerned parents, machine-gun chuckles.

Kolton?
Too little, too late—here it comes!
Hyperventilate.
Onslaught of memories.
Going, going, went there today.

I pulled myself out.
I mean, I really did.
Penny and I worked tirelessly for two years, hour upon hour.
 Silence upon questions.
 Tears upon answers.
 Reality upon discussions.
 Pain upon honesty.

I dated other people.
I finished college.
I moved into an apartment with Jackson and another roommate.
I upgraded my part-time jobs to my first salaried job.
I drank myself into trouble, only to clean myself up sober for a week, two, sometimes a month.
Up, down, back up, back down.
Just like the lint fuzzies in Penny's office, circling downward in lazy spirals, stirred up by inspiration, and inevitably back down to rest upon the carpeted loops at ground level.
Ground level isn't so bad, though.
Like the lint fuzzies, I too am on ground level.
It's steady here on the ground level. I maintain friendships. I run, a lot. I sew and pour over puzzles. I work. I hang out with my family. I participate in life, and I've transitioned from burden of a sap to *pretty normal*. Most everyone likes me. Not everyone, but most. They give me their nods, their laughs, and their yeses.
On paper, I am wonderful.
None of it matters, though.
The paper upon which I'm printed *pretty normal*, the surrounding people who like me, it means nothing to me. And they don't like *me*. They like my chameleon self. I'm a human chameleon.
I know what to say in order to:
> be respectful and respected,
> be humorous and humored,
> be engaging and engaged,
> be charming and charmed.

I play both sides well.
But I don't care for any of it.
I still miss Kolton.
> Which means what?
> What *is* missing someone?
> What is it?
> I can wake up, free from the thought, make coffee, run through my morning routine, drive to work, still free from thought. Then a song comes on shuffle, or I read a line in a book, and his face is suddenly all I see, and I miss him.
> So, what is missing someone?
>> It's a thought frequency.
>> It's tapping into a memory bank.

And now I wonder, how far did he go?
How much of my memory bank did he consume?
If ideas and schemas branch off in the brain like underground roots of a plant, how many branches bear Kolton?
And what is it about the curiosity that comes with missing?
    Why do we wonder what that person is up to? Doing? Thinking?
    Why does that matter?
    How do answers to those questions bring any fulfillment?
        I have no clue.

All I know is when I stop to visit Kolton in my mind, I still yearn for *his* nod, *his* laugh, *his* yes. But we weren't sustainable Then. And we wouldn't be sustainable Now.

But knowing is nothing if you can't nurture knowing into feeling.

So, in the crevices of my mind where I visit the memories, I get to be young and seventeen. I get to miss him. I get to be immature and play into the refusal. I refuse to convert my *knowing* that Kolton and I would never have survived into a *feeling*.

Yet I carry a stunning sureness that if I were able to remove him from those crevices of my mind by feeling and admitting we were wrong, I'd be released.

Chameleon no more.
I could be real.
I could move up and on.
I could be free.
    But I can't forget.
    How can I forget something like us?
    So, in the dulling crevices of my mind, I wait.
    Wait for his nod, his laugh, his yes.
        I should let go, but not Today.
        Today is never good.
        Tomorrow will be better.
        Until, of course, Today slips into Yesterday, and Tomorrow becomes Today.
        But, as you know, Today is never good.

2015,
we all fall down.
♪

After Ben, there's a lot of one-month flings.
No one worth mentioning until Mark.
I'm so silly-excited over Mark, I think this just *may* be it.
Until, of course, it's not.
He's not.
And I'm not.
It wasn't it.
We finally break up right after the Fourth of July.
We don't talk after that, but I pine after him all the way through Christmas.

It's Christmas evening, the family stuff out of the way earlier this afternoon, and I'm a few glasses of wine deep, so naturally I check Mark's Instagram. A picture of him and some beautiful girl turns the wine in my stomach into a whirlpool. I swear her hair is longer, her teeth whiter. Her boobs are definitely bigger.

I don't want to feel like this.
Death by comparison.
I'm not going down like this.

Before giving it much thought beyond my urgent need for distraction, I unblock Kolton, and I text him.

I haven't seen him in years, but between breakups and during alcohol-induced points of piqued curiosity, I'll unblock him, text him some babble, only to block him again when daylight hits. He hates it. I love that he hates it.

BLUE WATER, *a year in the ocean.*

KOLTON   JORDAN

                     Do you remember much from when we dated?

Do you?!?!?!

                     Are you drunk? I'm asking that seriously

No are you?

                     No, I have to run in the morning. You didn't answer the question.

I said no I'm not...

                                   Meant my question
                                                 First *

Oh well the answer to that is yes too. I know you've been drinking tho I've hit you up all week. Now you decide to get back to me. Why?

                                         I was just curious.

Your such a liar. It's cool tho. What are you doing Jordan

                                               Reading

What

                               A Tree Grows In Brooklyn

Ahhh one of my favs lol. Can I see you?

                                                    No

Why did you hit me up tonight?

                     I'm wondering what you remember. Like if you had to think of 3 specific instances, what are the first memories that come to mind? I'm curious about your perspective to all of it. It was so chaotic for me. So much bad stuff happened during that time and it's just difficult to wrap my head around it sometimes. I'm curious if you feel similar or if it just doesn't faze you at all.

Honestly to me I fell lie other things were happening to influence that bad feeling you had I can't contribute all of that to dating me we may have argued but I don't think it was ever to the extent that it was perceived to be maybe you want to say that it didn't phase me but I don't believe that's the case

It's crazy—during that time—I truly believed that everything was your fault. And now when I look back on it, I really do see that it takes two to tango. It can never be just ONE person's fault. I was involved too. It was my fault too. I just don't think we ever fit—we brought out the worst in each other. For that, I'm sorry. I don't think I've ever apologized for any of the chaos but I'm sorry for my part in it.

At the same time what ever it was MAYBE love but if you don't want to call it that I understand. What ever it was, it was an incredible feeling when we were ok. At the same time it was destructive. I don't know. I enjoyed all of it I can say I never lied about my feelings which is something I can't say for other ppl I've seen at this point.

I loved you during that time. I admitted it to you once while we were together. I was rolling when I said it but took it back the following day. I remember that. But I've admitted it to just about everyone else since.

Don't think you loved me back though. I believe that you loved Jackie. You

> said it yourself. It was on your birthday my freshman year of college and point blank I asked you if you genuinely wanted to see me & hang out and you apologized and explained that you loved Jackie & that she was the only one you would ever love.
>
> None of the details matter now anyhow. I just wondered what you thought about our history. That's all. Like I said, I'm sorry for my part in it. For the chaos to you and especially your parents. I adored them both.
>
> I guess I was just seeking closure in some sense. I feel like I got it. Take care Kolton.

And I apologize for that I honestly have never been about anything I said at that point bc what ever it was I was thinking was fucked up from the drugs. I remember and was a part of something I don't do n won't do ppl have died I know I'm sure you know but Patricks brother died from that

> Appreciate you saying that. It means a lot. I had NO idea about Patrick's brother. Wow. I don't even know what to say. I am so sorry.

Yeah kind of insane but I would just really like to see you. What are you up too

> Well not tonight but maybe soon. Going to bed now, night.

    Kolton and I just had a *real* conversation like mini adults. We allowed our thoughts and perceptions with open communication and consideration. Granted, we likely wouldn't be able to have this conversation face-to-face, but texting is still a step in the right direction. A built-in buffer of safety in digital

distance. We didn't sling red-hot fireballs of blame at one another. We didn't explode. We didn't shatter; not each other, and not ourselves.
   We...
      expressed,
      explored,
      opened.

BLUE WATER, *a year in the ocean.*

PART III: BLUE WATER,

a year in the ocean.

BLUE WATER, *a year in the ocean.*

Julianna Lembeck

salt

when you are hurting,
heal yourself with salt;

heal your mind
    through tears,

heal your body
    through sweat,

and heal your soul
    through the sea

© *Emina Gašpar-Vrana*

BLUE WATER, *a year in the ocean.*

AUGUST 26, 2016,
whiplash in my ponytail slash.

Your family moved to Channel Islands, not quite a stone's throw away anymore.
A lot further than Orange.
So, you haven't visited me, and I haven't visited you.
But we talk all year long, on and off.
I'm going through a rough spot with Jackson, with my drinking.
I date someone nearby to fill the time, but it's not serious.
I stop dating that one, date a few others.
I block you on and off to try and contain you in a way, in between all the dating.
I want to see you.
You say you want to see me.
Which should make this feel like any other year that's passed since we saw each other last.
    False promises.
        Anger.
            Block you.
                Unblock you.
                Repeat.
But I swear we're going somewhere new.
I can feel it in my bones.
We've got unfinished business.

And each time I unblock you (and once you get over the annoyance of being blocked in the first place), we get a little deeper, a little closer.

I'm drinking with Emily, a relaxed Friday night in. You and I are texting gibber jabber. I'm reading it all to Emily. We're laughing over you, over me, over the ridiculousness of it all.

Unexpectedly, you tell me you're driving to Orange tonight, tell me to come hang out.

This is a first.

I rally Emily. We change into cute clothes, freshen up our makeup, and holy shit, we're actually doing this. I tell you to come pick us up, and I cannot believe it, but this is it.

I am going to see you.

Five years.

And this is it.

I am going to see you.

You text me, telling me you're outside her apartment.

I scream a little, jump up and down, grabbing Emily's arm and squeezing it. She giggles, leads us out of her apartment, and locks the door behind us.

"Do you remember him from high school?" I ask her, as we walk out of the apartment complex.

"Kind of? You and I weren't super close then, so I know I've seen him, but I don't remember a whole lot," she answers.

"Well, he's hilarious. But kind of shy. So I don't know how he'll act in front of you. I can't believe this is even happening. I haven't seen him in *five* years. Five years!" I exclaim.

And there you are, car idling in the middle of the street.

We hop inside, me in the front and Emily in the back.

You and I don't embrace, or even touch. I'm determined to play nonchalant and not let on that minutes before I was jumping up and down, and squeezing Emily.

Your car smells like you.

Overwhelmingly like you.

"It smells like Black Ice and Cool Water in here," I comment before considering it might be weird for me to identify this right off the bat.

Without a word, you look over at me from the driver's side, a smile playing on your face, and you open your middle console to show me the cutout of a black Little Trees car freshener with *Black Ice* printed on the front.

We both laugh a little.

"Open the glovebox," you instruct.

I do as I'm told, and sure enough, I find a bottle of cologne that I recognized from years back. Cool Water.

"Knew it," I say with confidence.

"How?"

"Because I'm a sensitive sniffer and I know my scents. You wore that cologne back in high school," I answer without a shred of shame.

We're off to downtown Fullerton, and because we don't know what else to say, we turn to music.

"I wanna play a song. Where's your plug thingy?" I demand.

You surrender your auxiliary cord because you're already buzzed and feeling all sorts of pleasant and amicable.

I'm buzzed, too.

Wouldn't have it any other way.

♪
Music picks up where words fall short:
["Gold" by Kiiara]
♪

"Ohhhhh mannnnnn, sounds like a Jojo song," you chuckle.

But you know how we do.

    I tell you what I can't tell you through a song.

    I tell you what I can't tell you.

        Because I still need to tell you.

We pull into the downtown Fullerton parking structure and it's packed. You drive all the way to the top floor. Someone's waiting for a parking spot, but you've got an advantage on the angle. As soon as the car leaving backs out, you swoop in on the waiting car. They lay on their horn, honking and cursing you as they drive by.

I smirk from the passenger seat, slowly shaking my head back and forth.

"Fucking savage," Emily busts up from the backseat.

Out the car we go, downstairs, and into one of the bars, Heroes.

"You grab a table. I'll get us drinks," I direct Emily.

You follow me to the bar.

I'm waiting for the bartender's attention, and I can feel you behind me.

And then I hear you in my ear.

"I love you."

You spill it so simply.

I turn around to look at you, giving you a smirky smile. I roll my eyes and at the same time, roll my head as I gear up to sing along to the song blaring through the bar—"*Now everybody put your hands in the air—say yeahhhh yeahhh yeahhh*"—now tossing my head all the way back in full volume. I bring my head forward again, smiling a smirky, giggly, buzzed smile at you once more, finally turning my head back toward the bar.

When we love, we shine.

And it's blinding.

A high like no other.

This time, you place your hands on my waist, whispering in my ear again, "I love you."

I have the bartender's attention, so I whip around to face you once more, slashing my ponytail across the width of your chest. "What do you want to drink?" I yell.

"Jameson and coke," you say.

"Two vodka sodas and one Jameson and coke," I tell the bartender as I push your hands away from my waist.

Again, you're relentless. "I said I love you."

"Stop saying that." I don't even turn to meet your eyes as I pay for our drinks.

"Why did you have to bring Emily?"

I raise my eyebrow at you and frown your stupid question away. The unashamed look you give me in return echoes the same words you whispered seconds before. I skirt through the crowd, headed for our table.

It's nothing you haven't said before. In the past, you'd drop it in at this party or that. Only when you were drunk, of course.

And we'd wake the next morning and never talk about it.

But your proclamations of love, like a humming bird:

Enticing,

flighty,

and gone all too soon,

    for days, upon weeks, upon—yes—years.

Exquisite.

Impossible to hold onto.

Magic.

    Our love a little like magic.

    Or possibly it's the trick?

    Tricky, tricky magic trick.

Either way, magic wouldn't be magic if it happened all the time.

There's an m-word for the all-the-time happenings, too.

Mundane.

But we're a flighty magic. And I heard you. I know you love me in that flighty, magical, dark way of yours. I didn't have to hear it whispered in my ear. And I didn't have to see it echoed in your expression. I know this already.

We join Emily at the table, drink our drinks, dance our dance, and live out our happy, flighty magic.

Our laughter feels endless.

Expectations halted.

Responsibilities momentarily non-existent.

We're like kids, so alive, playing, laughing, singing, dancing.

My hair bounces in tune with my laughter.

I'm tickled by your presence, by your attention, by your quirks.

No one is starving yet.

Nothing is broken yet.

The magic runs rampant.

We've begun again.

SEPTEMBER 3, 2016,
hey, hi, how do you do? How do we do this?

    I'm in Newport, drinking on a Duffy boat with some girlfriends. We're texting, and you're telling me to come stay for the weekend at your parents'. I want to, but I'm nervous. Nervous about seeing your parents again. Nervous about what it'll look like to fumble back through our teenage romance as young adults. Nervous about being with you for a few days straight. Can we even get along that long? You're persistent, though, telling me to take the train.
    I believe you when you say you want to see me. But part of me wonders how much you talk just to talk, just to have something to say, to be a tease of action. I believe you want me to come and stay the weekend with you, but then again, there's an unbelieving part of me, too. What if you change your mind?
    We've been everything, and we've been nothing.
    So, I believe you. And I hesitate. All in one sweeping motion.
    Once off the Duffy boat, I Uber home to pack my bags and get a ride to the Irvine train station. Onboard, I settle into my seat, happily buzzed, wanting to be with you already.
    A few hours pass and the conductor announces Oxnard as the next stop. I unplug my iPhone charger, wrap it up, curl up my headphones, secure my bag strap over my shoulder, anxious and ready to get off as soon as the train slows to a stop.
    I call you, and you're already at the station.
    I find your car, put my bags in the back seat, and hop in the front.

Our talk is aimless as we navigate what it's like to be seeing each other again.

It's not exactly brand new.
I saw you just last weekend.
But this is different.
If we fight, I've got nowhere to go until my train home tomorrow.
We have to behave.

"I'm hungry," I tell you.
"What do you want to eat?"
"I don't know. Is there a Subway around here?"
"Yes."

You park, and we walk inside to order. After we both order, you pay and then tease at my TOMS.

"Nice shoes," you say.

"My TOMS? What's so funny about my TOMS?" I frown at you, giggling nonetheless. They're a perfectly standard pair of navy blue TOMS, nothing particularly special about them.

"Nothin' funny. Just sayin' nice shoes," you reply truthfully.

You're uncomfortable with how normal we're acting. I get it. It's odd. And it's a lot. A lot for me to be here. With you. Being normal. And happy. And light. And good. So, you're talking just to talk. Talking just to fill. Talking to distract from just how good and normal this feels. I get that.

Next stop is chasers and alcohol from your *homie* at the liquor store. We're like little giddy kids, laughing at this and that. Laughing at how heavily this store reeks of incense and spices.

At the register, I go to pay for my lemon-lime sparkling ICE's, but you come in from behind me and tell your homie to put it all on your card instead. Your homie gives me my card back.

A small gesture, but it's sweet and not at all expected.

We drive to your house, and it's homey and cozy and adorable. It's smaller than your last one, but even from the exterior, I love it already. I grab my bags from the backseat and we walk through a short swinging gate, an opening in the white-picket fence surrounding your front yard. The cement path leads up to your front door, and there's a vintage tin sign propped against the wall of your porch.

I tried to child-proof the house but they keep finding a way back in.

I read the sign aloud, shooting you a look with raised eyebrows and a smile that pulls up the corners of my mouth, threatening to spill into a full-blown laugh.

You smile back and laugh. "I know. Are you ready, though?"

I take a second to think but I'm definitely ready.

I've been missing your parents for years.

We walk through the front door, this new house immediately warm and welcoming, hugging me with the same hello as your old house, seven years ago. Scents of patchouli, pepper, and laundry detergent wrap me up as I realize, even two hours north in a different house, your home smells the same. Feels the same. Everything is tasteful, from the gray-white wooden floors to the wall decorations, some recognizable from the old house, full of life and culture.

We walk up a staircase, turn a corner, and head into your room. It's simple and clean, like usual. High ceilings, mirrored closet doors, endless shoes lined up on the floor on your closet, your bed made with a soft navy blue blanket and two gray pillows, a white dresser, your own bathroom.

I put my bags down in a corner between your dresser and closet. You look at me expectantly, asking the question again with your eyes: *ready?*

I nod, and we venture out of your room down a short hallway and knock on your parents' closed door.

My stomach flips in anticipation.

I'm nervous.

I haven't seen them since my brothers hopped their fence the summer before I went to college.

Are they still mad?

Do they think I'm a bad kid?

I so often thought of calling them over the past few years, but with nothing in particular to say, I held back.

Your dad opens the door, and an excited *huh!* pops out of his mouth as he pulls back and pauses, then rushes me into a full bear hug, embracing me wholly with his thin frame. I hug him back tightly with both arms, wanting to stay here forever.

Somehow, I manage to force back a flood of tears. I didn't know I'd been waiting for this moment. I've always wanted your parents' love. I've always wanted your home. I've always wanted your life.

Your dad releases me after a few seconds and stands back, his hands on both of my shoulders. "Oh, honey. It's so good to see you. How have you been?"

"It's so good to see yooooou!" I practically sing.

And then your mom's off the bed, coming over to hug me as well. "Honey! How are you!?" she yells in her raspy voice, with a hard laugh of joy, her height falling just under my head, her body soft and enveloping in our embrace.

Your mom and I catch up on all things practical—finishing school, working in digital marketing, where I'm living, their new house—until your dad suddenly jolts us out of the conversation in a delighted whisper. "Oh, honey! Look! He's back. Jordan, come here, look!"

Your dad peers out their bedroom window into the night, so I walk over to see where he's looking. From the light of the moon and a dock lantern, I see the outline of the dock extending into a body of water, and the silhouette of a tall bird with stick legs, an oval body turned upright, an s-curve of a neck, and a long, thin beak, perched on the edge of the dock.

"The bird!?" I ask in animation, thrilled at this game of find-what-I'm-looking-at.

"Yep, yep. You see 'em? That's our friend. Call 'em Jack. He's a heron."

"He's huge!" I chirp back.

"I know, I know. You should see his wing span. Maybe he'll flap open for us. And he only visits us at night. He'll just come and hang out!"

"He's cool," I say with bright eyes as I turn to face your dad, delivering my approval.

"He's *so* cool," your dad says as he steps back from the window, crossing his slender arms against his chest, all intertwined in his gray, worn flannel, gently nodding his head up and down as he meets my eyes with a smart smile.

"What's he even doing?" you jump in.

"Jus' bein' a heron. Doing bird things," your dad answers.

"Doing bird things," you repeat, chuckling a little. "Jack the homie, doin' big bird things," you add, chuckling to yourself even more.

Your mom likes that one and laughs, shaking her head left to right, tickled by your commentary.

"Alright, alright, I'll let you two get to bed," you conclude.

"Okay, okay. Well, thanks for having me over. It's so good to see you guys," I gush as I hug your parents once more.

"Anytime, honey," your dad says sincerely. "We missed you."

Back in your room, we make some mixed drinks, but we don't make a dent in them. Exhaustion calls us instead. I grab my pajamas from my bag and pause before changing. "Don't *look*," I say with hesitation and a giggle.

"Oh, okay," you say in exaggerated animation, rolling your eyes, laughing, and turning around.

I giggle, too, and change quickly.

I know you've seen me naked countless times, but still.

We brush our teeth and call it a night.

I take special care not to touch you under the covers.

I want nothing more than to cuddle up underneath your arm and steady myself against the length of you, but I don't want to seem needy. I sleep fitfully, waking up again and again, wanting to touch you, restraining myself instead.

It's a lot of work.

We wake up early and take showers. I put the tiniest bit of cover-up under my eyes and we go downstairs.

Cyler moves and clanks around the kitchen. He looks up, noticing me for the first time. "Jordan!" he squeals. "Well, you don't say. Long time, no see!" he snort-laughs as he wraps me in a brisk hug. His hair is the lightest brown, almost dirty-blonde, a sharp contrast to his bleach-blonde hair from years ago. It's even longer than the last time I saw him, parted down the middle, falling straight and scraggly at his shoulders, tucked behind his ears on either side. He's wearing a zipped-up bomber jacket the color of burnt peach and pants that hang a few inches above his ankles, exposing his plain-white tube socks tucked into a pair of beat-up Sperry's.

He offers me a cup of coffee, which I happily accept.

You offer me oatmeal before splitting off to a small outdoor atrium in the middle of the house to squeeze in a workout.

Your parents make their way downstairs, insisting I sit outside on the patio with them.

I follow them outside to the backyard, two large chairs seated around a rectangular coffee table on one side under a wooden deck in the shade, a patio table with four cushioned chairs on the other side in the sun. The patio overlooks the harbor and spills through a small gate that opens to a wooden dock, the one I'd seen the night before. Beyond the small gate, the wooden dock zig-zags in a tight z-shape down to the water. I spot a few kayaks, two singles stacked atop one another and one double.

I join your parents at the patio table, sinking into one of the cushioned chairs, the warm morning sun already kissing my skin to the Zen clinks of the wind chimes dancing lightly in the breeze.

We chat more about their decision to move here, so far from Orange. Your mom explains that she still makes trips down to Orange once a month to work a little at a jewelry shop and visit with friends.

You trail outside after your workout, and without a word, you clear my empty oatmeal bowl and walk it back inside.

A small gesture, but it's sweet and not at all expected.

When you come back outside, Nancy's insisting we take the kayaks out.
You look at me in question.
"Uhh, yeah," I gush, trying to contain my excitement.
We go upstairs to change clothes. Back outside, you ask me if I want to take the singles or the double.
"Let's do the double. Do I sit in the front or the back?" I ask.
"Front," you answer as you retrieve life vests and paddles from a huge, rectangular plastic container and then continue to push the double kayak into the water.
You coach me through a few tips on the correct way to hold and move the paddle.
I love your parents, but it's nice to be out of earshot for a bit.
We talk about everything.
We talk about your classes at the local community college and transferring to a four-year.
We talk about me finishing my undergrad, the work I'm doing now.
We talk about you wanting to move to Long Beach with Cyler.
We talk about my family a little, my dad and how he remarried.
In between all the talking is a lot of laughing.
An older gentleman headed the opposite direction passes by on a paddle board. He calls to us, "Nice to see couples laughing together. Gettin' along. Ya rarely see that."
We both laugh in response and continue paddling.
I wonder if his stray comment grasps you like it does me.
It's all I ever wanted for us.
> Be together.
> Be in love.
> Be good.
> Be happy.

My cheeks flush hot and my smile hits my face wide and hard.
I'm ablaze.
Positioned directly in front of you, my face stays hidden from your view, and I'm heavy with gratitude for selecting the double kayak.
If only that gentleman really knew.
But in a sense, he obviously *did* know.
He saw what I can only feel.
He bore witness to the magic of us.
Those fleeting snippets when we're softly aligned.
He caught us in a moment.

We paddle all the way down to Seal Island, which is actually just a large dock covered with twenty or so loud, barking, sun-bathing seals. We stop to watch them, cracking up each time one of the seals does anything at all, because it's all funny. They take turns popping out of the water onto the dock, waddling their fat blubber around. Some climb straight on top of the others like it ain't no thang. And when the trampled seal coughs and barks after being climbed on, we practically burst into tears. They stick their necks out like they're on the Titanic. One of them shoves another into the water, and we double over in laughter all over again, shaking the kayak.

"Wait. Are you sure these're seals? Or are they sea lions?" I wonder aloud.

"Huh, shit, never thought of that. Seals. I think…" you wonder back.

"Well, then what's a sea lion?"

"I don't really know. Maybe they're the same thing."

"No, they can't be the same thing. They have to be different."

"Well, then what's the difference?"

"I don't know. But now I want to know. Let's look it up when we get back."

We continue paddling toward where the channel opens up to the ocean. I tell you I need to pee, suggesting we find a bathroom before making the trek back home. We park the kayak on a small strip of bare sand, climb up the side of a few enormous rocks, and land on a bike path that leads to a public bathroom. You wait for me to pee, and afterward we return to our beached kayak.

I begin to search the sand for seashells as we talk about nothing in particular.

You join the hunt, but instead of shells, you pick up a few smooth, thin rocks.

"Peeeerfect for skipping." You nod your head up and down in anticipation.

Your rock skips once, twice, *three* times, rippling the water gently.

You look back at me with a celebratory smile, awaiting my praise.

I consider withholding, but I'm impressed, so I give in halfway. "Yeah, yeah, yeah. Good at everything. I didn't forget," I smirk.

I find a perfectly whole seashell, although it's tiny, smaller than my pinky fingernail. I pick up a few additional rocks, white with orange tints, and one clear piece of weathered glass.

"You ready to head back?" you ask.

"Sure. Can you hold these for me since you have pockets?" I ask offering up my treasures.

You extend your hand in easy agreement.

"Don't break the shell. It's perfect. No cracks or anything," I warn.

"Not gonna break it," you reassure me as you gently drop the treasures in your pocket, securing them with a Velcro flap.

We push the kayak back in the water and begin paddling back toward your house.

"Were you nervous about me coming to stay? We haven't hung out this long in years," I begin.

"Yeah, a little. Didn't really know what to expect. Thought it could go one way or another."

"Same."

"But I've changed a lot since high school. I'm a lot calmer."

"You seem calmer."

"Well, I mean, yeah, I'm calmer in general, but I pop off a little harder now when I drink."

"That wild blood. You can contain it, but only for so long. Then you gotta release it."

"Yeah, true," you chuckle in agreement.

"I'm the same way. Feel like I leveled off, but when I drink, there's still some wild anger down there, a little scary sometimes. Even to me. I'm sure you remember."

"Oh, I remember," you laugh easily.

"But I'm calmer in other ways, quieter. Different than in high school."

"Man, oh man, high school," you reminisce.

"I don't miss anything about it." I wrinkle my nose.

"I do," you reply. "I really whiffed after high school. All caught up in drugs. Not the business. That was stupid. And now I'm behind. Everyone's, like, graduated and shit. Working. And I'm stuck in schooooool. Again."

"So what? Even the kids who graduated still don't know what to do with themselves."

"Yeah. But at least they're done with school."

"Well, the trick is to just begin, no matter where you're at. You just start. Plus. It's a big deal you even came back from all the hoopla you were doing." I aim to sound encouraging instead of preachy.

"It was bad." Your voice drifts, tucked away in separate memories.

"Dude, honestly though, what were you thinking? Heroin? I mean…" I trail off, my curiosity hijacking the conversation.

"I wasn't, really."

"But why would you try it in the first place?"

"I don't know. I did drugs all the time. Didn't seem that bigga deal."

"What was it even like?"

"Warm. Floaty. Calm. All at once. Like the best high you've ever had. There's nothing like it. You're just happy. But then you come down and you've got to get back up. You gotta stay high. Enough is never enough."

"How poetic," I say flatly.

I don't press further on the subject.

I know the feeling, though.

The irony stifling but almost funny.

I know what you mean.

I feel that way sometimes.

With you.

Loving you is like that.

Warm. Floaty. Calm. All at once. Like the best high you've ever had. There's nothing like it. You're just happy. But then you come down and you've got to get back up. You gotta stay high. Enough is never enough.

How ~~poetic~~ pathetic.

"Do you think we meant to?" I ask.

"Meant to what?"

"Fuck each other up."

"No." I hear you thinking in your pause. "We were just…we were just young."

"We're still young," I respond.

"Yeah, but we're older."

"Yeah." And I leave it alone.

We continue paddling up the canal. Boats of all sizes flank us on both sides of the canal, bobbing gently, anchored to the docks. We read a few of their names aloud as we pass on by: *Horny Hooker II*, *Why Knot?*, *Catch My Drift*.

An unexpected sense of peace washes over me.

Like things are simple.

> As simple as the double kayak beneath us.
> As simple as the sun beaming from above.
> As simple as the calm, cool canal water ahead.
> As simple as the wide, wild ocean water behind.

And we're going to be okay.

> Not necessarily together, although my heart still jumps and aches a little at the thought.

But just us, as individuals; we're going to be okay.

I'm going to be okay.

You're going to be okay.

I feel calm and okay.
Almost as if our past has been completely absolved.
> Not forgotten.
> Not even close.

Just cleansed.
> Like dipping the memories in the ocean, exfoliating them with gritty salt, freeing them from their fatal, emotional potency, untangling the anguish from the memories themselves, explaining how we didn't mean all the things we said and did; we didn't mean all the meanness.

Is that possible?
Can that happen?
Can we be us as we are Now?
> Two emerging adults, humans nonetheless, talking about what happened Then, saying sorry Now, and stumbling into reality at our own pace.

And still be us as we were Then?
> Two pulsating teenagers, alive with the push and pull of separate agendas, feeding the scripts of our own narratives, the stories we crafted about our lives.

Can both be true?
> Then & Now?

And okay?
Can both be true and still okay?

Back at your house, we shower separately. We want to do something today, although we don't quite know what yet. As I get dressed, you plug your laptop into the speakers on your desk and make us some mixed drinks.

"Put on whatever you want," you offer.
Letting me select the music?
Don't mind if I do.
A small gesture, but it's sweet and not at all expected.
I play "In My Mind" by Maty Noyse, and I'm already feeling giddy. Happy and relaxed.
Next on my playlist is "Closer" by The Chainsmokers ft. Halsey.
The lyrics spill through your room, and the part where the guy says something about hoping to never see the girl's friends again finishes.
You meet my eyes, laughing.
"You like that part, don't you?" I ask, already knowing your answer.

"Yeah," you release your rolling chuckle and shake your head up and down.

"That part reminded me of you," I concede.

"Like before this, today?"

"Yeah," I answer matter of fact.

"I actually kind of like this song. Wasn't this the one on the VMAs?"

"Yeah, I think so. Halsey's the girl singing. I *love* her music," I gush.

"Yeah, he, like, actually bit her shoulder at the VMAs," you laugh as you begin moving your head, feeling the song.

In the music video, a couple drives up the coast overlooking the ocean.

"Ooooooh, know what we should do?" you ask suddenly.

"What?"

"Drive up PCH. There's this spot that kinda looks exactly like that," you point to the video.

"Perfect. I'm down. Lezzzz gooooo!" I'm buzzing already from our drinks.

We take shots before we leave, and then we're off.

And so it goes.

We drive up the coast, both of us buzzed and happy and lovey, a giggly mess of a couple, but we feel like a couple. I don't think we've ever had so much uninterrupted laughter between us. Who would have thought we could be trusted together for over twenty-four hours?

I want to listen to "Closer" again, so I blast it through your car stereo, and I'm singing along out loud. "Out loud" is an understatement. I'm belting out the lyrics and swinging my head like it's an on-stage performance.

Music picks up where words fall short:
["Closer" by The Chainsmokers ft. Halsey]

But you know how we do.
    I tell you what I can't tell you through a song.
    I tell you what I can't tell you.
        Because I still need to tell you.

The drinks loosen us both up, and we're touchier than we were before. I'm snapping pictures and videos of us. Something about the need to capture that which can't be captured.

Arriving at the strip of coast you had in mind, you pull over, we take a few swigs of the Henney you brought, chase it down with some Coke, and hop out. It's an incredible view indeed, the cliff pouring out to the sky ahead and the ocean below.

There are lots of people meandering around this lookout spot, so I ask someone to take a picture of us, and when I take my phone back to review it, I'm stunned by the happiness beaming from both of our faces.

Drunk and happy, you drive us back to your house, which is when my blackout sweeps over me. The last thing I remember is you racing up the 1-freeway, empty farming fields flashing by to our left, windows halfway down, music blaring, you rapping your songs to me, me just smiling and giggling like this is a fun game.

Morning smacks me upside the head with a slamming headache and a dry mouth. I'm hungover and feel like absolute death. I try to remember the details from the day before. Yep, *day*. As in, did we even make it to evening? Oops. Day drank ourselves into oblivion.

You toss and turn a little, so I know you're awake, too. I turn my body to lie on my side, facing you, although your eyes are still closed.

"When did we get home yesterday?" I whisper.

"Sixish," you mumble, eyes still closed.

"Did your parents see us?" I panic.

"Not really. You just went upstairs and went straight to bed," you answer, slowly opening your eyes.

"So we didn't talk to them?" I'm still concerned.

"I did a little. Jus' told 'em you were tired and then came upstairs with you," you explain as you slip your arm around the top of my waist, pulling me closer to you.

I know what that means.

You want what you want.

But I want what I want, too.

Closer means sex, which you want.

And sex means closer, which I want.

So, we have it.

It distracts from my hangover for about seven minutes, but then you finish on my back, and now I have to shower. Everything is fine until I close the bathroom door, immediately breaking into a cold sweat. My heart beats too quickly, and I'm dizzy and sweating and feel like fainting. In slow motion, I quietly collapse to the bathroom floor. My strength drained, I can't pull myself back up. I begin to panic because I need to shower but I physically can't move.

I think of calling for you, but I'm entirely naked and sick.

Too vulnerable.

Too much.

I don't want you to see me like this. I know you've seen me like this before, but still. We *just* started getting along again. And although you've seen my naked body through rippled sheets and dimmed lights, seeing my naked body in the loud light of the bathroom is different.

Too vulnerable.

Too much.

I still can't move, though, my hangover ripping through my body like poison.

I have no choice.

"Kolton," I whimper.

You open the bathroom door, wide-eyed with worry.

"A towel," I whimper again, my knees folded into triangles, one stacked on the other and tucked towards my naked ass. I have one forearm leaned against the closed toilet seat and my other arm steadies me against the bathroom floor.

You grab me a towel, and I lightly hold it against my chest, trying to shield my body.

"I don't feel good," I deliver next.

"Do you want something to drink?" you ask, concern laid out openly across your face.

"Please," I whisper.

"'Kay, hold on," and you disappear.

I feel like I need to puke, but when I try, nothing comes up.

You come back, offering me a sparkling water and unscrewing the cap for me. I sip a tiny bit.

"Do you still want to shower?" you ask.

"Yeah, I need to."

You reach over me, rip open the shower curtain, and turn the shower on.

"Thanks," I say.

"'Kay," you say, pausing to look at me with question before turning around and closing the bathroom door.

I slowly sip more of the sparkling water until I feel steady enough to climb into the shower. I hold the wall the entire time, sprinkle some shampoo in my hair, rinse it out, rinse my back, and I'm done.

You're back in bed. I crawl in, towel and all.

Typically, I'd try to restrain myself, but right now, with my body demolished and my mind threatening to slip into an anxiety attack, I need comfort.

"I know you don't like cuddling all the time, but I feel really sick, and I just need to be held for a little," I inform awkwardly.

You look at me in surprise but quietly oblige, allowing me to snuggle under your arm.

With the pressure from my swaddling towel, the blanket, and your body beside mine, I calm and breathe a little easier.

After about five minutes, I begin to drift back to sleep, but before succumbing fully, I unravel myself from you, turning around to be alone once more.

After a few hours of sleep, we wake up again, and it's afternoon.

"Do you know where my keys are?" you ask me as you sift through the top of your dresser and pick through the pockets of the jeans you wore yesterday.

"No. You can't find them?" I respond groggily, feeling much better than this morning.

You continue rummaging through your room, coming up empty handed.

"Did you check your car?" I think out loud.

You look at me, pause, and head downstairs without a word.

Two minutes later, you're back up the stairs, and I hear the clinking jingle of a few keys.

I meet your face with a smile, but you sigh heavily and shake your head back and forth.

"What?" I press, confused.

"Left 'em in the ignition. Battery's dead," you say, and I can hear the frustration in your voice.

"That's okay. We'll just get some jumper cables. Cyler can help us or something." I try to be helpful, but you don't respond.

I feel you leaving me, retreating into your head instead, feeling bad about drinking that much and driving, about forgetting your keys in the ignition, about draining the car battery. You don't like that part of yourself. I get it. I have the same part. I don't like it, either.

We go downstairs to eat, and Cyler greets us, tells us your parents are gone for the day, off at the farmers' market. You relax a little, we take the kayaks out once more, and then it's time to drop me off at the train station.

On the train ride home, I think about the day before. I think about us. You shouldn't have been drinking and driving; we both know better. It was all so careless. We should be more careful. But it was all so fun. It was all so selfish. But it was all so real. It was just us, in all our dark, selfish, glorious fits of laughter.

I think about my regular life, my life without you. I think of how depressed I'd been just a few years back. I think of my parents, and how neither of them helped me. I think about them leaving me. I think about them leaving my brothers. I think about them choosing drugs over four children, so alive, so full of potential. I think about how perfect life had been before my parents decided to screw it all up. And I think about growing up, and how hard and lousy it can be, and all the people who've already hurt me. I think about being good, working toward a good life, but remember how quickly good can flip to bad. I think about the good things I've done. I think about the bad things I've done.

When you and I first met years ago, I knew after one week we'd be bad and not good. It felt good at times, but I knew it wouldn't be that pure kind of good.

But then again, what had *good* done for me?

> Good was a beautiful family of six, straight out of a PG movie behind a white picket fence, gone bad in the flip of a year, nuclear implosion from the inside out.
>
> Good was nothing but bad waiting to happen.
>
> Good was hard to maintain and easy to turn upside down.

I feel bad and guilty about you drinking and driving, but another part of me indulges in the anger and retaliation. You're my *fuck you* to the world, the *fuck you* I don't dare say aloud with my girlish mouth that's supposed to be sweet and cheery, not angry and ugly.

You shake the world of its order, and sometimes I want to shake it, too. I want to be part of that, dismiss the world and all its delicate order with the flick of a finger, a deep, throaty laugh, or drunkenly raging up PCH for the fun of it.

And I hear the devil's serpents and God's angels rumble back to life.

> The serpents slapping their thin tongues against my ears:
>> *Care-less-ness.*
>> *Care less.*
>> *Freedom.*
>> *Power.*
>> *Screw 'em all.*
>> *Life is yours for the taking.*
>
> The angels singing in surround-sound:
>> *Care-ful.*

Julianna Lembeck

Care more.
Conscientious concern connects you.
Life is only life when shared.

OCTOBER 5, 2016,
you're doing that thing you do.

The plan is made.
I'm getting in the shower, preparing to drive up for the weekend.
And then my phone pings with a new text.
Before I even look, I already know it's you.
    Because I had a feeling you might do that thing you do.
I almost read it with a smile of pure amusement.
Of course you suddenly have an interview the day I'm supposed to come and stay with you.
Of course there is something separating you from me.
It's scary to have others rely on you, isn't it?
Terrifying to think others may *need* you for something, huh?
And, oh, how you love that one.
Need.
Needy.
You threw that one at me last weekend. You were playing *Call of Duty* the day I was supposed to leave for the train, right after you found your keys in the ignition. Right before kayaking. You were playing your game, and I kept pushing your chair with my foot, trying to get your attention.
"Pause your game," I whined.
"Can't," you chirped back, eyes still on the game.
So I pushed and tried to swivel your chair a bit more to bug you, still wanting your attention.

Between sessions, your game wrapped up for a second, so you turned your chair and looked at me directly. "You're being *needy*."

But when I met your eyes, I didn't see a statement.

I saw questions and worry pouring from your eyes instead:

Do you need me yet?
I'm not quite sure I can show up in the way you need me.
I'm not there yet.
I don't know what that looks like.
I'm not ready.

And even though your statement taunted me, your unsaid questions begged me to maintain strength, begged me not to let you in, begged me to remain separate from you for as long as possible. Quite possibly for as long as forever.

I shoot you a text back and let you off easy. *Good luck with the interview.*

We're getting close to danger, though.

We're getting close to the point where I just may need you.

All fun and games until someone falls back in love.

Ring-a-round the rosie,
A pocket full of posies,
Ashes! Ashes!
We all fall down

♪

OCTOBER 29, 2016,
Halloweeney & Vee.

I'm happily hungover, that small window when the hangover hasn't fully set in yet and the buzz is still kickin' from the night before. And one of my favorite things to do in a happy hangover is call you. You answer, and I'm making you laugh a little, so I know I've got your guard down.

"I'm coming to see you," I tell you, not asking.

"When?"

"Now. I'm taking the train. Just pick me up at five," I instruct.

"Honestly, you can't. I have to work with my uncle a little, plus I'm gonna be smokin' and chillin' all weekend."

"I don't care. I'm still coming," I say unfazed.

"I don't think you'll be able to handle all the chillin' though," you chuckle.

"The train gets in at five. Don't be late."

"You can't wear anything but underwear the whole weekend."

"'Kay, whatever. I gotta pack. Call you when I'm in. Bye."

After hanging up, I feel my hangover creeping on heavier. I look at the clock, realizing I only have twenty minutes until the train leaves, and it takes at least eight minutes to get to the station.

Shoot! I'm coming, I think determined.

My heart races from the thrill of it all.

I giggle like an idiot as I throw some clothes in a bag, a new pair of jeans, a tight, gray long-sleeve-shirt, sandals, a straightener, black yoga pants. My if-you-won't-love-me-emotionally-at-least-you-will-physically essentials pack.

I race down the freeway, park my car at the Irvine train station, and hustle across the bridge to await the Northbound train.

I barely make it.

But, of course, I can do nothing but make it.

It's you.

It's me.

It's us, and I have to make it.

Two minutes to spare.

I relax as I wait for the train to arrive.

Once onboard and settled into my seat, I laugh.

I didn't plan to call you this morning.

Just last night, I slept beside someone else. No one notable. Will probably never see him again.

And this morning, when I returned home from No One Notable's house, I called my fake weekend boyfriend so I'd have a breakfast buddy.

Barely clean of both their pheromones and testosterone, and now seated on a Northbound train to Oxnard.

To you.

While texting yet another fake boyfriend, another time filler, telling him I'll be back in town Sunday night.

It's all kind of funny to me.

Like a juggling act.

Each time-filling, fake boyfriend a ball in the air, and perhaps you're the unicycle.

And it takes all of you.

I can only have any of you if I can have all of you. All at once. I can't hold any one of you with stillness. That would shatter the juggling act, ruin the performance, tripping me off the unicycle of you while all the balls come crashing down. None of you are enough on your own.

Sometimes, I'm tempted to ride away with just you, thinking you and I might be enough, but then I remember what propels us forward in the first place: a revolving circle. Revisiting the same points on the circle again and again and again. *Ring around the rosie*, right?

So, I remember you're not enough on your own, and I play into the performance, juggling all my fake boyfriends at once, you the epicenter of it all.

And it's alright that it's all wrong.

It's a delicate mess, but I'm keeping everything in place.

I can't have just them. I can't have just them, and I don't *want* just them. The cleaner the fake boyfriends are, the more something deep and dark inside of me bangs against the parameters of my body, itching and scratching to get out and *Fuck. Them. Up.*

Un-turn the corners of their smiles.

Cackle at their sweet dreams.

Tear open their unbroken skin.

Poison their confident minds with ping-ponging indecision and self-doubt.

Give them a bubble where they can love and be loved, only to burst it open, free falling, heart shattered, empty handed.

And then there's you. You, in all your dark glory. You're a darkness, a mind shift. And me, too, remember? It takes me to see you. *It takes two to tango.* It's not just about you. It's about me, too. It's about the broken in us. The broken pieces of us spawned from darkness and ugliness, the stories we tell ourselves about our lovability, or lack thereof. Yes. I find parts of me in you, insatiably fascinating parts that are also alarmingly grotesque. I both love and hate these parts of me.

All these unlovable parts we both accept and repel in each other.

We accept these qualities because we share them.

We repel these qualities because we know we can be better.

I think this is the closest I've come to understanding us.

Us, us, us.

Because it's not about just you, or just me. It's about us.

It's about those pieces, those parts, alive and breathing, inside both of us, that only someone with the same pieces can see, understand, tolerate, and sometimes even love in someone else.

Us this time.

It's us this time.

Us, in all our dark glory.

I see us in my mind.

    We're walking.

    We're shuffling.

    We're walking.

        It's not a red carpet.

        It's a dark carpet.

        It's maroon, like the drip of new blood.

            Gangstas don't run, they walk.

            And bad bitches don't glide, they sway with hips that seduce, and heels that slap, like the reminder of a cracked neck.

                Steer clear.

                It's us.

                Us, in all our dark glory.

It's the grotesque parts of both of us that latch onto one another and spin; it's the way we spin.

It's the way we hold our circle.

It's a dark circle.

We take what we want, always more than we need, and it's about us and no one else. And we think it's hilarious. We find it so manically funny we can't even interact with anyone else. They won't get it. We draw others' attention with our magnetic charm and dizzying laughter, befuddling them up and down with our wild and polarizing differences, but we don't let them in. They don't see our similarities, never detecting the iron string connecting the dark, dank crevices of our cores. We're doing them a favor, keeping them out and us in, because there's no winning in our dark circle.

It's dark, but it still feels like love inside our circle.

Or at least, me to you.

I love you.

I love you so much I feel like my heart might explode sometimes.

A few hours later, I'm still thinking about us and our dark circle when I hop off the train, looking for your car.

I spot it, throw my bags in the backseat, and come to sit beside you in the front seat, fully prepared to soak up the touch and love I'm craving, not colored with the hesitance of my last visit. I loop my arms around your arm closest to me in the passenger seat, touch the pressure of my head upon your shoulder, releasing it all after a second or two.

"Hiiiiiiii," I giggle up at you.

"Hiiii." You glance over at me with a low chuckle.

"What have you been doing all day?"

"Watching the games with my bro. I like that thing." You point at the layered, black-yarn choker adorning my neck.

"My choker?" I ask, still disoriented enough from my hangover to not care whether you liked it or not. The fact that you *do* leaves me absolutely giddy, though.

"Yeah. It's sexy," you answer.

"I like it, too. Feed me, I'm hungry," I insist.

"What do you want?"

"Subway. Aren't you excited to see me?"

"Yesssss," you draw out the confirmation, accompanying it with another rolling chuckle.

"Did you miss me?" I ask through a laugh, not caring about the answer, just happy to be asking silly questions of ruffles, lace, and fluff. Just happy to be here with you.

"Yessss," you draw out again, another chuckle.

"What are we doing tonight?"

But I've already stopped listening because, as I glance at you from the passenger seat, the world shifts in slow motion, and I see us from an almost removed point of view. I see us circling each other. And your face. I see every precise angle of it, like a photo burst. From the sideways glance you shoot me, to the glance trailing degree by degree back to the road. The way your lips protrude from your face with the perfect amount of pucker and settle just so.

It's all I can do to stay seated and not crawl into your lap like a kitten.

I can feel myself come alive under your attention, in your presence. All the shiny parts of me come out to play. I'm sweet, fun, carefree, loving, laughing, waving through the wind of life, giggling and bubbling along the way. Sprinkling love here and there, like liquid gold, shimmering and shining, boasting a big, toothy smile and gentle echoes of sweet, soft, lovely laughter.

We stop to pick up wine. As we stand in line to pay, the cashier waves you over to check out, and then the next available cashier waves me over separately. I smile and veer to my left, trailing behind you. "Oh," I stutter out, "I'm with him." And I hand over my bottle of wine to your cashier, smiling all the way. The other cashier sizes us up, pauses a beat, and waves on the customer behind us.

"That fool couldn't believe you'd be with me," you say as we walk outside toward the car.

"Do you see how cute I am? I don't blame him."

"Nah, it's probably because I'm blaaaack," you say almost contemplatively, as if turning it over in your mind alone rather than discussing it with me.

I honestly forget. I forget all the labels. It occurs to me we've never talked about the fact that you're half black and I'm white. To me, it's never mattered. We started out as kids, and it was never an issue back then. I forget what others might see of you. I just know what I know of you.

I know you from the smile that spreads slowly, blooming from the right-side corner of your mouth. I know you from the coiled curls that lie close to your head. I know you from soft, open purse of your plush lips. I know you from the scent of Cool Water. I know you from your six-foot-one height and thick, well-proportioned build. I know you from your scarred hands, your scarred eye. I know you from your huge sweatshirts and crisply clean jeans. I know you from the thickness of your forearms, the beat of your music, the nod of your head, the exclamation at a basketball or football game. I know you from your rolling chuckles of laughter. I know you from all of these things. I forget all labels. I forget anyone can see you any differently than I do.

"Can you please put your seatbelt on?" I ask you in the car.

"Uh-uh. I don't wanna wrinkle my shirt. I be lookin' fresh, baby, can't ruin that," you sass back.

I turn my head back to the windshield and raise my eyebrows in an exaggerated sigh of exasperation, trying to hide my smile.

We get to your house, and you head straight for the TV. Cyler's home, but your parents are gone, so it's just the three of us. I tell you two to figure out what we're doing tonight while I shower and get ready.

Upstairs, I primp and prod, rinse my face clean of makeup, only to doll it up once more. I straighten my hair the way you like it, throw on my new pair of jeans and the tight long-sleeve-shirt I brought, and don my black choker again.

I come downstairs perfectly put together but don't get much of a reaction from you. You and Cyler have already dug into the beer, eyes glued to some sports game.

"I'd like some wine," I announce reasonably. I like when I have reasonable things to say so I can be saying things. There are a million things in my head I want to say, ask, analyze, talk about with you, but I pick and choose accordingly so as not to run you down. Plus, you said yourself you'd be *chillin'* this weekend, so I remind myself not to bug.

"So, did we decide what we're doing tonight?" I ask aloud as you pour my glass of wine.

"Bro-lee. What did Daven say?"

"Who's Daven?" I interrupt.

"Just a kid we met at a bar out here," you answer.

"Well. I texted him asking what's going down tonight. He texted back asking what we're doing," Cyler explains.

You and Cyler think this is hilarious and bust up laughing. Cyler heads into the kitchen and helps himself to a glass of wine, too. Neither of you answer my question.

"Sooo....?" I remind you both that I've asked a question, partway scowling at the semi-high smiles on your faces.

You look up at me, lips parted, pause, lift your eyebrows, and widen your eyes until you burst into another giggle and turn back to the TV, only to answer my question with another question: "I don't know, Bro-lee. So, what are we doing?"

"Good God, I leave you guys for like thirty minutes and you still haven't made a decision," I tease in fake exasperation and amusement.

Idiots…

You and Cyler exchange glances and crack up all over again.

I'm somewhere between still hungover from the night before and buzzed from the wine. I don't care what we do.

The two of you put your genius minds together, finally deciding on driving out to Ventura.

"I'll just drive. I won't drink that much," you inform us.

We embark on our adventure toward Ventura, although we haven't decided on a specific place. I search *bars* in Ventura on Yelp, and decide on a random one. We park, and as we near the address, we discover a huge mansion with a wooden, wrap-around porch and a long line trailing outside.

"Is this it?" I ask.

"I don't know. Looks like it. Everyone's dressed up," you answer.

Sure enough, this is the right place. The mansion-turned-bar is enormous and crawling with people in Halloween costumes. I'm too buzzed to care that we're dressed in regular clothes.

Once inside, the first order of business is drinks. I hold your hand as we push through the crowd to find the bar, Cyler trailing close behind. We pass a staircase on the left and what looks to be a living room to our right with people littered all over couches. Fog machines sit in various corners, and although it's dark inside, there are alternating strobe and neon lights flashing everywhere. We find the bar, and I yell over the crowd, asking Cyler what he wants to drink. I ask you, too, but true to your word, you're not drinking any more for the rest of the night. I'm slightly impressed. Cyler and I cheers our drinks, and we all meander through the party, scoping out the scene. People are everywhere, some areas more crowded than others, a dancefloor crammed body to body from each wall.

"I have to pee. Come with me," I direct you.

As I make my way up the wide staircase, following its square turns here and then there, I see the line to the girls' restroom spilling outside its door.

"Look, that's the line up there. I'm going up, but wait for me out here. Okay?"

You nod back, and I make my way for the line, sipping happily on my drink.

Inside, the bathroom looks like a Lana Del Rey music video with pale pink walls, sectioned off with square tiles and faucet sinks that look like they're from the '70s with handles like sprinklers. There are only two stalls, so we all stand close together.

Oh, the girls' bathroom.

Where female love is briefly shared warmly and openly.

The girl in front of me lets me cut in line for no reason at all, just to be kind. As one of the stalls opens up, I twirl around to face her, gently squeezing each of her arms, thanking her. "You are the best! I'm Jordan, by the way." I smile as I drop my hands from her arms.

"Veronica, or, well, Vee," she replies.

"You're the best, Vee!" I squeal as I tuck away in the available stall.

"You're beautiful," she calls out sweetly. I catch it over the stall, despite the high chitter-chatter all around us.

"I love you!" I gush back, meaning it in my way.

She's gone when I'm out of the stall, but I love her all the same.

I'm halfway surprised to see you at the bottom of the staircase, waiting for me obediently.

"Where's Cyler?" I ask.

"I can't find him, he just wandered away."

"Weird."

You're not worried and not intently looking for him, so neither am I. We stumble into an empty room, save for a pool table in the middle and a few tables lining the perimeter. We grope the pockets, but the pool balls are nowhere to be found. You search a few nooks and crannies around the tables to no avail.

A young couple meanders through, looking around the room, and before they walk away, I seize the opportunity and ask them to take a picture for us. There's no wiggling out of it once I've involved an innocent bystander. You have no choice but to oblige the photo.

I thank the girl who took the photo and look at it immediately. I look small standing beside you like that. The photo has a moody, hazy look to it, showing up in dismal shades of browned yellow corners and dipped in a heather-gray pixelated fog.

We go downstairs, wander outside, and search for Cyler. If we find him, great. If we don't, fine. The outside patio is just as large as the maze inside but wider, more open. People are still everywhere, so we acquaint a corner atop a wooden deck where we have a slight vantage point of the crowd, gazing over heads, trying to see if any of them belong to Cyler. He's still nowhere to be found.

"I want another drink," I insist, as the night plays forward.

I get another drink and decide upon another bathroom break.

As I slap-happy-clippity-clap down the stairs, with drink in my step and a smile on my face, I see you waiting yet again.

Good boy, I think to myself.

And there she is again.

Vee. Veronica. Her!

"You!" I squeak in a fit of laughter, as if I'm reuniting with a long-lost best friend instead of a girl who let me cut in the bathroom line twenty minutes prior.

We hug like it was the normal next thing to do, and then squeak about nonsense.

In my flurry of giddy, she remains even-keeled.

I love this about her, and I want her near.

She's easy-going and laidback, like someone who lives life joint-to-joint, meal-to-meal, smile-to-smile, no care in the world.

She takes to me, or takes to me taking to her, and joins us as we walk back outside.

She has a guy friend with her, not a boyfriend, and no one notable because as soon as he delivers his name, I've already forgotten.

The lazy search for Cyler continues, and by now it's sort of funny. With Veronica in our mix, I'm able to detach from you ever so slightly. I become less aware of you, less focused on your level of attention on me, and more aware of my giddy adoration for my new-found friend.

I begin to ask her questions as I take note of her. She's dressed as a vampire in all black. Her blonde, shoulder-length hair falls in loose, tousled waves. She dons a black cape, a black corset that pushes her boobs into a bouncy arrangement, black fishnets, and black Mary Jane heels with thin straps secured across her ankles. Her temperament feels calm, on the verge of confident, nonchalant, loving, easy to be with.

I can't name the way I feel toward her.

Something close, safe, distinctly female about her.

I love her in a quick and instant way.

I feel like I could take her anywhere with me.

If we move through the crowd, I lead.

But I also throw my hand back to hold hers as we make our way through the party.

I keep forgetting it's a party.

I feel like it's just me, Veronica, give me a few seconds and then I remember you're there, too, and, oh yeah, her bland friend. And, of course, the lazy search for Cyler. But I forget the rest of the party is there. To me, it's all a backdrop of costumes, shapes of people, loud music, and the colors and shades of blue neon lights and fog. I'm having fun. And I'm having fun for no particular reason, either. It's all just…fun.

Eventually, Veronica and her friend have to leave. We say our goodbyes and exchange numbers even though we'll probably never see each other again.

Suddenly, you beeline it for the back of the patio behind a pop-up island bar, where three chairs line up against a wall, all three occupants smoking cigarettes.

One of them is Cyler.

"Bro! What are you doing, man?" you ask, excited to find him.

"Bro! I've been here. What are *you* doing?" Cyler breaks into a laugh.

"Let's take a shot!" I throw in my two cents to this joy fest.

"Jordan, *yes!*" Cyler agrees with silly enthusiasm.

Cyler and I leave you to the chairs and make our way to the island bar in the middle of the backyard to order tequila shots with lime chasers.

"One, two, three, *cheers!*" I yell into the crowd as I clink Cyler's shot glass.

We squeeze the limes in our hot, stinging mouths and wince at each other. Then we burst into laughter like this whole life is a game and we're winning.

We're still laughing as we find our way back to you. You're right where we left you in one of the chairs by the wall, calmly sucking on a cigarette.

"You want to know how I found you, bro?" you ask.

"How?" Cyler takes the cigarette from your mouth and takes a drag.

"That jacket." You exhale, blowing smoke upward into the night sky.

Cyler's wearing his burnt-peach bomber jacket. The same one he wore when I first visited last month.

"The jacket, bro." Cyler nods his head slowly, smiling ear to ear, and the two of you burst into laughter again. The pointless laughter wraps me up, and I begin to laugh, too. Cyler laughs harder, the three of us a choir of inebriated joy.

Fuckin' burnt-peach bomber jacket.

NOVEMBER 2016,
candied darkness.

You're ignoring me again.
You've disappeared again.
With every minute that passes, I unravel.
Every second is a spiral.
Spiraling into emptiness.
I spin, trying to figure out why you're ignoring me.
Spin, spin, spin.
I don't know what to make of your nothing responses.
Silence makes chaos look easy.
> I would rather sit in a whirlpool of our circular chaos, alternating between gulping water and gasping for air, than be stuffed in a cube of nothingness, where the floor is covered with broken glass that cleanly slices the pads of my heavy feet.
> I'd rather a fight.
> I'd rather a blow-out.

You do me no good.
Yet I spin, again and again.
I'm spinning for you.
I'll never please you.
Which is unpleasing to me.
So, you're a safe spin.
I can spin out with you for eternity.
You rejecting me.

Me rejecting reality.

It's the perfect spin.

Did I lose you once more to the candied darkness you disappear to? Where it's alright for it to be all wrong? Did you know you were going back there? Did you fight it? Or did you surrender with a sigh of relief?

Sometimes, you are so stripped of emotion that I can't help but find myself surprised when you slip interest into something. It could be anything, really—the softness of a towel, a funny commercial, the fluffiness of a pancake. The mundane of mundanities, but somehow it still surprises me that you possess this ability to have the emotion, and to then go the extra step to verbalize it.

Back to your candied darkness. I could be right. I could be wrong. You could be ignoring me because of the insanity of our dynamic. It's so dizzying, so circular.

So dizzy you can't stand.

Can't stand up.

Can't stand me.

So, you stand down.

> *Ring around the rosie,*
> *A pocket full of posies,*
> *Ashes! Ashes!*
> *We all fall down*
> ♪

And does it matter? Does it ever matter? The thing about circles—you will always revisit the same point, again and again. Maybe that's why there's no panic this time. I know I will see you again. I know, all too well, this time is never the last time; it will only have been *the last time we spoke until the next time.*

I never know what you want from me. Perhaps nothing at all. And yet I'll scream love at you anyhow. Maybe that's why you hate me. I'm giving you things you don't want, didn't ask for, don't believe in, and won't accept.

Is the reality that none of this is real? Is the reality that we exist in my head and there only? Parts of me answer *yes*. Parts say *no*. And parts say *it will never matter—get out now.*

You know I'll stay and think about it, though. I won't stay forever. I'm good at leaving. I'm good at coming back, too. You know both. And so it goes.

DECEMBER 2016,
holding, getting, gaining.

I call you again.
You don't answer.
I believe you'll answer someday.
But I sense it will be a while.
Sometimes we need time apart.
Because our togetherness is dizzying.
Why can't I let go?
    Holding, holding, holding.
    What am I getting?
    What am I gaining here?
    Is it painful?
    Yes.
    But clearly not painful enough.
    Holding, holding, holding.
    What am I getting, getting, getting?
    What am I gaining, gaining, gaining?
I block your number again.
So I can believe it's my choice not to be hearing from you, giving me the smallest peace of mind.

Julianna Lembeck

Two months of silence and you finally come back around. Round and round, here we are. You say you were busy and you're sorry for not getting back with me. Not much more than that, though.

I drop it because I've got other priorities in mind, like getting along long enough to see each other again, and we resume like nothing happened. Because it's true—it's exactly what happened. Nothing.

[Wednesday, January 4th 7:07PM]

KOLTON   **JORDAN**

                               How was your day?

A days a day. What about you?

                     So dramatic over there. It was fine, really busy this week

That's good

                           You in a weird mood?

Yup

                                 How come?

Do we really need to get into this right now

                     Don't be like that. I'm just asking. It's fine if you don't want to explain.

No I don't. What are you doing?

                     Just getting home, deciding what to eat. Any ideas?

Make a salad lol

                     You want to hear a funny story?

Shore

                     It's too long a story to text out

Uh oh. My phones broke lmao jk I just

don't feel like getting on the phone

> You never do

I know. Texting much more specific and to the point. No fuckery. Plus I'm drinking

> Mmmmm

What if I needed to stay with you. What would you do about your other rocky relationship

> Lol you ARE my only rocky relationship

Mhmm

> You really have been drinking

Haha

> Most texts I've gotten from you in a while

Haha damn blowing my cover

> All you need to do now is be nice and then I'll KNOW you're wasted

Am I nice right now

> Yeah you are I guess

I usually scare white folks

> What is your preoccupation with black & white lately? You brought it up a few times when I was with you last time too.

It's crazy right now jojo

I know you can't understand or even begin to understand bc obviously you're white but it's real

Julianna Lembeck

> All the fools think now that trump is in office they can do and say what they want but that's where I might get myself in trouble bc I come from a better "white family" than 90% of the idiots doing and saying dumb shit. N I'll beat some ones ass. But I'm still perceived as just another ignorant black male bc of my appearance.
>
> But it's all gravy. This is life.
>
> Anyways where are you what's your story??

>> I didn't know you felt so strongly about your race. No need to play into other people's ignorance though. Keep focused on your own responsibilities & don't pay them any mind.
>>
>> When I look at you, I never see black. I always just see you? Idk, hard to explain. But I forget the labels.
>>
>> I'm home now & it's a long story. It's silly, I'll tell you another time.

> True but you know "me"
>
> And have for a long time
>
> But most people see dark skin and scars as a negative
>
> And to be honest I haven't felt this strong about my race until as of late. Because everything that's going on I had to
>
> It's also another long story I'll explain it to you tomorrow when you're here.
>
> Or Friday actually, so two days

>> Don't get caught up in other people's

> ideas of who you are. Who cares. Everyone lives in their own little worlds anyway, so just figure out how to make your world work for you & don't pay any mind or energy to other people's little worlds.
>
> Kolton, you've got it all. You're smart, you read people well, you're attractive, hilarious, extremely charismatic, fun & lovable. You have all the potential to be and do whatever you please. For whatever reason, I don't think you believe that.

Thank you!

Seriously that's one of the nicest most genuine things I've heard in a while.

I know deep down that's me I'm just stuck right now. N I don't care what any thinks of that.

BUTT, what time will you be arriving Friday

> You'll unstick yourself when the pain of being stuck becomes bigger than the pain of getting yourself unstuck.
>
> I won't be able to make it up Friday. I'm having dinner with one of my girlfriends Friday night.

Whiffin'

> By Friday you'll forget you wanted to see me anyway

Lmao or I'll be blocked who knows

> [sunset pictures]
> I took these yesterday morning.

Those are nice

> It's past my bedtime. Sleep well :)

LOL!

What ever dude

Why do you always do that your so sketch

I don't even care just don't ask me why I don't respond sometimes

Talk to you some other time

This is what I honestly can't stand about you

[6:07AM]

> What did I even do...? Go to bed? I literally don't know what could have possibly upset you from me saying goodnight? Wtf?

It was just dismissive

> I didn't intend for it to sound that way. I think your reaction was exaggerated though.

Probably

> You could just own it, apologize and then that'd be that.

Yeah, I'm sorry.

> Thank you, appreciate it. Hope you're having a good morning. It's raining here, I know you like that.

Yeah it was raining all day here yesterday

Our texts continue back and forth over the next few days. Friday night comes, and I'm having a wine night with Emily, texting you from behind my shield of drunken carelessness and indifference.

And you're not quite responding.
You are.
But you aren't.
I try to grab your attention:
> *I'm coming to see you.*

But it's no use.
All the same, you don't answer.
Until 11:00 this Saturday morning:
> *Sorry I fell asleep*

I'm hungover from the wine last night, gripping my last bits of carelessness and indifference:
> *Talk to me for 5 minutes*

As expected, you pull:
> *On the phone hold on I just woke up*

Straddling the fine line of caring and not caring, I push:
> *K, call me after*

After six minutes of no response from you, I push again:
> *...*

And you:
> *Where are you?*
> *Why'd you say you were coming to see me*

Transparent as glass, I answer, simple and honest:
> *To get you to respond.*
> *It didn't work.*

You tease:
> *lol*

I am so close, though. I know I'm close. I know your response patterns. You're right there. You're right by your phone. You're answering right away. I'm so close to your voice, I can practically hear it through your texts. We haven't spoken on the phone in two whole months, only texted back and forth.

Unfazed and determined, I push again:
> *K call me really quick*

Pull. You keep pulling:
> *What why*

Determination fueling my persistence, I keep pushing:
> *Just. Because*

You pull again, but only to make sure I'll push again:
> *I might fall back to sleep*

And push again, I do:
> *Perfect call me for 5*

That's not even long
Stop being so difficult
One final test, you pull once more:
I wouldn't need to call you if you would have came up like you said
Knowing I'm close, I push once more:
Omg call me
You surrender:
lol
And then you call.
And then I come.
And so, we begin again.
Something about you makes me forget.
    Forget all the problems you present.
    Forget all the times you haven't answered me.
        Forget as one day turns into a week.
        Forget I have to block you to keep my sanity.
            Not so that I never hear from you again.
            But so I don't have to face the fact that I'm not hearing from you. Again.
                Twisted as I am.
                Twisted as you are.
                Twisted as us.
When it comes to you and me, I can't decide what I love more:
    Remembering.
    Or forgetting.

JANUARY 12, 2017,
stupid happy.

It's been a long week.

And I'm thinking of you.

We didn't disappear this past week. You could have stayed. You could have gone. You've done both.

As if you read my mind, you text me to ask when I'm coming up, as though we'd already made the plan, even though we haven't.

It's only Thursday, but I'm coming.

I need to see you.

I send an email to my boss explaining how I'm not feeling well and won't be in the following day.

Almost two hours later, it's 11:00 p.m. and I've arrived. We hit 7-Eleven to snag wine for me and beer for you. And then we settle into our Thursday night like it's a Friday, swapping stories and pictures. I'm always snapping pictures of the sky, and so are you. You and your Oxnard skies. Me and my Newport skies. When our differences strike me confused, as they often do, I hold onto similarities like this, reminding myself of the large things in life that grant us small pockets of amity. We talk and laugh ourselves all the way to sleep around 2:00.

The next morning comes, slow and peaceful. I remember you mentioning something about needing to run errands today.

"So, what do we have to do today again?" I turn to you and ask through shining eyes.

"Oh, man, you're gonna love this. Alright, so we gotta get my books for class, then I have to go by this doctor to check on my TB shot, and then I need to stop by our storage unit to get my social security card. I can just do that one with my dad, though."

A day chock-full of practical plans. I couldn't be more excited. Makes us feel more real.

The whole day smiles before us.

Your mom's in Orange, your dad and Cyler at work, so it's just the two of us.

You make me breakfast, a perfect dippy egg and a slice of Jewish Rye sourdough toast.

After picking up your textbooks, we still have to stop by your doctor's office. I tell you I want to squeeze a run in before it gets dark. It's just before 3:00 p.m., so we've only got two more hours, and the doctor's office doesn't close until 6:30, so we head back to your house once more, opting for my run first.

"I'm gonna come with you," you tell me.

"You mean to run?" I laugh.

"You think that's funny?"

"Yeah, I do."

"You think I can't run?"

"I didn't say that. I just. I just think it's funny. I don't know. Whatever. Come with me, then."

"I will."

"Okay, then. Just don't cry like a little bitch when I run circles 'round your ass."

"Ohhhhh, okay, Jojo. Run circles 'round my ass. You swear…"

"You smoke cigs and weed. You're gonna be hacking and coughing the whole way…"

"Nah, you'll see. Big Slice's still got it."

"Mmmhhmm. Well, I was kinda planning on seven miles."

"Seven, huh? Easy. Done."

"Allllllrighty, then," I conclude, skepticism highlighting my voice.

By the time we change into workout clothes and hit the pavement, I'm downright giddy. I never pictured us exercising together, or running errands together. Doing healthy things. Practical things. Things typically reserved for normal couples.

You keep pace until you can't, telling me to just go on ahead.

I continue running until I hit the stoplight that dumps into a parking lot, giving way to the beach. I follow the path to the sand. It's a bit of a ways to the water, so I trudge through the sand until the ocean sits twenty feet in front of me.

It's the middle of January at sundown, and no one else is on the beach. The wind whips lightly against my moist face. I forget the chill as I take in the wide-openness of this entire view. I'm grateful that I have my phone, tracking all my runs on my Runkeeper app, because I need to capture this. Capture this moment. This sky. This beach. This water. This calm. These clouds. These colors. A picture isn't enough, so I take a full 360-degree video of all that is before me.

With the sun making its exit, the brown-beige of the sand looks darker, almost wet. It's covered with lopsided polka dots, past visitors signing their permeable presence in footprints as they passed through. The ocean water shimmers and shines in alternating layers of movement, flat and reflective as a mirror right where it meets the sand, a bubbly, pure whitewash at the lip of each wave, a dark, dimpled blue-green-black just beyond that, and then flat and shining once again where the ocean meets the sky.

And, oh my God, this sky. It's enormous. The base layer, only taking up but a tenth of the sky, is a soft, humming yellow, blurring into whispers of salmon-orange, which eventually give way to intermingled shades of red-orange, like a Big Stick popsicle. The colors hug the islands' silhouettes that sit atop the ocean in the distance. Above the Big Stick layer, swirls of soft yellow and red-orange, along with pockets of fiery, golden-yellow burst through in scalloped clouds; a falling sun's goodbye.

And that's just the base layer. That's just where the falling sun shines through. Above the base layer, the horizon rolls into an ensemble of blue-gray clouds. These blue-gray clouds then merge into patchy purple-gray clouds with coughs of barren blue blinking through. This is by far the thickest layer, claiming more than half the sky.

We get two reminders. Two. Every day.

At the beginning of the day.

At the end of the day.

Two reminders of infinite possibility.

Two reminders of those things that are bigger than us, beyond ourselves.

I finish recording my video, and then you're calling me.

"Where'd you go?" you ask when I answer.

"The beach. I turned at that light. Where are you?" I respond.

"Dying. I'm gonna turn back home," you machine-gun chuckle.

"'Kay, I'm going to go a little further and I'll meet you back at the house," I laugh lightly.

I sit and breathe in the sky and ocean for a few more minutes before trudging back through the sand, back to the path, and finally out on the street again to finish the seven miles.

As I complete my run, I'm walking down your street toward your house and I hit stop on Runkeeper to end tracking. The sun has gone down completely, and it's dark. I see a pair of headlights driving towards me. I look at the oncoming car curiously because it's moving slowly, and I switch to a dead pair of eyes in case the driver gets any ideas. I place my thumb on the lock button on the side of my iPhone, knowing all I'd have to do is press it five times to have 911 on the line at the screen-swipe of a finger.

The car pulls closer, and I see it's you. Jesus.

You flip the car around. I walk toward it and get in as naturally as if I'd been expecting you.

"What are you doing?" I ask.

"I was wondering where you were," you answer simply.

"You came *looking* for me?"

"Yeah, Jojo, Oxnard isn't Newport."

"Please." I roll my eyes with a smile.

But I can't believe you came to look for me. You could have just called or even texted. Yet you hopped in your car and came to look for yourself.

I try not to ruin the moment by acknowledging it. Instead, I silently tuck the details away in my mind.

We're back at your house now, and Cyler is just getting home from work. Cyler grabs his backpack from the backseat of his car, puts it on his back, slips both his hands around the straps, and books it across the street to catch up with us.

"What are you guys doing?" Cyler singsongs in his high-pitched voice.

"Went on a run, Bro-lee. Whatchu think 'bout that, huh?"

"Bro, a run? Well now, that's impressive," Cyler beams up at us.

"Bro, Jordan spanked me, though! Had to put some space between us so people didn't think we were runnin' together. She was kicking my ass," you explain.

"Jor-dan! You can run!?" Cyler says the first part of my name in a squeal like a girlfriend would if I told her I slept with three guys in one night. Unbelieving. Tickled.

"Well, faster than him. Which obviously isn't very fast," I tease.

"Ohh man, it's the ciggies, Bro-lee. Too many ciggies. My lungs just about gave out on me. So, what are we doing tonight?" you prompt.

"I don't know, Bro, what *are* we doing?" Cyler answers.

"Something low-key. I'm all tired and shit now," you respond.

"We could always go to that little brewery down the street," Cyler offers.

And it's decided.

After showers, we head straight to the brewery. When we walk in there's a huge, beautiful tricolored Bernese mountain dog lying on the floor beside its owners. I slowly approach the dog, carefully putting the back of my hand closer to his nose. The dog pauses and then bursts into a gnarly round of barks, standing up from the floor only to back me up, not quite nipping at me, but showing me away from his owners. I back up quickly, straight into you. You grab me securely, maneuvering me on the other side of you, and look me up and down.

"You okay?" you ask me as you shoot the dog owners a dirty look.

"I'm fine," I reassure.

I'm offended more than scared.

Don't dogs usually sniff out the *bad* people?

You and Cyler order Stout beers, which I've never tried, so I order one, too.

There's a worn deck of cards atop the little wooden table we're sitting at, so we unpack them and begin playing Poker. Sort of. You two try and explain the rules of both versions to me. I think I get it, but I'm buzzed and happy from the beer, plus I don't care to win. We switch to another game, similar to Bullshit, but it's almost impossible with just three people. All of us start cracking up as we attempt to continue playing.

I love our tripod.

We're the lightest, most giggly triangle I've ever met.

After we finish our beers and games, we head out to pick up pizza and jalapeño poppers from Toppers Pizza, your favorite. You park on the inside curve of a cul-de-sac, a spot not designated for parking where no curb even exists because you do things like that. I laugh, because I love that you do things like that. Cyler's unfazed. The three of us head inside, and Cyler's telling the hostess we're here for pick-up while you head to the open island with sides and dressings, scoring six packets of ranch.

And we're out.

Back at your house, some basketball game lulls you and Cyler to the living room couch, but no matter. Your dad's home, so I chat with him about work, where I'm living, life's practicalities.

When you and I eventually steal away upstairs, you're the cutest kind of sleepy, even though it's only 11:00.

"Oh, mannnnn," you sigh with heavy, happy sleepiness.

Within moments, we're lying down in bed, and although I'm turned away from you, you come up behind me and coax me open. We have sex, shower quickly, and we're back to bed.

I turn away from you once more. As I do, you come up right behind me again. I pause with a moment of confusion. We just had sex. What do you want?

You drape yourself all around me, cuddling me into you.

I'm fully cocooned.

I think it's the only thing I've ever wanted.

I think this is it.

I think this is what I miss most when I'm missing you.

We fall asleep like this.

Cuddled.

Cocooned.

Close.

Saturday comes slowly. We sleep in, and the day unfolds uneventfully. You're playing *Call of Duty* after two hours of football games, and I'm growing more and more impatient.

"Come lay with me," I insist.

"Come on, Jojo, I don't want to do that. That's so soft when guys like doing shit like that."

"What? What is wrong with you?"

"What do you mean? It's lame. It's soft."

"Seriously, Kolton? You're so ridiculous sometimes."

"Why?"

"You just are. That was mean."

"How was *that* mean?"

"It's just mean. I like laying down together, and you're saying you hate doing it? It's just mean."

"It's not mean. I just don't like doing it. How's that mean?"

"It just hurts my feelings. Makes me feel like I'm gonna cry. I don't know. It's just insensitive."

"Are you serious right now, dude? How can something I said make you want to *cry?*"

"I'm just saying it hurts my feelings. You're just so cold sometimes."

"Nahh, how can something I said make you want to cryyyy? Like, what? That's so dumb, dawg. I just hate when people hold me responsible for *their* emotions."

I don't respond but instead begin to pack my bags, call an early end to our visit.

"You're gonna leave?"

"Yep."

"Seriously?"

I don't answer. I move to your bathroom sink, zipping my black makeup bag closed, placing my deodorant, perfume, and face lotion back in my ditty bag.

Cyler hollers up the stairs, "Broooooo-leeeeee!" There's some commotion as we hear him clamber up the stairs, and seconds later, he's in your room.

"What's crack-a-lackin', guys?" Cyler immediately breaks the ice, not knowing he was mediating to begin with, jumps up, and lands back-first on your bed, propping his head behind him with his hands.

You two banter back and forth, and the room softens as I feel our tension dissipate.

You two talk about evening plans, going out again.

When Cyler leaves the room, you shoot me a look. "So, you're staying or what?"

"Shut up," I clip back with a smirk.

You smirk, too, eyes back on the game.

You finally wrap up your game, I get ready, and then we're all drinking downstairs. When we leave the house, Cyler requests some Stevie Wonder, and you oblige because he's your Bro-lee.

We hit Ventura, scope out a few bars, and decide on one with a pool table.

After ordering drinks, you and Cyler make your way to the back of the bar, waiting for the pool table to open up. All sipped up, you're paying all sorts of attention to me. I steal off for the bathroom, and when I come back, you and Cyler are playing pool.

I get comfy on a stool near the pool table and sip away happily.

You're good at pool.

I'm watching you, and you keep looking back at me, watching you.

On Cyler's turn, you come over to me, making your way to stand between my legs.

"What do you think you're doing?" I smile through glossy eyes.

"Standing with my lady."

"Your lady?!" I practically spit, throwing my head back in laughter, feeling a little swirly from the alcohol. When I bring my head back to normal, you're sitting there unmoved, steady, and you pause dramatically, shifting your eyes from left to right.

"Yeah. You done?" you ask in play-seriousness.

"I'm done." I try for a serious face myself.

"So, will you be my lady?" You gaze straight into me, holding my eyes in a way that makes me hold my breath.

I stare back at you in circles, a small, circular smile playing across my face, but I don't answer.

I don't know that I ever *stopped* being your lady.

Don't you know?

"Bro, your turn," Cyler calls from across the table.

"Gimme kiss." You hang your cheek subtly in front of my mouth. I kiss you quickly and you go back to your game.

Stupid happy.

It flips through my mind again and again.

Stupid happy.

I'm stupid happy.

You're back onto me.

You're loving on me.

And I'm stupid happy.

Just like years and years ago, you insist I go with you everywhere.

    With you to the bathroom.

    With you to talk with your bro-lee.

    With you to get another drink.

    With you for another game of pool.

    With you, with you, with you. Everywhere.

        And it's everywhere I want to be.

        With you, with you, with you.

Stupid happy.

JANUARY 21, 2017,
levity; light as air, breath, and laughter.

We hang again this weekend.
We're getting ready to go to Lazy Dog for dinner, drinking ourselves silly in your room.
You're telling me about your English class and how lame your teacher is because she uses class to talk about her own life. I'm drunk and feeling all types of sassy, so I'm taking everything you say out of context.
"They always have their own personal experiences that they bring up in class. I just think school's a fat joke," you start.
"What if I wanted to teach school? You think I'm a fat joke? What if I wanted to teach school, and share things I cared about? And wanted them to understand, too?"
"But that's not like…school. That's a different type of school."
"Well, what is that, then?"
"Like I just said," you reiterate.
"*Like I just said,*" I mimic.
"You don't just go in there and try to teach people life lessons relating to your personal experience. That's not what English is about. English is about…English is about something completely different."
"What's it about, then?"
"It's about the English language."
"No, it's not."
"Then what's it about?"

"It's about…It's about themes. It's about bigger pictures. It's about. Well, I guess it's about everything you hate—words. And what all those words and themes mean to create the bigger picture. It's about the universal. Which, of course, you wouldn't understand."

"I'm not knocking it, I'm not, you know? Take math for instance. Math has a certain point. But what you're talking about is life…that's life."

"Yeah, it's life," I deadpan. "Can you get me a drink?"

"English. Math. History. They're all just— "

"We're never gonna get to dinner," I whine. I don't even know what we're talking about anymore.

"They're all just staircases to the bigger picture, which is life," you say, happy with yourself for finding your point.

"So, what's life, Kolton?" I bounce back at you.

"Life is…being on good terms with your own life, first off. Doing something that fulfills you in whatever way."

"What fulfills you?"

"It doesn't matter. That's not…that's not a relevant question to the topic of what life is."

"Okay, I'm over this conversation, and we still need to go to dinner." I pour myself another drink since you're distracted with your philosophy lesson.

"Dude," you chuckle. "You need to calm down right now."

"No. You're bugging me."

"Well, *you're* bugging *me*," and after a pause, "Oooooh, am I bugging you?" You switch your tone to mock mine in animated exaggeration.

I'm staring at you, trying to look angry and keep a poker face. "*I'm bugging you?*" Like it's the most ridiculous thing I've ever heard.

"I'm bugging you right now? Am I bugging you right now?"

"Yeah." I answer.

"Oh, I am?"

"You are," I confirm again.

"Oh yeah, I'm bugging you?"—a degree louder, like your voice is climbing that staircase to life you were trying explain a second ago.

"Are you being me?" I ask, finally realizing we're not fighting. We're playing.

"Yeah, I'm you right now," you say quickly and quietly in your normal tone, then switch back immediately to playfully mocking me. "Oh, I'm bugging you? Am I bugging you?"

"What are you gonna do? Leave?" Now I'm you.

"Pft, ugh. Yeah, *maybe!* I can if you want me to," you spit out, still pretending to be me.

"Do you want to leave?" I say calm and steady, still playing you and your voice.

"No!" you yell back and switch quickly back to yourself. "I'm you still," you remind me, and then right back to mocking. "*No!*"

"So, whadda you wanna do then?" I ask back, pausing and surrendering to the laugh that's just behind my lips, dropping my poker face altogether. "Suck my diiiiiick?" I say in a high-pitched tone, and we both burst into laughter.

"Something like that."

We get to dinner, and the drinking continues. To my surprise, you tell me something about me having it all together, saying I'm where most people our age want to be.

I never knew you thought that.

You dismiss it from the conversation as quickly as you dropped it in. "Yeah, yeah, yeah, well, we don't need to get into that. That's enough deep talking for today."

I let it go, but not without turning it over in my mind, examining it.

I thought I was here with you:

    Crazy.
    Needy.
    Wild drinker.
    Likes to talk…a lot.

And with the slip of a few sentences, I'm better informed.

Because all the while, I've been here with you:

    Together.
    Kind.
    Wild drinker (yeah, that part didn't change).
    Loves me silly…don't know why.

I'm reminded that everyone paints the world around them a little differently. Every single person is living out their own narrative. Every person tells themselves a different story about why this happened and how come that.

We may all reside on the same planet, but we're seeing a million different realities play out before us—every. single. day.

We're telling different stories.

I forget that sometimes.

Mine?
> Love lost:
> Hasn't been found yet.
> Want it more than anything.
> Yet will continue to try and prove I can do life without it.

Yours?
> You think you screwed it all up.
> Beyond repair.
> Everyone left you behind.
> And you can't catch up.

With so many different stories floating around, it seems an act of pure wizardry, of sorcery, during these brief moments when any of us can peek beyond our own storylines to remember the characters in our lives have stories of their own.

When we wake up the next morning, I'm a little hungover from such a boozy dinner. We decide to kayak and sweat it out a bit. After forty-five minutes or so, we head back to your house, docking the kayaks, and as we're walking up the ramp to your backyard, you lift your right arm and sniff your armpit. "Woo-wee. I'm smellin' a little stankay. Need to get a shower."

"Oh, grooooosss!" I tease.

"You probably stink, too," you clap back.

"Not as bad as you."

Back inside your house, we head straight for your room.

"Wait! Before you hop in, I've got a good one for you." I start laughing in anticipation before I can even finish my sentence. I pull out my phone, looking for the post I want to read you.

And, found.

I begin reading aloud like I'm engaging a class of students:

"How to shower like a woman: Take off clothing and place it in sectioned laundry hamper according to lights and darks. Walk to bathroom wearing long robe. If you see husband along the way, cover up any exposed areas. Look at your womanly physique in the mirror—make mental note to do more sit-ups, leg-lifts, etc. Get in the shower. Use wash cloth, long loofah, wide loofah, and pumice stone. Wash your hair once with cucumber and sage shampoo with forty-three added vitamins. Wash your hair again to make sure it's clean. Condition your hair with grapefruit-mint conditioner. Wash your face with crushed apricot facial scrub for ten minutes until red. Wash entire rest of body with ginger nut and jaffa cake body wash. Rinse conditioner off hair. Shave armpits and legs. Rinse off. Turn off shower. Squeegee off all wet surfaces in shower. Spray mold spots with Tilex. Get out of shower. Wrap hair in super absorbent towel. Return to bedroom wearing long robe and towel on head. If you see husband along the way, cover up any exposed areas."

Your light chuckle begins breaking up my narration, but I continue on.

"How to shower like a man: Take off clothes while sitting on the edge of the bed and leave them in a pile. Walk naked to the bathroom. If you see wife along the way,shake wiener at her, making the *woo woo* sound."

Your chuckle breaks my narration again, and I stumble through my own laugh, determined to continue on.

"Look at your manly physique in the mirror. Admire the size of your wiener and scratch your butt. Get in the shower. Wash your face. Wash your armpits. Blow your nose in your hands and let the water rinse them off. Fart and laugh at how loud it sounds in the shower."

My smile could split my face, it's stretching so wide. I wipe a tear of laughter from my eye, breathe, and laugh once more, trying to collect myself, determined to finish reading.

"Spend majority of time washing privates and surrounding area. Wash your butt, leaving those coarse butt hairs stuck on the soap. Wash your hair. Make a shampoo mohawk. Pee. Rinse off and get out of shower. Partially dry off. Fail to notice the water on the floor because curtain was hanging out of tub the whole time. Admire wiener size in mirror again. Leave shower curtain open, wet mat on floor, and light and fan on. Return to bedroom with towel around waist. If you pass wife, pull off towel, shake wiener at her, and make the *woo woo* sound again. Throw wet towel on bed."

You're out of breath, and I'm crying.

The laughter holds us, or rather—
> contains us,
> encompasses us,
> wraps us up,
> gently slaps us on the back in camaraderie.

Life is light.
We are light.
We are so light.
> Light as air.
> Light as breath.
> Light as the laughter that holds us.

Light as levity.
So good. It's all so good.

Julianna Lembeck

Like a kaleidoscope, turning 'round and 'round.
We're spinning 'round and 'round.
High on this life.
Soaring. And deserving. And everything.

FEBRUARY 2017,
missing, memories, loss.
Things to think of when you're not thinking of me.

    What goes up must come down.
    So, of course, after we share some levity, you pull away, giving me nothing but silence.
    You wanna know what the key to keeping you is?
    Nothing.
    As in, the absence of anything.
    Nothing.
        You love nothing.
        You like to say nothing.
        Like it even more when *other* people say nothing.
        Your favorite thing to do is nothing.
        You prefer to think about nothing.
        You deal with nothing.
        And you want me most when I give you nothing.
        That's it. That's all you want.
        That's all I have to do to keep you.
            And of all the things I *can* do, the one thing I can't do is…
            Nothing.
            I can't.
            It's not my style.
                Oh, but I try.
                I try and give you nothing.

I try and muffle my everything so I can give you nothing instead.
It works for a little while.
But then a little while ends.
So, here we are.

♪

Music picks up where words fall short:
["Old Money" by Lana Del Rey]

♪

What are you?
What am I?
What are we?
Where are you?
Where am I?
Where are we?
You're a sticky kind of dark.
I'm a warm bruise.
We're a black circle.
I don't know where you are, but I can make a good guess.
Because I'm going there, too. I can feel myself slipping.
Slipping away to the candied darkness where you yourself love to disappear.
The candied darkness, where it's alright for it to be all wrong.
All wrong, but it's still somewhere to go, somewhere to be.
The candied darkness is comfortable. Familiar. Soothing. Crack the irony—it feels safe.
When I go, I reside there alone.
It's a place I've frequented often as I've grown up.
    It's a place of retreat.
        It's my place.
        To be dark.
        Sad.
        Crying.
        Empty.
        Disheveled.

Un-showered, unmotivated, unimpressive.

This dwelling, this dark, dank cave of nothingness, is as much a part of us as our moments of sheer joy and laughter.

You've never been here with me.

At least, not to *my* candied darkness.

You have your own.

I'm sure yours looks different than mine.

But it's essentially the same thing.

It's a place for the living dead, a place to carry out your own flavor of silent suicide.

It's a place of dwelling where no dealing has to be done.

It's a place to check out and drown piercing pain points with endless something or other—you name it:

Fast food, sweets, alcohol, drugs, video games, harder drugs, Netflix, excessive sleep.

Anything that dissolves feelings and takes up space.

I go there today.

To ignore my feelings.

To ignore the pain of missing you.

And, mostly, to ignore the fact that you want to ignore *me*.

When you're ignoring me as such and I'm still missing you like this, I have no choice but to visit you in my memories.

A slight unease settles over me as I browse through old pictures of us.

In the pictures, I see the patterns.

    I see us on repeat.

    I see our circle.

    Years and years.

        Where did the time go?

        Why can't we let this go already?

        Aren't we supposed to fix things as we grow older?

        Shed the problems, cure the directionless thing?

        Doesn't a year gone by force people to grow up?

        Why are we still spinning on the same circle we were at seventeen?

        How are we here?

        Again.

I don't need a picture for some of the memories. Some are simply feelings.

> Like the time we went bowling with your family. It was nice, just being part of a family, even if it wasn't truly mine. I felt pride watching you excel at yet another activity. As if you needed to contain any more talent in that body of yours. It was incredible. And we all laughed. And it was all okay. And then we went back to your house. And we all ate dinner around that large glass table. And the food was good. And it was all okay. Cyler was there, and I fell in love with the way you two played, such an unlikely pair.

So much of it was simple like that.

Your old house in Orange, a calm, serene acre of land, with plentiful snacks, cran-grape juice, and a soundtrack of your mom's raspy laugh, your dad's voice dripping like honey. It was just all okay.

And now it's not. Because your family doesn't live there anymore. And we're older. And things lose their romance. And romance is all there is in this life. The fairy dust. The love. The enchantment of it all. That's all there is. And if that's gone, then what's left?

It's just not all okay anymore. The world is bigger, scarier, and doesn't move unless you push it. And most of the time, pushing is hard. And mostly everyone pushes for the wrong reasons. But it's so simple. Don't they all see? It's just so simple.

Be a family. Love hard. Laugh all the time. Talk to each other when you're mad. And then love hard all over again. And stay together.

It's that simple.

I'm convinced those are the only things worth pushing for.

I was borrowing time in your family's cocoon back then. A cocoon I hoped I could work myself into someday, somehow. With you. With your parents. With your eccentric brother. I thought I could be part of it, once and for all.

I couldn't.

It all got ripped out from underneath me.

You. Them. The whole shebang.

Orphaned once more.

Gypsy on the run.

I lost back Then.

And I'm losing again Now.

How can I explain loss?

Losing is losing, and there are only so many ways someone can explain that. Or perhaps it can be explained into infinitum.

But it never stops being loss.
It never stops being an absence,
    a hole,
    a need,
    skin missing the tingle of touch.
You can name it whatever you want. It never stops being those things, though.
Shouldn't I have known this time around?
Known I was going to lose again?
And that this wasn't going to be that funny after all?
Was I playing coy?
Thinking we could write this off as innocent fun?
What was I thinking when I allowed us to hang out back in September?
    We're not talking running with scissors here.
    We're talking drunkenly skipping with a hand-grenade.
        All fun and games until someone falls back in love.
And now what?
I have this urge to separate myself from you. Move on from the nonsense that is you.
Break the cycle, right?
But where would I go that doesn't have you written into it?
You pop up everywhere.
I stumbled upon this quote on Pinterest:
What you resist persists.
It's been following me around ever since.
    Haunting me.
    What you resist persists.
        What am I resisting?
        Am I resisting you?
        What about you, though?
        What's under all that is you?
        What is it?
        What am I resisting?
        I can almost hear Penny's voice in my head...
            The pain.
                The pain.
                    The pain.
                        The pain.
                            The pain.
        The loss.

        The loss.
          The loss.
            The loss.
              The loss.

        Okay.
        Okay.
        The pain.
        The loss.
            So, how do I embrace the pain?
            And lose you once and for all?

[Thursday, February 9th 4:14PM]

KOLTON   JORDAN

Yoooo

[Surprise, surprise.]
[Suspense suspended.]
[36 minutes later]

Not going to say hello?

                                                                       Hi there

Can you come up today

                                                                           No

Ok

[6:54PM]

You said the words not me don't be a sour puss

                                              Said what words?

Lol "I'm signing off…blah blah blah"

                            Oh that. Well I'm not being a sour puss.

I have work tomorrow.

Well that's good, alrighty.

[Friday, February 10th 10:50AM]

So are you signed off?

[14 minutes later]

Lasjdflkjaslkghahrkehlk;jaflkdjflk

What was that?

Something I wanted to tell you

Thank you for sharing. Glad I didn't miss out on that.

Ok so...back to the real question

I'm not signed off. I was frustrated.

So ur coming up today? You should leave early like 11:30 to beat traffic

You are something else my friend

[11:13AM]

Hurry!

[11:16AM]

??

[11:22AM]

Bueno?

[11:26AM]

Alright fool

[11:29AM]

> I can't just dip out of work at 11:30. Are you already sippin' over there?

Why not? No I haven't got out of bed yet lol

> You're in BED still. Jesus

Yupppppp

> I can't come this afternoon I have to work

Whiffin'

> I could tonight but then again, you change your mind multiple times a day

I do?? Lol or you do

> Both probably

You probably have like a dinner date after work and then something else so you would get here at like 10 or what?

> I'm not sure

Um ok...

> Woah woah woah now. No brattiness allowed. I'm saying I'm not sure what time I would get there

When are you able to leave

> After work. I'll call you.

Agitjoijals;kdjflkjasldk;jf

Hurry up

I call you after work, and, naturally, I'm coming up to see you this weekend. I keep you on the phone for almost the entire drive.

I knew we'd talk again like we are now, and I didn't have to wait long this time. I wonder why you pull away in the first place. Sometimes I think I know. Other times, I forget.

Right now, I'm wondering what if…

What if you're just dangling me like I've dangled others?

What if I'm just filling your time, filling the space where your pain usually sits?

What if you feel so slow and wide that you haven't yet realized you're dangling me?

What if you haven't even processed us yet?

What if you actually don't know…

how close I am to you?

how far away I am from myself?

how high you're dangling me?

how crushed I'll be when I finally accept we'll never be together for real?

Just wondering.

The weekend passes uneventfully, and it's already time to make my way home.

I make you talk to me on the phone during my drive home, surprised that you actually oblige. With twenty minutes to go until I'm home, night has fallen, and the moon is enormous tonight. Enormous and beautiful. Round and glowing a creamy white against the night sky. I'm thinking about the week ahead, remembering Valentine's Day is three days away. It falls on a weekday, so I know we won't be spending it together, but I decide to poke at you anyway.

"Dude, you have to look at the moon tonight. It's huge and looks so cool. P.S. What are we doing for Valentine's Day?" I ask.

"When's Valentine's Day?"

"Tuesday," I giggle.

"Well, *that's* not gonna happen," you spill with a hearty laugh.

"I know. I'm just giving you a hard time. Are you gonna at least say Happy Valentine's Day?"

"Nope." You laugh again playfully, and follow up quickly, "I'm kidding. Yeah, of course, I'll say something."

"Alriiiiiight. Well, I'm just pulling up to my house so I'm gonna let you go. Make sure you look at the moon. Don't forget."

You just chuckle.

"What's so funny?"

"You," you answer, and then you mimic my words, *"Don't forget."*

"Laugh all you want. And then bite your tongue and tell me I'm right once you see it."

"I will, I will."

The day comes to an end, and I know you have a math test tomorrow, so I wish you luck.

And...

KOLTON	JORDAN

[Monday, February 13th]

[Tuesday, February 14th]

[Wednesday, February 15th]

[Thursday, February 16th 1:02PM]

    What's good hombre?

[4:59PM – Missed call from you]

But see, the thing is I don't want to just be a Thursday. I'm this huge amount of a person Monday, Tuesday, Wednesday, and even when I can't see you Thursday, Friday, Saturday, Sunday. I'm a person all those days, too.

And I was a person this past Tuesday on Valentine's Day, when you couldn't even accommodate with a text.

And now it's Thursday, and you're ready to pick me up again.

And you want me to just jump back in, right?

No conflict, right?

No sadness allowed, right?

No anger, right?

No faulting you for anything, right?

You didn't do anything, right?

    Well.

Right.
>You can always be counted on for *that one*.

I hate myself a little more for being in this, but I'm not ready to get out yet.
Nothing does it quite like you, Kolton.
Nothing brings me up.
Nothing brings me down.
Quite like you.
And sometimes, it's just quiet.
It's not a fight.
It's not a push nor a pull.
Sometimes, like this week, I just get nothing.
Sometimes, and not often, just often enough to be sometimes, you just deplete me.
>It's when the anger is gone.
>And I'm just sad.
>And maybe a tad bit fearful, too. Maybe some of that.
>Fearful that we're not all I made us up to be.
>And you're just a person. And not my thing.
>And if you're just a person and not my thing, but I still feel the way I feel, then where does that leave me?

Julianna Lembeck

MARCH 2017,
why are we doing This?

    My roommate's home with me. I have you on speaker, so she hears the whole thing, hears us unfold, witnesses how the plan takes form, how a few words turn into actions. After you and I hang up, I say almost defensively, "I don't even know why I go up there. It's not like I get anything from him."
    My roommate answers back matter-of-factly, "I mean, I don't really see it, but obviously you get something or you wouldn't be driving two hours to see him."
    Two hours.
    Yikes, well, when ya put it that way, all out loud and everything.
    Two hours.
    How did that escape me?
    And that's just one way.
    Two hours back, too.
    All me, both ways.
    You don't lift a finger.
    Listing excuses for why you can't visit me here.
    Pale in comparison to the reasons it should be you.
        I'm the one with a real job.
        I'm the one who pays my own rent.
        I'm the one with only two days to get it together on the weekends:
            Clean the apartment. Dishes. Laundry. Sweep the floor. Another load of laundry. Grocery shop. Meal prep. Check emails. See friends. Run.

Yet I choose you.
Two hours up.
Two hours down.
There and back.
For what?
Why do I go?
What am I getting from you?
Why can't I let this go yet?
I keep waiting.
    Always waiting.
    Turning nothings into somethings.
    Turnings slivers of niceties into signs.
    Squeezing meaning out of every look, every text, every word, every interaction.
        Am I making you up?
        We're still the magic, aren't we?
        Aren't we?
        Because right now I'm not so sure.
But clearly none of that matters. Enough.
None of it matters *enough*.
Because I just need to see you.
    So, I'm coming.
    I'm on my way.

♪
Music picks up where words fall short:
["I Won't Bend" by Dawn Golden]
♪

[Wednesday, March 8th @ 11:38AM]

<u>KOLTON</u>   **<u>JORDAN</u>**

Why do you have feelings for me I'm having a hard time figuring it out?

        What's there to figure out? It's a feeling. I can't explain it.

        I love your humor, your personality, your

> confidence. I just love being with you and around you, talking with you. You're not a bad person, Kolton. There is a lot to love. I think you just don't see it, believe it or allow it. Do you not believe me when I've explained how I feel towards you?

I do I just don't see why

Or how

> Because of the way you treat me?

Lol no just everything

> I don't think I understand what you're asking then. What are you asking?

Just why and how you have feelings for me

> I just tried to explain that? Are you saying it doesn't make sense?

No it does. I just don't see how you could have those feelings.

> Why not?

Just because of everything

I don't see how anybody could feel that way about me

> Why would you say that?

Bc I've been a shitty person

> Okay. Well you and the rest of the world. People do shitty things all the time. You don't have to stay stuck there. You can choose to be good and feel good. It's up to you.

That's true.

> Don't overthink it. Just try and be a good

person every day. That's all any of us can do

I don't really care how you take this or if you think it's soft or sounds weak but I've never felt dumber or less confident in myself than I have recently

> That honestly just broke my heart a little. Kolton...you just have to rebuild. It's possible though, I promise. Not without hard work but it IS possible.
>
> You are NOT dumb. You're just going to have to spend some time exploring what this life means to you and how you see yourself in it, what type of interests and work pulls at you. That's okay though. That's part of growing up. If you think for one second you're the only one figuring that out, you're wrong. All of us have to figure this out and it can be challenging but it can be fun too.

Yeah I know just letting you know where I'm at and why I don't communicate as much as I maybe should

> I appreciate the insight here and you sharing where you're at.

Yee

> Meanwhile I found this video of us
>
> [YouTube video of Clingy panda cub won't let nanny go!]

Lol that's perfect

While I'm trying to watch a game

> pahah oh man or playing CoD

[Thursday, March 9th @ 10:38AM]

I have a date tonight

> Oh

Lol

With my bong

> My stomach just did that weird floppy thing when I read that. I was like wtf.

Thought you'd be able to figure out I was kidding

> I was gonna say. You haven't even taken ME on a date

I don't go on dates lol

> Whaaaaaaat

Lol

> That's all you got over there?

Yup what are you doing now

> Bowling omg I'm so horrible

Haha. We'll have to go sometime I'll show you how it's done

> That's a date then

No it's just going bowling

> Why are you so against taking me on a date?

I'm not but it's not a date

> Bowling is a date

No not everyone bowling is on a date. It's just called "going bowling"

BLUE WATER, *a year in the ocean.*

                                         Oh fucking kay

Lol dang you got the attitude going are
you drinking

                No just over you giving nothing as per
                usual. I don't understand why you are
                the way you are with me.

You always say I'm giving nothing I
don't know why it gets so serious.

We're just talking.

Everything was cool then you tell me I
give nothing I guess bc my responses
weren't long enough

                Why do you talk to me? At all?

Why do you always do this

                Answer me. I answered you the other
                day when you were looking for
                answers.

                What do you want from me?

I want to be able to talk to you without
this happening every week

                Nothing is happening...

The same series of questions is
happening and it does every week

                Do you realize you've never told me
                you like me? Or care about what's
                going on in my life?

That's bullshit sorry

                              Not bullshit

Wow here we go again you're doing all
this bc you want me to tell you
something. Like when you want me to
tell you I miss you or I want to see you

after I already did

> You are being so simple minded. It's so much more than that. It's everything. It's how I feel, how open I am with you, how honest and vulnerable I am with you and how you don't budge in return. You hold back in every aspect, communication, affection, effort.
>
> It comes back to my question. Seriously what do you want from me? Nothing is what it seems like.

I don't know then I seriously can't worry about this. We have such a long history I don't know how you don't understand.

> Long history doesn't mean anything about how you currently feel. I have a long history with Aslyn and Britney, yet not close with them at all. History doesn't mean anything.

I'm tired and this will never end

> The end.

Goodnight sleep well

   I hear the words from your texts in my mind again and again:
You always say I'm giving nothing I don't know why it gets so serious.
We're just talking.
Why do you always do this
I want to be able to talk to you without this happening every week
I don't know then I seriously can't worry about this
What is This, Kolton?
Huh, what's This?
You mean anything beyond nothing?
Is that the This you're referring to?

I thought This was our passion, our love, our hate, our push, our pull, our why, our iron string, our laughter, our understanding, our compassion, our tolerance.

I thought This was exquisite, unconventional, charming, secret, real.

I thought in This, we at least had each other.

But you sit cities away and act cold.

>Untouched. Unfeeling. Bored. Unamused by the world or any of its color.

She created This herself, you think to yourself.

Your thought is a release,
>shakes you free of the uncomfortable responsibility of a feeling,
>the guilt-ridden heaviness of leaving me worse than when you found me.
>That wasn't your intention.
>Your intention is you.
>To cruise on through life, just being you, for you only.
>Not being you for anyone else.
>Not bumping into anyone.
>Just out for yourself.
>And you're a simple man—not asking for much, are you?
>Just looking for the pad, the Benz, the blunt, and the music.
>Sprinkle some sports and sex in there and you're golden.
>Nothing less, certainly nothing more.
>And can't we just all leave you alone, right Kolton?

Well, wake up.

You don't get to go through life untouched.

You don't get to meander on through, aimless as you may be, and manage not to move people, places, and things. Move them in the literal sense, not the profound. Your living, breathing being has an effect. But you're cradled, cut off in the furthest extent from the impact you have on the world around you.

You blunt it out, not feeling a thing.

You act like the house in which you dwell, the bed in which you sweat and sleep, the blunt you disappear with, the laughter you spill my way, the pressure you exert on my skin, the pleading in your eyes—you act like that all comes out of thin air.

It doesn't.

Let me break it down for you.

Your parents pay for the house, pay for your bed, loving your sorry ass the whole, long way. The blunt comes from the minimal amount of money you're making as a security guard, which you hate, but it was either get a job or forfeit the house and the bed. The laughter you spill is ours. We create that together. The pressure you exert on my skin is yours until it transfers to me, and then it's mine. The pleading in your eyes is all yours. Again, it's something you share with me. I can't take away the pleading in your eyes. It will always belong to you. But even so, it still moves me, infiltrates my thoughts, changes my day. What are you pleading for? Help? Love? Meaning? More weed? Who's to know?

Do you see now?

Your intention can always be you.

But you'll still move people, places, and things along the way.

You can't evade the responsibility of being a human.

>Whether you own it or not.

>Whether you *feel* that or not.

And I didn't create This alone.

We *both* created This, Kolton.

We.

We, as in the both of us.

Not just me.

You missed my birthday.

But, I mean, no worries. It was on a Monday, after all, and as I've come to learn, those days tend to be off limits, right?

Right.

So, I'm not too surprised or thrown off when you text me Thursday saying, *Happy belated bday sorry I was really busy this week. What are you doing this weekend?*

I was angry Monday.

I was angry Tuesday.

I was angry Wednesday.

Angry in all that nothingness from you.

You have such a finite amount of yourself to give.

I'm terrified of running out of you.

When I run out of you, when you disappear as you do, I'm left in the dark.

I'm wound tightly in our dizzy daydream, so when I run out of you, I collapse, fall to the ground, fall apart. As my responsibilities grow, I find myself running out of other things, too. Like the power and sheer force it requires to pick myself back up from the fall. I don't have the internal resources for it like I used to. It takes me longer to come back around, longer to smile and feel okay, longer to like to myself again.

But when your text hits my phone today, the anger flips as the giddy possibility of seeing you takes over. I flip from angry-sad to giddy-excited as quickly as a baby distracted by peek-a-boo after a tantrum—with giggly smiles and blushing bounce returning to my face as soon as your own face is revealed once more, my doting eyes still dewy from tears only seconds before.

I should let this all go.

I know I should.

It's dangerous.

I hate myself a little more for being in This, but I know I'm not ready to get out yet.

So yes, I'm coming to see you.

When I get to your house tonight, you're already sipped up on the Henney, though, *super* sipped up.

You're FaceTiming with Georgie.

Georgie, as in from high school.

Talk about blast from the past.

I didn't even know you two were still friends. The past few months, you made it sound like you didn't talk to anyone from high school. In fact, I think it was, *I don't want to talk to any of those fucking douche bags,* if I do recall. Of course, I figured it was *them* that didn't want to talk to *you* after your whole heroin-inspired sabbatical from life.

You two are shooting the shit. You take special care not to let him see me. I don't know why, exactly. I don't know if it's that you don't want to explain, or if you don't want news spreading to the old crew. Embarrassed? Ashamed? Maybe talking to other girls? Who honestly knows.

I mouth for you to go grab me a cup from downstairs, so I can at least try and get drunk enough not to be annoyed.

You talking to Georgie makes me think of everything from high school—everything I'd slowly but surely lost. First my parents, my steady ground. Then you. Then Aslyn. After the holiday fallout in 2012, things were never the same. Aslyn and I fell into radio silence and haven't spoken since. Didi and I drifted apart as time went on, and when she moved back to California after college, she didn't even tell me. Britney naturally faded out, too.

But I did get Emily. I never would have guessed it'd be down to her and me—best friends, nonetheless—but with each passing year, our friendship continued to bloom with mutual respect, trust, and loyalty that didn't exist with the others.

When I think of the girls and our chaotic relationships with each other and everyone around us, my heart aches. Not just for myself, but for all of us. Everyone was sad and lost. How could any of us have been good friends to one another if we weren't good to ourselves? While I miss certain things about each of them—Aslyn's larger-than-life personality and sassy humor, Didi's laughter and carefree vibes, and Britney's ridiculous music and screw-it-let's-just-have-fun attitude—I do mostly feel relieved. The friendships worked back then but would never work for me now.

Shouldn't the same apply to you?

I cling to you like us working out might fix the past, reconcile my adolescence.

But you'll never be all the things I lost.

You're downstairs for twenty minutes, now shooting the shit with Georgie on the phone and Cyler in the kitchen.

I drove two hours for This?

I drove two hours to be completely ignored (as in, more than usual)?

I drove two hours for you to take Georgie's call, his FaceTime call nonetheless, when I have to fight tooth-and-nail for you to take mine?

This is what I came for?

I don't want This anymore.

I don't care who created it—me, you, us.

Screw This.

Screw you.

I. Don't. Want. This.

I don't want you.

When you come back upstairs, in one hand, you have your phone held out in front of you, still FaceTiming Georgie, and your other hand? Empty. No cup. Your Henney'd eyes meet mine and I see you remember what you forgot.

Me. The cup.

But it's so much more. You know that, too. You know you've forgotten so much more. You continue to come up emptied handed again and again and again and again and again and again.

 Again
  and
   again
    and
     again

                    and
                            again
                                    and
                                            again.
Do you hear it?

> *Ring around the rosie,*
> *A pocket full of posies,*
> *Ashes! Ashes!*
> *We all fall down* ♪

I hear it, and I'm bored.
I'm bored of your empty hands.
I'm bored of my spiraling madness of sadness.
I'm bored of you.
I'm bored of me.
I'm bored of This.
I don't want to crawl into your lap like a kitten.
I don't want to solve The Great Mystery of Why You Don't Love Me Right.
Something inside me busts.
The juggling act collapses.
It's me or you, Kolton. It's *me* or you. I either continue hating myself and stay. Or I decide to finally hate you and leave.
I must be wearing the decision on my face, though, because I see it reflected back in your eyes.
I leave.

[Saturday, April 1st @ 12:32AM]

KOLTON	JORDAN
Wow	
	I'm sorry you spent the time to drive I can reimburse that for you

[10:16AM]

Julianna Lembeck

> ?

[12:21PM]

Why did you leave

> Because you were preoccupied

Bc I took a phone call?

> Because you were completely ignoring me and talking to Georgie about fucking some chick in the ass. And when you went downstairs to get me a cup, you were hanging with your brother forever. I honestly don't know why you invited me. Just for sex maybe? Idk.

I was just messing about that me and georgie just mess around like that

> Cool well I gave you all night to mess around for as long as you want, all weekend actually.

I don't understand why

> Yes you do

I don't but ok

> Call me

What's so important that we need to get on the phone about?

> So you're absolutely stoked to take Georgie's call even when I'm there and you won't even call me. I don't understand you Kolton. I really don't.

I had a feeling that's why you left you got mad I was on the phone

That's crazy

> Yeah, I'm just so crazy.

> I don't think you care about me as a person. You just aren't very respectful towards me.

I think you're constantly looking for something to complain about

> I'm really not

I think you are

> I would love to just get along and also not feel like shit around you

Well if I make you feel like shit maybe we shouldn't be doing this I'm not into making people feel shitty

> K.

> Are you relieved?

Are you?

> No I like when we're getting along

Yeah right you always want to complain and fight about something

> How can you say that? Why would I WANT that? I don't understand why you always make me the bad guy. All I've done is be good to you.

You seriously left last night because I wouldn't pay attention to you? Sit there and stare at you? You want me to just be a little bitch and roll over and be like uhhh yeah Jojo, what do you need? Man, fuck that. I ain't never gonna be that pussy and you wouldn't like a pussy like that anyway.

> Wow. Just wow. I've got nothing left to say.

Nothing left to say.
That's a first, I think to myself.
I laugh gently, quietly, because although it was *my* thought, it was *your* words.
Or would have been, if I didn't block you again.

I feel numb.
The last thing you said haunts me:
> *You seriously left last night because I wouldn't pay attention to you? Sit there and stare at you? You want me to just be a little bitch and roll over and be uhhh yeah Jojo, what do you need? Man, fuck that. I ain't never gonna be that pussy and you wouldn't like a pussy like that anyway.*

Well spit some truth and paint me honest, why don't cha.
You're right.
Yes, right Now, you're right.
Because right Now, I don't want the kind of someone who will pay me more attention, sit there and stare at me, ask me what I need.
Right Now, there's a hurt part of me that yearns for all the hurt in you, all the hurt you bring, all the hurt we create. Paradoxically, it's actually safer this way, more stable, because the most painful part was the first time you let me down, which was a week into us dating all those years back. But after that, I knew I'd stay for a long time because I knew the worst was behind me. I knew what to expect. I was prepared to endure. Back Then, you'd perhaps been my second real heartbreak, after my mom. And I kept you around to guarantee you'd be my last.
So, for Now, I want you, because loving someone with no love to give is predictable, steady, comforting, and consistent, whereas loving someone with the capacity to love you back also has the potential to trip you up, sending you straight into Disaster's drooling mouth.
Love withdrawn breaks the body, mind, and heart in ways love that never was never could.
So, yep. For Now, I want you. The you who plugs away at that delayed AA degree at your local community college, working as a security guard on the weekends and playing *Call of Duty* or smoking blunts in your spare time. Also, the you who tolerates my drinking debacles, withstands my rapid, hop-

scotch mood swings, swallows my meanness, knows me inside and out, makes me laugh harder than most, and shares your family with me.

I want you Now, which makes This acceptable.

But Now turns into Then as soon as what I want changes.

So, I'm not worried that I want you Now.

I can change that.

Julianna Lembeck

APRIL 2017,
the sun shifts without you.

  When the anger at you anger floods in, I surprise myself by how quickly I can force it to settle, all on my own, because I get it Now.
  I get it, I do.
  I think of the random texts you sent me that one Wednesday morning when you just couldn't understand how I could have feelings for you. That conversation had truly shocked me. It was everything I thought in my head but never knew for sure.
  Your words ring through:
> *Why do you have feelings for me I'm having a hard time figuring it out?*
> *I don't see how anybody could feel that way about me*
> *Bc I've been a shitty person*
> *I've never felt dumber or less confident in myself than I have recently*

  I know you don't try to intentionally hurt me.
  In fact, I think you may have tried to love me as much as you could.
    I've seen it in your texts.
    I've seen it when you let me stay with your family for the weekend.
    I've seen it in the way you share any attention at all, when you're already so low.
    I've seen it in our laughter.
    I've seen it in the silly errands we run together.
    I've seen it in the way your tired body fell into me after we drank beer and ate pizza.

You're stuck. When you're not in school or working, you retreat to your candied darkness to forget you're in a rut. You drink. You smoke. You play video games. You do whatever it takes to forget.
Which has nothing to do with me.
And everything to do with you.
I can't pry your fingers away from the shards of broken glass you're clutching. Broken glass from the window overlooking your glory days of high school, when life was daylight. A time when things flowed abundantly for you. Indulgences had you wrapped up.
Life in the daylight of a daydream.
 Impossible?
 One would think.
 But it was indeed the life you lived.
Endless flow, a clean whip, joint upon joint, homies, a pad, a silly-happy dog, fresh clothes, talent to toss around, responsibilities at a minimum, stunning looks, thick confidence, and of course, if you happened to find yourself one baddie down? You just replaced her, baddies a plenty back then. Me, Jackie, Megan—take your pick.
But time has passed.
And the sun shifted without you.
Leaving you in the shadows of where the daylight used to live.
And you haven't moved.
You just keep waiting for the daylight, wishing it to come back.
You're mad at yourself.
You're disappointed in yourself.
You have this inflated confidence that ebbs and flows;
 sometimes it's there,
 sometimes it disappears entirely.
You gotta retreat inward to forget, tuck it all away.
You believe you've screwed it all up beyond repair, and that happiness will always and forever be reserved for those deserving, which certainly doesn't include you anymore.
And it's a lot. Thinking you deserve everything and nothing all at the same time. I've thought the same thing before, asked myself the accompanying questions.
 Am I everything or am I nothing?
 Am I good or am I bad?
 Am I my accolades or my mistakes?
Kind of feels like being on a bender.
 Up, up, and away.

High on this life.
Light as air.
Soaring. And deserving. And everything.
> Only to come down, down, down.
> Low lows.
> Heavy.
> Drowning. Diet of despair. And nothing.

I get all of that.

I only know because I've done it myself. I go to the candied darkness sometimes, too. Nothing but outlined dreams unfulfilled, and hearts strangled alive by black ivy made of luck that never was and a thumping heartbeat of tragedy. A sorry place, the candied darkness, layered in dust from fragments broken and never fixed, creaking with rust from dwellers' tears that never cease.

When I go there myself, I don't intend to hurt anyone by leaving, retreating, forgetting, but sometimes I do. I'm not proud of it, but again, I get it. And during those times, I know it's about me and no one else.

In the candied darkness, people come and people stay.

Far fewer ever go.

The key to staying is to forget you're there at all.

And the trade off to forgetting you're there?

You don't get to belong anywhere.

> So, the dwellers drink, smoke, eat, numb themselves.
> The dwellers find other dweller lovers.
> And they stay.

I know you go there often. I would come and get you, but you know there's only one rule in the candied darkness, where the troubled unlovables dwell.

Only the dweller decides to stay or leave.

No one can take them out.

So, I can't go in there to get you.

If I did, I might never come out myself.

And sometimes when you come out, remembering where you've been, freshly bundled in your own hurt and hate, it quite honestly offends you that I dare try and love you in this state, the troubled unlovable you are. Naturally, you remind me why I shouldn't. You remind me how horrible and nasty you can be. You remind me how scary you are, right Kolton? And you do things, or do no things at all, to make it impossible to stick around.

Another past conversation drifts to mind.

> *God, you were such an asshole back then*, I had said.

Well, what if I still was? What if I'm still like that? What if I still have those asshole tendencies? you taunted through your Henney'd tongue.
Give it up, Kolton. I'm not scared of you, I responded.
I'm just sayin'…I might still be like that, you tried to convince us.
Mmhhm, I dismissed.
I get it.

Jackson's doing worse and worse.
He hasn't had steady work in over a year.
His skin is broken where he picks it apart.
Living with him is weighing on me.
Pile, pile, pile.
Pressure, pressure, pressure.
I love him, but I also want to strangle him.
Living with him strikes me upside the head with the family bullshit.
It's the devil's serpents.
But instead of hissing sweet surrenders in *my* mind, they've slithered into *his*.
It's hard to watch.
I see him.
I see him losing control.
I see him surrendering to them, to the devil's serpents.
I see him giving in to giving up.

> I see the McDonald's, Del Taco, and Jack N' The Box bags littering his bedroom floor.
> I see his Rottweiler, Whiskey, collecting dirt in her fur, stillness in her joints, depression in her drooping eyes.
> I see his bare mattress, stained a light yellow-brown from the cigarette smoke that clings to it, a stray sheet wrestled in dirty bundles.
> I see trays filled to the brim with ashes.
> I see clothes strewn across the floor among the fast-food bags.
> I smell his room's rankness sifting through the hole in my closet upstairs, only separated by a thin piece of plywood. I don't know where that smell comes from. The meth? Lack of hygiene? No idea.
> I smell the dog crap piling up in the backyard when I throw something in the garbage.
> I hear his explosive anger in the slam on our door to move a car blocking him in the driveway.

I hear the hate seething through the chorus of his complaints—*fuck this, fuck that, fuck Dad, fuck work, fuck people on the road, fuck the government, fuck the neighbors.* Etc.

And I certainly feel him.

I'm beginning to panic.

I try and talk to you about it.

 What did your parents do when you kept using and using?

 How did you finally get clean?

 But you don't want to talk about it.

You can barely support yourself, let alone me.

Pile, pile, pile.

Heavier, heavier, heavier.

Disaster bangs through my mind, the memories clanking like metal on metal.

 Clank, clank, clank.

 Memory, memory, memory.

 Dust bunnies, dishes in the sink, dirty bathtub.

 Disaster, disaster, disaster.

 Disaster's come back for more.

 It already ate my old house in Orange.

 It snacked on my family, spitting them back out mangled and chewed apart.

 And now it's come back for more.

 Disaster's trying to eat my apartment.

 Disaster's hungry.

 It's chomping down on Jackson.

 It's coming for me.

  I.

 Gotta.

 Get.

 Out.

Change typically meant Disaster.

And Disaster was something I'd learned I couldn't fix.

Then.

 Disaster was something I couldn't fix back Then.

 Things are different Now.

 I can fix this for me Now.

 I hold a job Now.

I earn money Now.
I am not a child Now.
I make my own decisions Now.
I am responsible for myself Now.
I love Jackson. But Imma 'bout to strangle him.
    Pile, pile, pile.
    Pressure, pressure, pressure.
    Anger, anger, anger.
    Infuriated all the way to action.
        I see myself in him.
        I see you in him.
        I see him retreat to the candied darkness.
        I see him live there.
And enough is enough.

I want to take him with me. I want to save him. I want to save you. I want to save us all, but I know Now. I get it Now. I can only save myself. That's all I can do. Which is enough work on its own.

My mind silently screams at even the slightest of irritations in my life—a car cutting me off, someone walking too slowly in front of me, a baby's tantrum during lunch breaks at the mall, an unreturned text, the grocery store being out of the only peanut butter I like, someone sitting in my spot at the local coffee shop.

In my mind, I hear myself loud and clear.
    Move!
    Get out of my way.
    Excuse me, *move!*
    Move!
    Move!
    Move!
Until I finally flip that around.
Scream it back at me.
    Move!
    Move!
    Move!

Move. Move away. Move to a new place. Get out of this situation. Separate myself. Jackson is not my responsibility. I can't fix him any more than I can fix you. I can love him and still move away from him. I can do both.

Julianna Lembeck

MAY 2017,
the magic. Oh, oh, oh.

I did it.
I pushed myself.
I moved into my own place.
I work on letting you go.
You ask me to come up and visit you, and I can't bring myself to do it.
    Because the two hours finally seems like two hours.
    Because the thought of watching you play *Call of Duty* makes me cringe.
    Because, honestly, I don't want to.
So, one weekend I visit a girlfriend in San Diego.
Another weekend I decorate my new studio.
And another weekend after that, I even meet someone new.
    I kinda, sorta fall in love all over again.
    In that immediate, urgent type of way.
    It feels exquisite, unconventional, charming, secret, real.
    It feels like…
    Magic.
Wait.
It feels like *magic*.
The magic I thought belonged to only you and me…
I'm remembering.
With you finally removed from my tunnel vision, I'm remembering.
There's been other magic.

Yes, I remember now. I've felt it with others.
And it dawns on me.
If I've had the magic with you, and with him, and with others in the past, then perhaps...
I've been the magic all along?
    Oh, oh, oh.
    I'm the magic.
    Duh.

Julianna Lembeck

JUNE 2017,
we're easy to name and hard to hold.

I text you out of the blue.
Kolton, I have a question for you
Jordan, what's your question?
Do you think I'm actually crazy?
No. Not really. Just when you drink
    And that's it.
    I know you're right.
    I already knew that answer.
    I mean, it's that simple.
        How?
        How is it that simple?
         What about all the years of everything that wasn't simple?
        What about the fire?
            What about all the pitch black?
            What about everything that got scorched?
        What about the floating?
            What about being stuck in limbo?
            What about the living that wasn't actually living?
        What about the blue water?
            What about the secret world that was ours?
            What about the pockets of peace we created, despite ourselves and against all odds?
                Odd, aren't we?

I don't have the answers I'm looking for.
Because at every point and turn, it was all real to me.
    We really did love a love that burned us both, burned things and people around us.
    We really did float around in limbo—aimlessly, miserably, separately. And we really did sift through all of it in blue water, cleansing ourselves, exchanging apologies, and perhaps seeing each other for the first time.
Odd, aren't we?
What are we?
We are so much.
We are
    a feeling,
    a story,
    a song,
    a smell,
    a circle,
    a quote,
    a tear skimming my cheek,
    a frustration untangled, only to be tangled again,
    a raindrop on my outstretched fingertip,
    a facial expression spread wide, wild and alive,
    a laugh living belly-deep and sounding of youth,
    a crack in the sky as the sun subsides, sayin' See ya tomorrow,
    a wave in the ocean, crashing cyclically, every shade of blue.
We are
    all those things,
    which are easy to name,
    and hard to hold.

JULY 2017,
I miss you when you're sober.
But only when I'm drunk.

Haven't seen you in months now.
    When we text, it's patchy and lacking.
    I can tell you're high from your dull, slow responses.
    I miss you when you're sober.
    I miss that part of you, the alive-and-kicking part. The challenging part about being alive is trying not be eaten alive by all the other living things—fear, doubt, insecurity, life, adulting. All of it.
    I still miss you when you're sober, though.
    Perhaps I was one of the few who ever got to meet that delightful part of you.
        Giddy and free and confident.
        And the talent. Oh, the talent.
        Magnetic.
    I miss you when you're sober.
    But only when I'm drunk.

AUGUST 2017,
*you tell me to turn off my emotions,
but don't you know that's what keeps you around?*

I read your text again, thinking it over before I respond.
> *I'm just not trying to get put on the burner seat and talk about feelings all the time when I don't want to talk about that stuff. I don't believe in all that feeley shit. And you always say you get that but nothing changes. The last time we talked that's exactly what happened so I mean how do you not understand?*

I don't believe you.
I can't tell if you believe you, either.
You say you don't believe in feelings, but your anger alone betrays your disbelief.
Where do you think anger comes from?
What do you think it's made up of?
> Sadness.

You're sad.
You can't accept love because you mistakenly think you never had it.
You did, though.
You had so much of it.
You had Megan's, Jackie's, mine.
But you still couldn't feel it, couldn't accept it, didn't see it.
So, you wanted more.
More girls. More attention. So you had em'.

Yet somewhere amongst the flavors of long legs, short legs, blonde hair, brown hair, bubble butts, olive skin tones to Filipino mocha. Somewhere amidst all that female, all that estrogen, all those wild personalities, you created some love within you—messy as it was.

Indirect. And hungry for all of us. But love all the same.

But we are female.

And for that reason alone, you'd never trust yourself to love just one of us at a time.

Because inevitably we'd have to let you down, wouldn't we?

Isn't that the story you've been proving your whole life?

Your biological mother put you up for adoption.

Left you in the hands of strangers, eager to love you and let you grow.

The hand-off.

From biological mother to your parents.

Arrested development.

Stunted and stuck.

And you'll never let it happen again, right Kolton?

Never trust dem females, bloated with emotion, unruly, unreliable, and wild.

So, you point the finger back at us when we demand more than your indirect love.

You set out to prove your narrative, cheating on us all the same, stirring up the ugly in us, the craze of an unrequited love.

And, oh my God.

Look at those females.

Megan, Jackie, me, so many, many more.

Aren't we unreasonable?

Aren't we insane?

And we were.

But it takes two to tango.

And tango we did.

All of us.

Ashes, ashes, we all fall down.

We all loved in ways that didn't add up.

And we all hurt.

I'm going to stake my claim here and say, besides your parents and your brother, I loved you the hardest, the longest, the deepest.

But even all the love in me can't overturn all the demons in you. I can't wait as long as you can hold out.

So, I'm laying down. Quietly. Surely, we all have a threshold. Maybe you've finally uncovered mine. And of course I'm sad. But it's different than before. The sadness is for you, not so much for me. I know I'll be okay. And surely you will, too. But I'm sad I believed in you and the possibility of your love more than you did.

I type my response back to you:

The irony is you tell me you don't want to talk about feelings and I should feel less and not let my feelings dictate my day or my choices but that's what sends me back to you every time.

So I suppose I'll heed that advice & leave you alone and lay this whole "us" thing to rest once and for all. I love you whether you know what to do with that or not. You're doing really well right now, take care of yourself.

You respond immediately:

You should do what ever is best for you.

I say nothing else.

What's best for me is removing you. And you know that, too. Because you've written your story and crafted yourself unlovable, time and time again. You do it so well. So, I'll let you have your narrative, proving yourself correct once and for all.

I call Jackson regularly now. Our relationship shifted instantly once I moved out. The hate and anger melted like ice on a summer sidewalk.

I'm driving, so I call him. I don't know how often he's using, but I've found bubbles of coherent conversation speckled throughout the last few months. Right now, he sounds pretty normal, so I go ahead and ask him, "What does it mean if someone keeps reaching out but they don't want to talk about anything real, or they don't want to talk about their feelings? What do they want? Why do they keep reaching out? What are they getting out of it?"

"Which someone we talkin' about here?" he asks.

"Okay, it's Kolton."

"I thought it might be."

Yet Jackson enters the conversation with me, equipped with a patience that surely isn't deserved, knowing what he knows about us, and leaves anger outside. "Kolton can't tell you what he wants from you because he simply doesn't know himself."

"I just don't understand. I mean, I just don't get it. Why does he bother talking to me at all? I'm far away, and we haven't seen each other in months. So it's not like he's getting sex on the reg. I don't know. Okay, this is stupid, but at the end of the day, do you think he loves me?" I feel foolish for asking, but I'm hoping Jackson, also a drug-addict, also a male, might be able to provide some insight.

"I hope not. At the same time, I know that would hurt you, but I really hope he doesn't love you. You'll never be happy with him." His answer surprises me.

He's right.

So, the answer doesn't matter.

I know.

Jackson knows.

You probably know, too.

We all know.

Jackson continues, "You like Kolton because he's like Dad. He'll never give you all the love and attention you want."

I cry a little, thinking aloud. "I know. And it's not good. Because I'm working hard to become okay with who I am, and some days, I still don't feel like I'm there. I know I can be emotional and super sensitive, and I'm working on keeping that in check, but I'm also embracing these qualities for who I am. My greatest strength, my greatest weakness kind of thing.

"But being with Kolton when he can't even support me if I've had a hard day is crazy-making. It makes me literally feel crazy. Like I'm a problem. Like there's something wrong with me. And that's not the case. I just need someone to listen and be patient because I always come back around. I always calm down. Even Dad is better with me now."

"Yeah, but Dad's also sixty-two. You don't want to be waiting around until you're sixty-two to have someone pay attention to you."

"I know. Even if Kolton were to be with me, I'd still be alone. That's the catch. I just don't understand how he can say he doesn't want to talk about feelings. I know he has them."

"Kolton just thinks he's a gangster. Thinks he's hard. Saying he doesn't want to talk about feelings and acting like he doesn't have any? That's not hard. That's pussy-shit. Being ready to support and love your family? Now, that's gangster. That's the hard stuff. Kolton's just immature. He's not there yet. He doesn't know anything yet."

How in the world does my *little* brother hit upon the heart of the matter so precisely?

How does he understand This so accurately?

Because, forget not, this other little love of mine, my youngest brother, goes missing with the drugs, too; disappears to the candied darkness, too.

"The weirdest part of all this is when I'm missing mom, or sad and worried about you and what you're struggling with, those are the times I reach for Kolton the hardest," I say.

"That makes sense, though, because you love all of us, but we all struggle with the same things, and sometimes we're not there to love you back. And you don't want to be alone. No one wants to be alone. It's hard," he explains.

And we come full-circle.

From family to significant others, it's all the same thing.

It's love.

And it can be hard.

All the same thing with one caveat.

Loving *you* is a choice.

Julianna Lembeck

SEPTEMBER 2017,
it ain't me.
♪

I've never waited so long for someone.
Never let my heart break again and again like I did for you.
I accept the fact that I can't accept This anymore.
I think of you with a gentle tenderness.
I know you'll miss me from time and to time,
    and more than likely, you won't know why.
I'll tell you why, though:
    Because everything else will taste bland and flavorless.
    Nothing will be as loud as us.
    And although it was absolute chaos, you'll miss the noise.
    You won't be able to sit still in the quiet.
    You'll miss our magic.
A vision of us channels through my mind's eye:
    You're sleeping, your face smooth with innocence and calm, somewhere safe and away.
    I reach out my hand, fingers curled ever so slightly, and graze the side of your cheek.
    I know it won't matter. You're tucked in deeply with drunken stupor.
    I don't fully want to leave but know there's certainly no staying.
        I know this is it.
        Not that I could explain it to anyone else.

It's just a knowing, sitting in the middle of my being, hard and unshakable.
You'll awake, dry and blurred, fuzzy and in pain.
Your head will be loud with a hammering headache.
Your hands will clasp upon themselves when you reach out to grab for me, finding an empty bed.
Your mind will absently dismiss the emptiness, focusing on fixing the headache instead.
Days will pass.
   And then a week.
   Maybe two.
   And one day, out of seemingly nowhere—
   your heart will catch up, and it will pinch.
   And you'll think of me.
   And you'll miss me as the quiet sets in.
   You'll miss the noise.
   You'll miss the high of our laughter.
   You'll miss me smiling into you.
   You'll miss the craze of my belief that we could be something someday,
   that the both of us were born to love,
   worthy of it.
   You'll miss the potential I saw in you, so alive you almost believed it, too.
   You'll miss it, and I won't be there to put an end to the missing.
   You'll just keep missing.
   And I'll be gone.
   I'll have written you out of my heart,
   forced you out of my mind,
   taken you out of my smiles.
   You'll just keep missing.
   And all you'll be to me is an ancient narrative, a song I used to sing.

Music picks up where words fall short:
["It Ain't Me" by Kygo, Selena Gomez]

Julianna Lembeck

Brings me to tears.
Putting this all to rest.
Isn't that all I ever wanted?
To put us to rest?
    Yes.
    And no.
Because at least we were always a place.
If nothing else, we were a place.
    Somewhere to go, to be, to sit.
    Somewhere where all the anger made sense.
    Where all the chaos was cozy and predictable.
Being with you allowed me to replay all the reasons someone would leave me.
    Irrational.
    Too much.
    Emotional.
    A sensitive black hole.
        (I believe you actually coined that last one. Has a nice ring to it. Touché.)
    Someone who gave too much.
        And when it didn't work out,
        gave again,
        but the wrong kind of give.
    Gave up.
Suppose there's some peace in This ending.
But it's lonely all the same.
It leaves me without you.
    How can I be without you?
    You've always been in the background.
    Something to turn to when all else fails.
    A safeguard.
    My security blanket.
    My favorite excuse for being mediocre, unlovable, unloving.
    Someone to point at and say, "He did this."
        With you gone, my finger can only point to myself.
            Point to myself.
                Perhaps that's been the point all along.
I think back on the day I started to know This was over.

I remember we were in your car.

We had finished running your errands, and as we neared your house, I thought to myself:

This is it.

This is as far as we go.

The thing is, we could keep doing This, again and again—me driving up to visit you on a weekend, you not making an ounce of effort; me throwing love at you only to have it drip away unabsorbed, piece by piece; your parents tucked away securely on the sidelines should we need the neutrality; your brother around for comic relief; co-existing in Channel Islands in the first place, far removed from anything that resembles reality, at least *my* reality, *my* life, away from *my* friends and all the things that make up the life I've built over the years.

My reality. My life.

In order to be with you, I have to relinquish all that. I've been willing to do it for a weekend here and there, but I'm not willing to do it forever. At some point, you would have had to fit in, mesh with my life, too, and you won't.

But I can't live here with you in the blue water.

I've got to get back.

> Which is why This is as far as we go. You see? We can go again and again but only This far. We can't go further than This. We won't make it past the Ventura county lines, not to LA, not to Orange County, certainly not to my place, where the rest of my life waits for me to return. We can only exist in this city, far removed. We can't build beyond that. We won't be able to; This is as far as we go together.

So, on that day, in that moment, as we neared your house, I felt the familiar pang of knowing.

> You know what I know.
>
> I know what I know.
>
> We both know.
>
> > We aren't sustainable.
> >
> > We weren't built for the long haul.
> >
> > We weren't enough for one another.
> >
> > We weren't going to make it.
>
> Knowing This slices my heart apart,
> > puts the pang in my stomach.
> >
> > It just breaks me to my core.
> >
> > I had hoped for so much.

I had expected so much.
I wanted it to be you.
I wanted to be saved.
And in return, I wanted to save you too.
The fairy tale.
I wanted it to be us, but...
You know what I know.
I know what I know.
We both know.
    We aren't sustainable.
    We weren't built for the long haul.
    Oh, how I wanted it to be us.
    It wasn't.
    And so it goes.
It's time to get out now.
Out of the blue water.
Of all our time together,
this year in the ocean
was my favorite.

BLUE WATER, *a year in the ocean.*

ACKNOWLEDGEMENTS

A special thanks to Joshua Berman, for helping me believe I could start this book.

A divine thanks to Alison McKinnon, for helping me believe I could finish this book. You stuck with me every step of the way and "saw" this book completed before I did.

An enormous thanks to my editor, Nina Denison, for your sharp eye and soft heart. You took my words and made them better. Where pragmatism meets magic—that's the place you work from.

A great thanks to Ms. Betsy Amster, for seeing the potential in my story; even before I was ready to claim it as my own.

A deep thanks to Patti Huber, LCSW. You held tremendous amounts of space for me in therapy as I cracked open, year after year, session by session.

Thank you to my best friend and *BLUE WATER*'s first fan, Amanda Meyer, for never leaving me at the party—literally and figuratively. Your friendship over the last decade has kept me going amidst life's challenges.

Thank you to my mom, Anna Blackburn-Lembeck, for breathing life and heart into our family and home during those foundational years. Thank you for the tireless work of seeing me, hearing me, and reflecting back my strengths. You taught my brothers and I how to be warm, kind, and loving.

Thank you to my dad, John Lembeck, for TCB'in (taking care of business). You led by example in embodying one of life's secrets—if you fall down, get back up. Thank you for being a stone's throw away while allowing me to develop the surprising strength that only comes from doing one's *own* soul-searching.

Thank you to my brothers, Joshua Lembeck, Jacob Lembeck, and Lembeck, for always caring, eventually forgiving, and simply being

---

Thank you to all my high-school companions—best friends and party acquaintances alike—for the thrills, the laughter, the memories, and the lessons.

Thank you to "Kolton," for the wild ride, the music, and for helping me discover the true source of life's magic. Thank you to your parents and family too—for borrowed time in a loving home.

ABOUT THE AUTHOR

Julianna Lembeck is the Founder and CEO of Taurus, a holistic mental health app. She graduated with a B.A. in Psychology. Possessing a knack for the art of expression, she was naturally drawn into the world of digital and content marketing after college, helping brands tell their stories.

This is her first book. She believes stories heal because they carry what otherwise might be a private or taboo experience into the mainstream and collective consciousness, helping transmute stigma and shame. This allows room for understanding and acceptance of challenging events, setting the stage for true healing and forgiveness.

Stay connected with her at https://www.juliannalembeck.com/

Learn more about the taurus at https://www.tauruswellness.io/

REFERENCES

Anonymous. 1800's. *Ring Around the Rosie*. American version.

Anonymous. 2009. *How to Shower Like a Woman/Man*. Accessed January 19, 2017. https://www.ebaumsworld.com/jokes/how-to-shower-like-a-woman-man/80517426/

Burton, Roderick (widely known as Dolla). "I'm F***ed Up (Main Version – explicit)." Zomba Recording, LLC. Spotify, 2008.

Casady, Sierra and Casady, Bianca (widely known as CocoRosie). "Rainbowarriors." The Adventures of Ghosthorse & Stillborn. Touch and Go Records, 2007. Spotify.

Collins, Armon and Johnson, Corey and McElroy, Derrick and Nachowitz, Eligh and Scoffern, Corey and Whitaker, Josh and Woolfolk, Tommy (widely known as Living Legends). "She Wants Me." The Gathering. Legendary Music, LLC, 2008. Spotify.

Croft, Romy and Sim, Oliver and Smith, Jamie and Quereshi, Baria (widely known as The XX) and Wallace, Christopher (widely known as Biggie Smalls). "The XX- Intro Feat. Biggie Smalls Juicy." Beggars (on behalf of XL Recordings Ltd, 2009 / Young Turks Recordings); LatinAutorPerf, UMPG Publishing, UMPI, UNIAO BRASILEIRA DE EDITORAS DE MUSICA - UBEM, LatinAutor - UMPG, ASCAP, LatinAutor, Sony ATV Publishing, and 14 Music Rights Societies, 2013. YouTube. Retrieved from https://www.youtube.com/watch?v=Ftfcxn4P3PM

Gašpar-Vrana, Emina. *Salt*. Accessed May 9, 2018. https://www.instagram.com/p/Bij92chA1-B/Copyright 2018 by Emina Gašpar-Vrana.

Gørvell-Dahll, Kyrre (widely known as Kygo) and Gomez, Selena. "It Ain't Me." Kygo AS, 2017. Spotify.

Grant, Elizabeth (widely known as Lana Del Rey). "Old Money." Ultraviolence (Deluxe). Lana Del Rey, under exclusive license to Polydor Ltd. (UK). Under exclusive license to Interscope Records in the USA, 2014. Spotify.

Hicks, Andre (widely known as Mac Dre) and Cuthroat Committee. "Song For You." Treal TV#2 Soundtrack. Thizz Nation, 2006. Spotify. (With original music from Mitchell, Joni. "Blue." Warner Records Inc., 1971. Spotify.)

Hicks, Andre (widely known as Mac Dre). "All I Want To Do." All Boo Boo. Thizz Nation, 2003. Spotify.

Holland, Brad (widely known as Ian Carey Project). "Get Shaky." Spinnin Records, 2009. Spotify.

Johnson, Matt and Schifino, Kim (widely known as Matt and Kim). "Daylight." Grand. Matt & Kim, Inc., Under exclusive license to FADER Label, 2009. Spotify.

Mathers, Marshall (widely known as Eminem) and Fenty, Robyn (widely known as Rihanna). "Love The Way You Lie." Recovery. Aftermath Records, 2010. Spotify.

Noyes, Madeline. "in my mind." Noyes Complaint. Republic Records a division of UMG Recordings Inc & Lava Music LLC, 2016. Spotify.

Päffgen, Christa (widely known as Nico). "These Days." Chelsea Girl. UMG Recordings, Inc., 1967 and A Polydor Records Release, 1967. Spotify.

Pall, Alexander and Taggart, Andrew (widely known as The Chainsmokers) and Frangipane, Ashley (widely known as Halsey). "Closer." Disruptor Records/Columbia Records, 2016.

Purdy, Joe. "San Jose." Take My Blanket and Go. Joe Purdy Records and Joe Purdy, 2007. Spotify.

Quin, Tegan and Quin, Sara (widely known as Tegan and Sara). "Nineteen." The Con. Sire Records for the U.S. Marketed by Warner Records Inc., A Warner Music Group Company, 2007. Spotify.

Saulters, Kiara. "Gold." low kii savage. EFFESS/Atlantic Recording Corporation for the United States and WEA International Inc. for the outside of the United States, 2016. Spotify.

Tortoriello, Dexter (widely known as Dawn Golden). "I Won't Bend." Still Life. Downtown Records, 2014. Spotify.

BLUE WATER, *a year in the ocean.*

Copyright © 2023 by Julianna Lembeck
All rights reserved

315

Made in the USA
Las Vegas, NV
04 January 2024

83869077R00174

BLUE WATER, *a year in the ocean.*

ACKNOWLEDGEMENTS

A special thanks to Joshua Berman, for helping me believe I could start this book.

A divine thanks to Alison McKinnon, for helping me believe I could finish this book. You stuck with me every step of the way and "saw" this book completed before I did.

An enormous thanks to my editor, Nina Denison, for your sharp eye and soft heart. You took my words and made them better. Where pragmatism meets magic—that's the place you work from.

A great thanks to Ms. Betsy Amster, for seeing the potential in my story; even before I was ready to claim it as my own.

A deep thanks to Patti Huber, LCSW. You held tremendous amounts of space for me in therapy as I cracked open, year after year, session by session.

Thank you to my best friend and *BLUE WATER*'s first fan, Amanda Meyer, for never leaving me at the party—literally and figuratively. Your friendship over the last decade has kept me going amidst life's challenges.

Thank you to my mom, Anna Blackburn-Lembeck, for breathing life and heart into our family and home during those foundational years. Thank you for the tireless work of seeing me, hearing me, and reflecting back my strengths. You taught my brothers and I how to be warm, kind, and loving.

Thank you to my dad, John Lembeck, for TCB'in (taking care of business). You led by example in embodying one of life's secrets—if you fall down, get back up. Thank you for being a stone's throw away while allowing me to develop the surprising strength that only comes from doing one's *own* soul-searching.

Thank you to my brothers, Joshua Lembeck, Jacob Lembeck, and Jonathan Lembeck, for always caring, eventually forgiving, and simply being nearby.

Thank you to all my high-school companions—best friends and party acquaintances alike—for the thrills, the laughter, the memories, and the lessons.

Thank you to "Kolton," for the wild ride, the music, and for helping me discover the true source of life's magic. Thank you to your parents and family too—for borrowed time in a loving home.

ABOUT THE AUTHOR

Julianna Lembeck is the Founder and CEO of Taurus, a holistic mental health app. She graduated with a B.A. in Psychology. Possessing a knack for the art of expression, she was naturally drawn into the world of digital and content marketing after college, helping brands tell their stories.

This is her first book. She believes stories heal because they carry what otherwise might be a private or taboo experience into the mainstream and collective consciousness, helping transmute stigma and shame. This allows room for understanding and acceptance of challenging events, setting the stage for true healing and forgiveness.

Stay connected with her at https://www.juliannalembeck.com/

Learn more about the taurus at https://www.tauruswellness.io/

REFERENCES

Anonymous. 1800's. *Ring Around the Rosie*. American version.
Anonymous. 2009. *How to Shower Like a Woman/Man*. Accessed January 19, 2017. https://www.ebaumsworld.com/jokes/how-to-shower-like-a-woman-man/80517426/
Burton, Roderick (widely known as Dolla). "I'm F***ed Up (Main Version – explicit)." Zomba Recording, LLC. Spotify, 2008.
Casady, Sierra and Casady, Bianca (widely known as CocoRosie). "Rainbowarriors." The Adventures of Ghosthorse & Stillborn. Touch and Go Records, 2007. Spotify.
Collins, Armon and Johnson, Corey and McElroy, Derrick and Nachowitz, Eligh and Scoffern, Corey and Whitaker, Josh and Woolfolk, Tommy (widely known as Living Legends). "She Wants Me." The Gathering. Legendary Music, LLC, 2008. Spotify.
Croft, Romy and Sim, Oliver and Smith, Jamie and Quereshi, Baria (widely known as The XX) and Wallace, Christopher (widely known as Biggie Smalls). "The XX- Intro Feat. Biggie Smalls Juicy." Beggars (on behalf of XL Recordings Ltd, 2009 / Young Turks Recordings); LatinAutorPerf, UMPG Publishing, UMPI, UNIAO BRASILEIRA DE EDITORAS DE MUSICA - UBEM, LatinAutor - UMPG, ASCAP, LatinAutor, Sony ATV Publishing, and 14 Music Rights Societies, 2013. YouTube. Retrieved from https://www.youtube.com/watch?v=Ftfcxn4P3PM
Gašpar-Vrana, Emina. *Salt*. Accessed May 9, 2018. https://www.instagram.com/p/Bij92chA1-B/Copyright 2018 by Emina Gašpar-Vrana.
Gørvell-Dahll, Kyrre (widely known as Kygo) and Gomez, Selena. "It Ain't Me." Kygo AS, 2017. Spotify.
Grant, Elizabeth (widely known as Lana Del Rey). "Old Money." Ultraviolence (Deluxe). Lana Del Rey, under exclusive license to Polydor Ltd. (UK). Under exclusive license to Interscope Records in the USA, 2014. Spotify.
Hicks, Andre (widely known as Mac Dre) and Cuthroat Committee. "Song For You." Treal TV#2 Soundtrack. Thizz Nation, 2006. Spotify. (With original music from Mitchell, Joni. "Blue." Warner Records Inc., 1971. Spotify.)
Hicks, Andre (widely known as Mac Dre). "All I Want To Do." All Boo Boo. Thizz Nation, 2003. Spotify.

Holland, Brad (widely known as Ian Carey Project). "Get Shaky." Spinnin Records, 2009. Spotify.

Johnson, Matt and Schifino, Kim (widely known as Matt and Kim). "Daylight." Grand. Matt & Kim, Inc., Under exclusive license to FADER Label, 2009. Spotify.

Mathers, Marshall (widely known as Eminem) and Fenty, Robyn (widely known as Rihanna). "Love The Way You Lie." Recovery. Aftermath Records, 2010. Spotify.

Noyes, Madeline. "in my mind." Noyes Complaint. Republic Records a division of UMG Recordings Inc & Lava Music LLC, 2016. Spotify.

Päffgen, Christa (widely known as Nico). "These Days." Chelsea Girl. UMG Recordings, Inc., 1967 and A Polydor Records Release, 1967. Spotify.

Pall, Alexander and Taggart, Andrew (widely known as The Chainsmokers) and Frangipane, Ashley (widely known as Halsey). "Closer." Disruptor Records/Columbia Records, 2016.

Purdy, Joe. "San Jose." Take My Blanket and Go. Joe Purdy Records and Joe Purdy, 2007. Spotify.

Quin, Tegan and Quin, Sara (widely known as Tegan and Sara). "Nineteen." The Con. Sire Records for the U.S. Marketed by Warner Records Inc., A Warner Music Group Company, 2007. Spotify.

Saulters, Kiara. "Gold." low kii savage. EFFESS/Atlantic Recording Corporation for the United States and WEA International Inc. for the outside of the United States, 2016. Spotify.

Tortoriello, Dexter (widely known as Dawn Golden). "I Won't Bend." Still Life. Downtown Records, 2014. Spotify.

BLUE WATER, *a year in the ocean.*

Copyright © 2023 by Julianna Lembeck
All rights reserved

Made in the USA
Las Vegas, NV
04 January 2024

83869077R00174